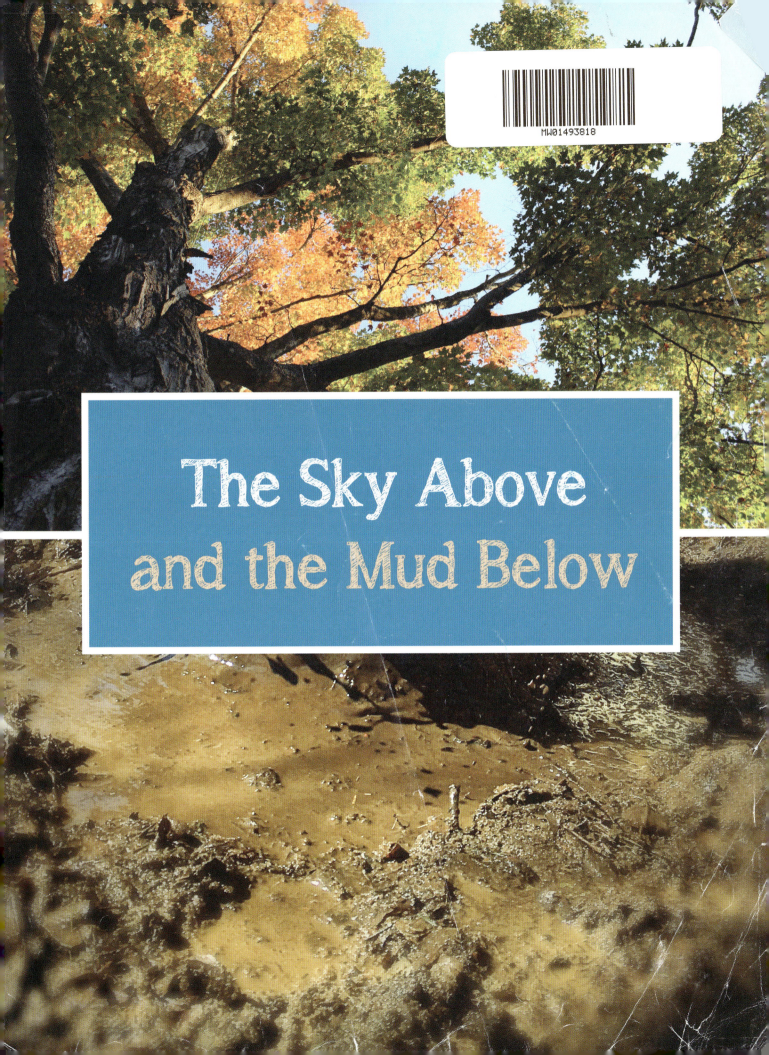

The Sky Above
and the Mud Below

Other books by David Sobel

Nature Preschools and Forest Kindergartens: The Handbook for Outdoor Learning

Children's Special Places: Exploring the Role of Forts, Dens,
and Bush Houses in Middle Childhood

Childhood and Nature: Design Principles for Educators

With Molly Steinwald
Beyond Ecophobia: Reclaiming the Heart in Nature Education

With Steven David Johnson
Play-Based Education: Connecting Classrooms and Communities

The Sky Above
and the Mud Below

Lessons from Nature Preschools
and Forest Kindergartens

DAVID SOBEL

Redleaf Press®
www.redleafpress.org
800-423-8309

Published by Redleaf Press
10 Yorkton Court
St. Paul, MN 55117
www.redleafpress.org

First edition 2020
Cover design: Erin Kirk New
Cover photograph © iStock.com/natalie_board
Interior design: Becky Daum
Typeset in Baskerville URW & Helvetica Neue
Interior photographs: All interior photographs by the newsletter contributors except page 7 by David Sobel; pages 9 (bottom), 11, 63 (bottom) by Dawn Jenkins; page 53 (top right) by Elaina Foxx; pages 63 (top), 67 (bottom), 70 by Willa Chandra; pages 66, 69 by Anthony Vincente; page 88 by Anne Emmerson Sorrell; pages 92, 94 by Anna Aragon; pages 95 (top), 96 (bottom) by Anthony Rogers; page 95 (bottom) by Eric Isaacs; pages 96 (top), 97 (bottom) by Lucia Torres; page 130 by Marilyn Diekman; page 131 by Melanie Connors; pages 170 (bottom), 171–174 by Geoff Griffen; pages 196–198 by Sue Thompson-Mitchell; page 222 (bottom) by Ruth Kagle.
Printed in the United States of America
Library of Congress Cataloging-in-Publication Data

Names: Sobel, David, author.
Title: The sky above and the mud below : lessons from nature preschools and forest kindergartens / David Sobel.
Description: First edition. | St. Paul, MN : Redleaf Press, 2020. | Includes bibliographical references and index. | Summary: "David Sobel's follow-up to Nature Preschools and Forest Kindergartens walks readers through the nitty-gritty facts of running a nature-based program. Organized around nine themes, each chapter begins with an overview from the author, followed by case studies from diverse early childhood programs, ranging from those that serve at-risk children to public preschools to university farm programs to Waldorf schools"— Provided by publisher.
Identifiers: LCCN 2020011011 (print) | LCCN 2020011012 (ebook) | ISBN 9781605546827 (paperback) | ISBN 9781605546834 (ebook)
Subjects: LCSH: Nature--Study and teaching (Early childhood)--Case studies. | Outdoor education--Case studies.
Classification: LCC LB1140.5.S35 S63 2020 (print) | LCC LB1140.5.S35 (ebook) | DDC 371.3/84--dc23
LC record available at https://lccn.loc.gov/2020011011
LC ebook record available at https://lccn.loc.gov/2020011012

Printed on acid-free paper

This book is dedicated to all the hearty and courageous
early childhood educators who are forging new paths
into the natural world with young children.

Contents

Without the help of a few people, this book would not have been possible. Thanks to:

Tricia Hurley, who created a phenomenal system for communicating with contributing authors and photographers, evaluating photos, and wrangling permission from parents to use pictures of their children. She was also a sounding board in helping me evaluate which articles were most important to include in the book.

Margaret (Peg) Smeltz, who has provided tireless energy in organizing our In Bloom: Promising Practices in Nature-based Early Childhood conferences around New England. These conferences helped us to identify some of the innovative practices shared in this book. Peg also did the preliminary graphic work to help figure out how to most appropriately present the fine work of all the contributors.

Ellen Doris, the cocreator of the Nature-based Early Childhood program at Antioch University New England. She has a fine ear for the *mot juste* and a fine eye for good teachers and good curriculum. I have enjoyed crafting a vision with her of what early childhood education could be.

Jennifer Kramer, my wife and colleague, who has joyfully joined me in many program visits and translates many of my ideas into brilliant practice with children and in teacher professional development workshops.

Elijah Sobel and **Tara Elliott**, my children, who were willing and gleeful participants in all our natural childhood experiments and adventures. They convinced me that natural childhoods should be available to all children.

Why *The Sky Above and the Mud Below?*

The sunlight slinks through the pine branches above, and snippets of blue, blue sky peek through. Or perhaps the drizzle slithers off the maple leaves, and the snippets of sky are a mottled gray. Up ahead, the drizzle and trail soil have conspired to create a beckoning mud puddle. Clad in rainsuits and wellies, the children squeal with delight as they tromp into the ankle-high depths. Let the wild puddle rumpus begin! The fluorescent lights, letter posters, and worksheets are forgotten. The classroom, at least for the next few hours, is a distant memory. The children and teachers submit to the thrall of puddle whumping with just the sky above their heads and the mud below their feet.

Most of the readers of this book won't recognize the origins of the book title, so a bit of explanation is called for. *The Sky Above, the Mud Below* was a 1961 French film that won the Academy Award for Best Documentary that year. The film documented a seven-month, thousand-mile Franco-Dutch expedition into the previously unexplored territories of what was then Netherlands New Guinea, where the explorers encounter the local indigenous peoples. There are exciting accounts of arduous bridge-buildings and crossings of dangerous streams, along with difficult climbs up rain-washed mountains. The native people in that part of the world live much of their lives in the elements with the sky above their heads and their feet in the mud.

Nature-based early childhood programs are similarly foreign to many explorers from the outside world. (Think well-dressed, sensible-shoed evaluators from the Child and Family Services department who have come to see whether your program meets state early childhood licensure guidelines.) "These children have no roof over their heads most of the morning, and you're letting them stomp wantonly in the mud? And some of them have their faces painted with squished raspberries! Is this safe? And what about this strange ritual of every child alone in the woods in a special place—are they praying?" They'll feel like they've entered a land almost as strange as the New Guinea jungles.

In a way, this book is an ethnography of nature-based early childhood programs. One of the goals is to explain why the sky above and the mud below are actually good for children. It helps to translate from the language of the woods and fields to the language of early childhood program approval guidelines. It describes outdoorsy curriculum that meets literacy, math, and science goals. It shows how tree climbing and fire building can be fun *and* safe *and* educationally valuable.

Like the French and Dutch explorers, nature-based early childhood pioneers are blazing new trails into the woods and fields of early care.

You're becoming experts in outdoor gear, peeing and pooping outside, plant identification, yellow-jacket-nest detecting, icy-slope negotiating, and communicating with parents about why their children come home every day with dirty clothes and a glint in their eyes. You're learning to articulate why counting with acorns and sticks is just as valuable, maybe more valuable, than counting with pennies. You're coaxing parents to join you out in the woods, away from the humming, overhead-lit school cafeterias, to explain how this playing in the woods will prepare children effectively for public school kindergarten or first grade. It's a tall order, but you can do it. Help is on the way from all the adventurous early childhood teachers who have contributed to this book. Follow them; they know the trails.

A NOTE ABOUT SOURCES

This book is a watershed, with trickles emerging from a wide array of sources and gradually converging into mountain brooks, then a few streams through fields, then a river with a slow but strong current. The many streams are early childhood educators who are working across the United States—from Santa Barbara, California, to Baltimore, Maryland; from New Orleans, Louisiana, to Montpelier, Vermont. All but one of them received a fellowship, funded by the George B. Storer Foundation as part of their participation in the Nature-based Early Childhood Certificate program at Antioch University New England in Keene, New Hampshire. The fellowship required them to document the naturalization of their early childhood programs. These ranged from programs for homeless and at-risk children, to independent schools, to public preschools and kindergartens, to university farm programs, to Head Start programs, to botanic gardens, to Waldorf schools.

Essentially, most kinds of settings—urban to rural, traditional to cutting edge—are represented. These efforts at getting children learning and playing outside can, and should, happen anywhere. As Joan Almon says in the movie *The Best Day Ever: Forest Days in Vermont Kindergartens* (2017), "All children need more nature, that's a given." And so we hope that this book helps you give the children in your care more nature.

I've taken these diverse sources of good ideas and woven them together into chapters. The first half of the book is about policies and practices to help you organize your school and classroom for the different demands of being outside in all kinds of weather. The second half of the book is about curriculum—all the basic things like reading, writing, arithmetic, science, gardening—and how you can address most of the academic and social-emotional goals of the early childhood curriculum outdoors.

I've written an essay at the beginning of each chapter that connects the articles to some of the current educational issues, themes, and emergent research. At the end of many of the articles, you'll find several state early childhood standards or Next Generation Science Standards (NGSS) and an indication in italics of how the activities in that article met those standards. We're trying to show very specifically how these naturalized programs cover all the requisite bases in some new, and perhaps better, ways. I hope this combination of thematic essays and nitty-gritty articles are a good synthesis of big ideas and brass tacks.

My thanks and appreciation to all the contributors to this book who are bringing more nature into children's lives. In many cases, they've moved on from these organizations, but they worked or interned at these early childhood programs when this book was being written:

Michel Anderson, Waldorf School of Baltimore, Baltimore, MD

Maryfaith Decker, Lime Hollow Nature Preschool, Cortland, NY

Audrey Fergason, Forest Gnomes at Natick Community Organic Farm, Natick, MA

Matt Flower, Urban Ecology Center, Milwaukee, WI

Melissa Frederick, Magnolia Nature School, Nauvoo, AL

Wendy Garcia, Cold Spring School, New Haven, CT

Megan Gessler, Natural Beginnings at Kendall County Forest Preserve, Yorkville, IL

Harriet Hart, Dandelion and Snail Preschool at Twinfield Union School, Plainfield, VT

Alicia Jimenez, Storyteller Children's Center, Santa Barbara, CA

Brooke Larm, MSU Tollgate Farm and Education Center, Novi, MI

Hannah Lindner-Finlay, The Gordon School, Providence, RI

Clare Loughran, St. George's Episcopal School, New Orleans, LA

Jennifer Newberry, Marion Cross School, Norwich, VT

Kestrel Plump, Sustainability Academy at Lawrence Barnes School, Burlington, VT

Wendy Robins, Explore Ecology and Open Alternative School, Santa Barbara, CA

Sarah Sheldon, Chicago Botanic Garden Nature Preschool, Glencoe, IL

Lauren Skilling, Amanda Hull, and Shannon Cramer, Hartland Elementary School Kindergarten, Hartland, VT

Janet Strader, Teton Valley Community School, Victor, ID

Katie Swick, AllTogetherNow! Preschool, Montpelier, VT

To echo Arlo Guthrie, it looks like we've got ourselves a movement here.

Part I
Getting Organized

CHAPTER 1

Before Taking Children Outside

Taking children outdoors is full of promise and laden with challenges, especially if they're used to school being indoors most of the time. Going outdoors means recess, and recess means outdoor voices, climbing on the monkey bars, and getting as far away from the teacher as possible. Going outside also potentially means the neighborhood dog will trundle in to nuzzle the children and disrupt your activity, the grounds crew will start mowing the grass right next to your outdoor classroom, the wind will blow the children's worksheets off the table into the poison ivy, and someone will have to pee as soon as you settle in under the big white pine. So much for just smelling the roses.

Whether you're starting a nature preschool from scratch or you're a kindergarten teacher who wants to get the children outside more, you'd be wise to focus on that old scouting mantra: be prepared. And being prepared means more than tucking your pant legs into your socks and bringing a first aid kit along. Here are the top ten things (roughly in order) you need to accomplish before you start to take children outdoors:

TEN THINGS TO DO BEFORE HEADING OUTSIDE

1. **Assess potential hazards in the environment.** Conduct a risk assessment of the outdoor spaces you'll be visiting. Are there yellow jacket nests, poison ivy, potential encounters with dangerous animals? (Later on, you'll learn about the big-animal drill they do in Victor, Idaho, where it's possible to encounter bears or moose!) You'll also want to look for broken limbs still hanging in trees, old barbed wire, and other potential hazards that children might not notice. Modest risks are good—they provide appropriate challenges that encourage learning for your children. It's your responsibility to allow for acceptable and appropriate risk (slippery, not-too-steep slopes). Hazards are things your children can't assess or manage on their own, and it's your responsibility to eliminate them or avoid them. Therefore, you have to spray the yellow jacket nest or not go in that section of the forest. Or, you can ask the maintenance staff to cut down the broken limb over your outdoor classroom meeting area. Use modest risks to your advantage; eliminate or avoid hazards.

2. **Differentiate between recess and outdoor learning.** Figure out how you will make it clear that outdoor time is different from recess. Yes, the children will have some free nature playtime, but there will also be circle time, story time, sit spots, and outdoor lessons. Outdoor learning time has the same kinds of expectations as indoor learning.

3. **Develop techniques for outdoor group management.** Developing a set of management techniques that will keep children both safe and engaged outside is important. Hannah Lindner-Finlay's guidelines in this chapter have got you covered here. Let me suggest an additional modestly stern but effective technique: The first time you take children outside, make it clear that you will walk in the front of the line, and no one will go ahead of you. Otherwise, everyone must come back inside. As soon as you pass through the door to the school yard, walk slowly and allow an energetic child or two to bolt past you into the inviting sunshine. Immediately use your whistle or teacher voice to call everyone back, and walk them

back inside. Then sit them in a circle and remind them about the rule that the teacher walks in front of the line. Tell them if they can't follow this one rule, then you won't be able to do outdoor learning. Ask them if they can follow this one rule. If they agree, try going outside again. If the children are successful, praise them and then engage them in an activity. If some children rush ahead, take them back inside again and say you'll try again tomorrow. Mean what you say—it works like a charm!

4. **Create risk-management plans for potential risky behaviors.** In addition to removing hazards, decide ahead of time what kinds of risky behavior should be encouraged or avoided. If there are small climbable trees, what will you do when children want to climb them? Do you allow the children to hop across the little stream? How will you visually create boundaries in the woods so children know where they're not allowed to go? Maryfaith Decker's protocols in chapter 3 on tree climbing, playing near water, and cold- and hot-weather guidelines are components of a risk-management plan.

5. **Identify the affordances of the environment that support play and learning.** Affordances are opportunities for engagement. Look for them while conducting your risk assessment of the landscape. A tree trunk on the ground, at just the right height, affords comfortable sitting. A pine-needled forest floor with no vegetation under a grandmother white pine affords a perfect circle gathering spot. Lots of dead branches on the ground afford fort building. The slippery slope affords problem solving: "How can we be sure that everyone can get up this slope safely? Can you help your friend?"

6. **Align outdoor activities with your curriculum standards.** Teachers at a public school nature kindergarten program in the Sooke, British Columbia School District were initially concerned about whether the children's academic progress would be compromised. The plan was to have the children outside in the morning and inside in the afternoon—inside in the afternoon so they could make sure they had enough time to address the academic aspects of the curriculum. But after the first three months, the teachers found that academic skills were just as easily developed outside as inside.

When I visited one of these classrooms, teachers introduced the letter *S* inside, and then everyone went outside. The children walked *S*'s in the dewy grass in the field. Once in the woods, they made *S*'s on the ground with sticks and pinecones. During circle time, they named things they'd seen that morning that started with *S*—sunshine, spruce, salmonberry, sand. Later chapters articulate clearly how such outdoor play activities—both teacher-led and children-initiated—meet the local early childhood curriculum standards.

7. **Learn phenology—the science of what's happening now in the woods and fields around you.** Nature-based early childhood teachers need to be knowledgeable about both child development and natural history. One without the other is not sufficient. It's why we have a Natural History for Early Childhood course in our program at Antioch New England. You should know some of the mushrooms that emerge in the fall and where you're likely to find them. You should know the difference between goldenrod and aster, and which berries are edible and which are toxic. Pokeberries (toxic) look a whole lot like blueberries (edible) to children. Can you tell the difference?

In the winter, learn how to tell whether a raccoon or skunk has been visiting the compost pile. Which birds overwinter in your area and are likely to come to your feeders? When do snow fleas start to appear, and how can you find them? When and where will the first wildflowers emerge in spring? What are vernal pools, what will we find there, and why are they important? And which birches are best for bending? (Don't know about this lost New England pastime? Read Robert Frost's "Birches.") Have a collection of natural history guides for your area in your indoor space so both you and the children can browse them.

8. **Know the personalities and dispositions of the children in your group.** Are any of the children in your care "runners" (children who are prone to taking off and not stopping)? You'll want to know the answer to this question before you head out into the field with no clear boundaries. Familiarize yourself with the children's fears and dispositions in more bounded settings before moving into more unbounded settings. Again, Hannah's guidelines later in this chapter nicely articulate moving children from indoors to a nearby outdoor space on the play yard and practicing rule behavior before moving farther afield. This will allow you to understand which children are afraid of worms, which children need to be close to an adult, which children might have trouble keeping their hands to themselves, and so on.

9. **Know the previous outdoor learning experiences of the group.** This is a corollary to the previous guideline. It's important to know if the children have prior experience learning outdoors. Did last year's teacher conduct a day in the woods? Do children already know about appropriate clothing?

Acclimated children need very different treatment than a group that is not outdoors savvy.

10. **Dress for success.** That means both you and the children. Being outside for hours in the winter in northern climates requires lots of preparation. Everyone is going to need really warm boots, rain or snow pants and jackets that shed water, and lots of layers of fleece and wool. No cotton or denim! Children also need backup clothes to change into when they come back inside. All of this clothing necessitates a really good clothes storage system inside. Audrey Fergason's guidelines in this chapter provide a good starting point for northern winters. On the other hand, being outside in Arizona in the spring means sun protection, scorpion avoidance, and lots of hydration. (Someone needs to create the Arizona version of Fergason's guidelines.) And get familiar with which brands actually perform—for example, which mittens children can actually get on when their hands are damp and cold. You'll need to tell parents what to look for at the secondhand shop or at the outdoor clothing store. One suggestion—investigate Polarn O. Pyret, a manufacturer of high-performing children's outerwear.

The articles in this chapter will get you started in your preparation. Hannah Lindner-Finlay gets down to brass tacks in terms of rules and guidelines. Audrey Fergason provides sage wardrobe advice. Wendy Robins explains the logistics necessary to ensure a good lesson in the garden. And follow Jennifer Newberry's very explicit guidelines for making your outdoor apron and what goes in it.

Strategies for Safe, Fun, and Focused Nature Explorations

GORDON SCHOOL

East Providence, Rhode Island

by Hannah Lindner-Finlay

When I first considered incorporating nature-based learning and play into my own curriculum, there were three big questions in my mind: How can I ensure that the children are safe? How can I encourage focused learning in nature? How can I maintain control in the "wild" outdoors? Through conversations, readings, and direct experience, I have learned simple strategies for establishing nature as another classroom. I am sharing them in the hope that they might make your work with children in nature easier and more fun.

BRING FAMILIAR ROUTINES OUTSIDE

- If you use a bell, chime, or call-and-response in the classroom to get children's attention, take that management tool outside. Practice using the tool and having children freeze or circle up on the playground. When children become adept at responding to the tool on the playground, take it with you to other nature spaces and practice using it there.

- Establish a meeting area in each nature space you visit. If your children sit in a circle during inside meeting times, then do the same outside. You might want to provide structure for your circle using logs, rocks, or poly spots.

- If you do morning greetings in your classroom, you can transfer this routine outdoors (even if it isn't morning). Children who have practiced passing a question around the circle inside will be able to focus while doing so outside as well.

DEVELOP NATURE-SPECIFIC RULES AND ROUTINES

- Consider how you want students to transition into each nature space. You may want different routines for different spaces. When I take children to visit the garden, we start with a nature concert. Each child gives me a "ticket" and then they sit in a circle, counting on their fingers all the sounds they can hear. When we go to the woods, children first go to their own "sit spot" where they can sit or build quietly while observing any changes since their last visit. Sit spots are followed by a circle time where students each share one change that they noticed.

- Visit each nature space before bringing children there, and try to anticipate important safety rules that children should know. For example, you might want children to ask permission before climbing trees or swinging on vines. You also might want to make sure that you have a stick safety policy approved by your school administrators. Make sure you can explain the purpose of these safety rules to the children so that they are meaningful.

ESTABLISH BOUNDARIES

- Before taking your children to a new nature space, identify important boundaries that you want them to know about. For the first several visits to the nature space, bring cones to mark "stop spots" that children should not go beyond. After the first visit, have children work together to put the cones in place. When you invite other children to visit the nature space, have your students teach the boundaries. As children develop ownership over the boundaries, they become more likely to remember and adhere to them.

- Consider how you want children to travel to the nature space. Will the children be allowed to run, walk, or crawl? Will you be playing a group game, moving in a clump, or walking in a line? It may be helpful to identify stopping and waiting points, assuming that children will be moving at different paces.

INTRODUCE NEW MATERIALS AND NEW IDEAS INSIDE

- If you plan to have children use bug boxes, penlights, magnifying glasses, or nature journals outside, teach them how to use these tools inside where there are not so many distractions. Model how to use these tools and have children practice themselves. When you bring the tools outside to a new environment, the children will be comfortable and confident using them.

- Nature is a wonderful, sensory-rich environment. If you want to cultivate focus, try to introduce one new thing at a time. It can be helpful to identify and explore essential concepts inside before taking them outside for focused learning. This makes it so that children are applying a familiar concept in a new environment.

PREVIEW AND MODEL NATURALIST BEHAVIORS

- Practice observation in the classroom and on the playground before taking children to nature spaces. Observe by describing, counting, categorizing, collecting, and drawing a variety of natural objects. Explore nature with all five senses—touch, taste, smell, sight, and sound. Developing a culture of observation will make your nature explorations rich with the kind of attention that inspires further inquiry.

- Model kind and respectful ways to interact with creatures in nature. Hide toy slugs, snails, insects, salamanders, and worms under rocks and logs in the classroom. Have children practice lifting up the rocks and logs, handling the small creatures, and returning them to their homes. Explain that creatures' homes should always be put back as they were found. You may want to set this up as a station in your sensory area so that children can continue to practice these skills.

PROVIDE OPPORTUNITIES FOR STUDENT REFLECTION

- Take photos and videos of children's work and play outdoors. Children may not always be ready to reflect in a meaningful way outside, but if you share documentation with them later on, they often have thoughtful insights to share about their learning.

- Before going outside, ask children to remember their last visit to nature. You may want to provide photos or other memory prompts from the last visit. This will help children to build on their previous learning and prime them for noticing patterns and changes in nature and in their own play.

The **GORDON SCHOOL** is a racially diverse nursery-through-eighth-grade coeducational independent school in East Providence, Rhode Island. In 2016 The Gordon School opened an Early Childhood STEAM Lab. Every three weeks, the students explore a new scientific domain through explorations that integrate science with technology, engineering, art, and math.

Providing Appropriate Clothing for Nature Preschool Programs

by Audrey Fergason

Forest Gnomes Waldkindergarten
Natick, Massachusetts

"Can I take my jacket off?" Dakota asks.

It's the middle of a rainstorm, but Dakota has already decided he likes playing unencumbered by his rain jacket, a thick plastic coat that doesn't breathe well in the 70-degree weather. Dakota is allowed to play without his jacket now on this warm September morning, but if it were colder, he would have had to keep it on.

Dakota's parents, like all the Forest Gnome parents, were given an extensive gear list before enrolling in the outdoor preschool program. The gear list was developed by the program's founders after three years of running the program; it is very brand-specific due to the differing quality between brands, with a focus on durability, warmth, and mobility.

FALL/SPRING CLOTHING GUIDE

WHAT TO WEAR

- Long-sleeved shirt
- Long pants
- Fleece or wool sweater
- Sun hat
- Sturdy walking shoes
- Waterproof rain gear (mud pants or puddle pants)
- Lined rubber boots if it has rained in the last three days

BACKPACK

- Water bottle

PLEASE PACK IN LABELED ZIP-TOP BAGS

- 1 extra underwear
- 2 extra socks
- 2 extra long-sleeved shirts
- 1 extra long pants
- Rain gear

WINTER CLOTHING GUIDE

WHAT TO WEAR

- Insulated, waterproof boots
- Wool socks, silk/synthetic liners a plus
- Base layer: wool, silk, or polypropylene long underwear top and bottom (no cotton!)
- Mid layer: long-sleeve wool or fleece sweater and fleece pants
- Over layer: Insulated waterproof jacket with hood and insulated waterproof pants
- Gloves: waterproof, insulated liners a plus
- Fleece or wool hat

BACKPACK

- Water bottle

PLEASE PACK IN LABELED ZIP-TOP BAGS

- 1 extra underwear
- 2 extra wool socks
- 1 pair of long underwear
- 1 pair of fleece pants
- 1 extra fleece or wool hat
- 2 extra pairs of insulated gloves
- 1 set of lightweight waterproof rain gear

About 80 percent of the parents comply and buy everything on the list, which includes items such as backpacks (retailing at approximately forty dollars) to puddle pants (approximately sixty dollars). To outfit one student in the Forest Gnomes program in wholly new items might cost a family close to four hundred dollars.

Cheaper options are provided, when possible, and the list includes local resale boutiques. But in the end, the price tag for the required gear might scare off parents who otherwise would be willing to enroll their child in an outdoor preschool.

Proper gear that fits well is imperative to enable a child to explore their outdoor world comfortably. Puddle pants and L.L.Bean rain jackets are expensive but also necessary to keep the children warm and willing to stay outside even in the middle of driving rain. Winter coats, wool layers, and socks are equally expensive but vital in our New England winters. It is difficult to observe frogs if you don't have puddle pants and almost impossible to explore the creek without watertight boots.

Mindful of these costs, we created a gear lending library for the present and future Forest Gnome families. Each current Forest Gnome family has been asked to donate one gently used item, and preschool staff continually visit thrift stores and resale boutiques for good-quality gear for our use. As of October, we have amassed quite a collection of fall items and are just beginning to see a few winter jackets, base layers, and snow pants come in. Items that are donated but are not the right fit for an outdoor preschool program are given to Cradles to Crayons, an organization that provides clothing to poor and homeless children in the surrounding community. More donations come in every day. Our admission application

is being changed to draw attention to our gear lending library, and the parent handbook has been edited to encourage parents to ask for help outfitting their child.

After the rainstorm passed, the children took advantage of the wet weather and the abundance of water in our rain barrel. They took turns loading a wheelbarrow and using various kitchen implements borrowed from our "bakery" in the sandpit. Once the wheelbarrow was successfully full, one child directed our oldest gnome in the movement of the wheelbarrow and the perfect placement for their "river." While the younger gnomes delighted in the cascade of water as they dumped the wheelbarrow, others grabbed pieces of tree bark and sticks and tried to dam up the flow. Still others tried to float leaves in the temporary stream. Fortunately, it was warm and everyone was wearing good boots. Plans were made to construct a bridge the next time there was a rainstorm, and everyone agreed that water made everything more fun.

"Teacher, I hope it rains tomorrow," were Dakota's parting words.

NATICK COMMUNITY ORGANIC FARM's Forest Gnomes Waldkindergarten (German for forest kindergarten) program was established in 2009. We are a nature program for preschool children in a classroom without walls, changing with the seasons. Our gnomes are outside in all weather, through the fall, winter, and spring. Grounded in the values of a traditional Waldkindergarten, our minimally structured program focuses on free play, where exploration and imagination guide our gnomes every day in our beautiful woods.

Best Practices in a School Garden

by Wendy Robins

ExploreEcology

Santa Barbara, California

Having twenty or more young children in a school garden can be challenging. There is a lot going on in addition to the day's lesson and activity. Weather (rain, wind, heat), animals (birds, rodents, insects), and things to pick up (dirt, sticks, leaves) can get the class off track very quickly. Establishing routines and having a plan and a backup plan are essential.

At my two schools, we almost always start our garden lessons at the picnic tables in front of a chalkboard: our outdoor classroom. I write and draw pictures of the day's objective. Many of the students are TK (traditional kindergarten) through first grade (ages four to six) and are beginning readers, so the first thing we do is sound out and then read what we will be learning about. We also take a moment to observe the weather (is it hot? windy? cloudy?) and acknowledge any other potential distractions (helicopters, hawks, another class walking by). It is important to be flexible and use these teachable moments.

Our first activity at the beginning of each year is a discussion to establish appropriate garden behavior. The children tell me their ideas of how to be safe and smart in the garden, and together we create our garden agreement, which is really just three rules, framed in a positive way.

GARDEN AGREEMENT

- Walk on paths. Watch where you walk.
- Respect everyone and everything. Keep us all safe.
- Ask before picking.

For the first half of the year, the garden agreement is reviewed before every garden activity. It gets repeated as necessary throughout the remainder of the year.

A typical lesson in the garden uses literature as a jumping-off point. I read aloud from either a fiction or nonfiction book related to the day's activity. Any supplies (clipboards, worksheets, pencils, magnifying glasses) needed for the class are assembled ahead of time and ready to go in a separate area. After the book, there's a quick review of our objective and then we're off to the garden to sketch, observe, or count. If our main activity is art based, we come back to the picnic tables to color, paint, or use glue.

When a lesson involves working in the garden (planting, harvesting, or using tools), the class gets divided into three groups and we rotate everyone through. I often have a classroom teacher with me, so she stays with the groups at the tables and I take the "working" group. I have found that the magic number for a working group is six—however we frequently have more than that but never more than nine.

It is okay to spend a short time in the garden in the beginning of the year, fifteen to twenty minutes, and then go for longer periods of time as the children become accustomed to learning and working outdoors. Even with a quick lesson, some children will finish early and ask what else they can do. Having a few extra tasks or activities available will keep everyone busy until it is time to clean up. Some of my favorite extra tasks include the following:

- Children can make a picture of themselves in the garden, their favorite flower or insect, and so on.
- Identify a type of weed and have the children collect them in a bucket.
- Clean tools.
- Look for or catch insects or lizards.
- Explore and have free time.

Being prepared will make your garden time successful. Having the lesson plan, materials, and extra activities ready to go are all essential. Be sure to be equipped for emergencies. Always have a first aid kit nearby as well as a list of children with allergies.

EXPLORE ECOLOGY is a nonprofit organization that oversees a garden-based education program in over twenty elementary schools in Santa Barbara County. I work at two schools, seeing children in grades TK–8 in the garden once each week for thirty to sixty minutes. Sometimes we have a structured lesson, sometimes we perform garden work, and always we explore our beautiful gardens.

Forest Teacher Tools

Marion Cross School
Norwich, Vermont

by Jennifer Newberry

TEACHER APRONS

One tool that saves time and keeps me efficient at taking anecdotal records is a teacher apron. I can record the important work that the children are doing in the forest. Parents love the stories of learning, especially when I can capture the exact words, pictures, or even video of their children in action.

With just a couple yards of fabric, you can customize your own teacher apron to fit your needs. I was fortunate to have my mom and her friend make six of these aprons. Each adult has one of these to wear on our forest days. One assistant wears her apron every day, even in the classroom. Here is a list of the contents of my apron:

- **Cell phone and/or camera.** We communicate with the school office through our cell phones. I take many pictures and capture video of learning.

- **Flip-book with quick games.** Attention can be redirected with a game. This has been helpful to have right at my fingertips.

- **Permanent marker and a 6½-by-4½-inch piece of cardboard with label paper attached with a binder clip.** This is used to take anecdotal records. I take the sticky label and attach it to students' files so that I can use it as a reference when writing report cards and communicating with parents.

- **Band-aids and antiseptic wipes tied together with hair ties.** Often I will notice that someone will need to have their hair tied back so they can see. Facial tissues are also a must-have.

- **Every adult has a list of our activities and the plan of the day.**

One fall afternoon in the forest, my students and I were transitioning from one core routine to another when I overheard the following conversation. Without my teacher tools, I wouldn't have been able to capture the beauty of it. This is evidence of the connections that these two students are making with the natural world.

> "Sometimes trees just tell the truth."
>
> —Josie, age six

Sally, age five, and Josie, age six, were both alert and relaxed, observing a tree and conversing with each other about all the things that they noticed about the tree. They decided that the tree was just like Josie and her twin brother, Ben. It had started as one tree and grown into two. Josie explained that they were in their mom's tummy together and were born just moments apart. Sally chimed in, "And now Josie is in our class and Ben is in Ms. Morse's class. They were together and now they are apart—just like that tree." Josie noticed another tree close to it and said, "Maybe next year we will be like that tree and be in the same class." This tree had started to grow with one trunk, then split off into two, and then joined into one trunk again. I congratulated them on noticing the similarities between Josie and Ben and the trees. Josie's matter-of-fact response was "Sometimes trees just tell the truth."

CONNECTIONS TO STANDARDS

COMMON CORE STATE STANDARDS

CCSS.MATH.CONTENT.K.MD.A.2

Directly compare two objects with a measurable attribute in common, to see which object has "more of"/"less of" the attribute, and describe the difference. Describe and compare measurable attributes. *(Sally and Josie compared the trees with the twins.)*

CCSS.MATH.CONTENT.K.MD.A.1

Describe measurable attributes of objects, such as length or weight. Describe several measurable attributes of a single object.

MARION CROSS SCHOOL is a nurturing kindergarten-through-sixth-grade public school located in Norwich, Vermont. There are currently two full-day kindergarten classes that go out into the forest for most of the day on Fridays. The Milton Frye Nature Preserve has much to offer, including natural streams to explore the properties of water, trails with a wide variety of trees that change with the seasons, and wildlife that depend upon both. These resources give children tangible ways of working with and in nature to increase their intimate connection to it. Some investigations might take the whole school year as we explore the changes that occur in nature over time.

CHAPTER 2

Scaffolding Nature Play

Whether you teach in a full-fledged, outdoors-most-of-the-day forest preschool or you're in a public school kindergarten classroom wanting to go outdoors half a day per week, you need to scaffold your outdoor time with children. Scaffolding refers to the structures you put in place to keep your children safe and to maximize the learning that occurs. Scaffolding is the schedule for the day, the rules for using sticks, the way materials are arranged for the cooking activity, your system for making sure everyone has the right outdoor clothing for that day. Each reader will be at a different place along the spectrum of exploring outdoor learning, so feel free to take the suggestions you need and save the rest for later.

In high-quality nature-based early childhood programs, I advocate for a balance between teacher-directed and child-directed learning opportunities. If your time outside is too open-ended or too overly directed, the quality of the experience for the children will suffer. Note that I am consciously making the decision not to talk about the balance between play and work, or between play and learning. This is to counteract the assumption that play is not work, or play is not learning. Instead, I am advocating for the mind-set that there are at least two, and really many, forms of playful learning. Child-directed playful learning is more free-form, exploratory, and often more physical. Teacher-directed playful learning is more bounded, focused, and goal-directed. They're both valuable, and the aha moments happen in both contexts. If you're in a highly teacher-directed academic school setting, I suggest introducing small amounts of child-directed play when outside. It's good to allow children to collect acorns and hide them the way the squirrels do. On the other hand, if you're in a free-form, anything-goes setting, I suggest introducing some teacher-directed elements—a story time at a certain point in the morning or a time for individual sit spots when each child is quietly by themselves.

Nature-based early childhood programs take many forms. On one end of the continuum are Forest Days programs where children, predominantly in public school kindergarten programs, spend half of a day or most of one day a week in the woods. In the middle of the continuum are nature preschools where children are outside approximately half of their program day. On the far end of the continuum are forest kindergartens where children are outside most of the day and often there's no formal, heated indoor meeting space. In all these permutations, I advocate for a balance of open-ended nature play with teacher-directed playful learning.

Take a look at the daily schedule for the Wednesday in the Woods day in the public elementary school in Hartland, Vermont (Powers 2017). This is a full-day kindergarten program with the day running from nine o'clock in the morning to two-thirty in the afternoon. Times are approximate. Note the balance between teacher-directed and child-directed parts of the day.

FOREST DAY SCHEDULE, HARTLAND ELEMENTARY SCHOOL, HARTLAND, VERMONT

- **9:00** Children assemble in the classroom, pack up small matching backpacks with lunch and water bottles, and dress in layers for the weather.

- **9:20** Enter the woods across the playing fields and pause for "Tree Stop" at the woods' edge. At this giant fallen tree at the top of the hill leading down to their outdoor classroom, kids sit, take in the view, sing a woods song, and discuss the day's plan.

- **9:40** Steep descent to the site, holding onto a rope tied from tree to tree, or tumbling on ahead.

- **9:50** Gather briefly around the fire pit.

- **10:00** Children and adults head to their sit spots for quiet observations. Then small groups gather with an adult to share what they noticed, changes they observed.

- **10:30** Gather around the fire for snack.

- **10:50** Child-directed nature play choice time. Belly sliding, wandering, building forts, tracking animals, gazing at the sky, making nature collections, vine-swinging, see-saw construction, and play. (All within the prescribed outdoor setting marked off with flagging tape.)

- **11:30** Teacher-directed playful learning with multiple offerings. Children have three or four choices offered by attending adults. Sometimes they are assigned to a group, usually they choose their preferred place.

- **12:15** Lunch around the fire circle.

- **1:00** Back up the hill, out of the forest, return to the classroom.

- **1:30–2:30** Back in the classroom. Writing and drawing in journals, teachers and children discuss morning happenings that get documented in the Wednesday in the Woods blog. (See the class blog at http://wednesdayinthewoods.blogspot.com.)

The rhythm of the day is a balance of child nature play and teacher-directed playful learning. The morning preparation, walk across the field, and Tree Stop are scaffolded by the teachers. Descending the hill is more child-directed (with teacher assistance where necessary) with some children sliding down or bounding down, others more cautiously using the rope handrail.

Sit spots themselves have this same balance—the requirement to stay in your sit spot is teacher scaffolding—but what happens there is child directed. Then there's a teacher-led discussion afterwards to reflect on changes, observations, and questions.

The heart of the morning is two sessions—child-directed nature play and teacher-directed lessons. As examples, one morning during nature play, I observed four girls cavorting on a vine swing and a group of boys carrying a very long stick and singing, "Hey, ho, we're sticks boys." During teacher-directed playful learning, one teacher did a math activity that involved constructing number sentences with numbers and operations signs (+, −, x, =) on oak tree cookies while another group followed a recipe for stick bread for baking over the fire. Another group made aluminum foil boats for floating down the stream. Both the child-directed and teacher-directed sessions provided valuable learning opportunities. The open-endedness of lunch and climbing back up the hill to the classroom is followed by the more classically academic drawing and writing in journals.

This same balance between teacher-directed and child-directed activity shows up at the micro level as well. When should teachers step in and when should they step back? Does this potential problem require my teacher management, or should I let the children try to figure this out? The virtue of teacher restraint is illustrated in the following description of an incident during a forest day in the Idaho woods. Teacher Jane Strader recounts that a group of four boys was exploring in the woods when she noticed that Cole, one of the boys, was "deading" ants—his term for killing them. She considered stepping in and giving him the lecture about respecting all the creatures of the forest but decided to hold back. After a few minutes, another boy, Jared, confronted Cole.

Jared: "Hey Cole, my dad says that if you kill an animal you have to eat it. So if you're going to kill those ants, you have to eat them."

Cole: "Yuck, I don't want to eat ants. They'd taste bad."

Jared: "I heard they taste kind of like chocolate watermelon. Sounds good to me. You should eat them."

After much cajoling, Cole decided to go ahead and eat an ant. Needless to say, it didn't taste much like chocolate watermelon, and, based on their unpalatableness, Cole decided to stop deading ants. Behavior modified, problem solved—in a much more genuine and perhaps permanent manner than if Jane had stepped in. Sometimes, letting the children solve the problem themselves is more effective.

The articles in this chapter represent this same balance between what Alfred North Whitehead called "the rhythmic claims of freedom and discipline." You'll notice that there are multiple articles about the same things, showing that children's underlying desires for the same kinds of activities pop up over and over again in different programs around the country. (See *Childhood and Nature: Design Principles for Educators* for a description of these recurrent play motifs.) Savvy teachers recognize these deep childhood desires to create structures, use tools, bake mud cupcakes, go on treasure hunts, and so on. They scaffold these activities by providing appropriate loose parts, collecting child-friendly tools, identifying locations that support these activities, and providing large enough chunks of time so children can be appropriately immersed. Here are some of the themes you'll find in the following articles:

- **Forts and structures.** The first three articles are about supporting children's fort making, shelter construction, and building inclinations. The fact that the programs are located in Maryland, Illinois, and California indicates that this is a universal fascination of children. It's the first step toward children making their own homes in the world.

- **Sit spots.** Sit spots are common in many nature-based programs. A sit spot essentially is a place a child has found for themselves in the woods—at the base of a tree, on top of a rock, in the midst of a fern dell—where they sit or stand quietly for a set amount of time without talking, just quietly observing the world around them. Children spend less time in sit spots in the beginning of the year and develop into spending longer periods later. (It's a little bit like meditation, but that's controversial in some quarters.) Jessica Newberry describes how she made this practice part of their routine on forest days and how she had to modify it for some children.

- **Mud kitchens and woodland bakeries.** This is another coast-to-coast and 'round-the-world phenomenon. Collect a bunch of aluminum cake pans, plastic cups, chipped dishware, forks, spoons, and spatulas. Store them on shelves or in an easy-to-open cabinet next to a supply of loose dirt or sand, and your mud kitchen is open for business. And expect that children are likely to eat a little dirt. But consider that a type of bacteria present in mud, when isolated and fed to rats, increased their serotonin and decreased their anxiety—making them able to navigate mazes quicker. Similarly, it may be that mud helps children get smarter. (See an article on why dirt is good for kids at www.npr.org/sections/health-shots/2017/07/16/537075018/dirt-is-good-why-kids-need-exposure-to-germs.) And in winter, when it's really too cold to be outside, Harriet Hart shows how you can bring the natural world inside to stimulate dramatic play.

- **Tools.** The last set of articles shows the resonance of this childhood fascination across ethnicities and socioeconomic status. Alicia Jimenez works at the Storyteller Children Center, a program for mostly Latino at-risk and homeless children in Santa Barbara, California. Sarah Sheldon works with mostly white children from well-off families at the Chicago Botanic Gardens in the Chicago suburbs. Both groups of children are fascinated with real tools. And, more specifically, Sarah opens up the diverse possibilities of brooms—of all shapes and sizes. Who would have thunk that such a simple household implement would offer worlds of play opportunities for children?

I see many of the recurrent themes in this chapter—special places, mud kitchens, fascination with tools—as examples of convergent cultural evolution. In other words, the same kinds of activities or cultural practices evolve in completely different places over time. Children in São Paulo, Brazil, and Saint Paul, Minnesota, are both inclined to build cabanas, or forts, without being influenced by each other. The impulse is coming up and out of children's genetic dispositions to make their own shelters when given the right materials and a suitable setting. When presented with lots of small flowers, children everywhere create flower tiaras. When presented with small streams, children everywhere want to dam them.

I've seen the same thing in regards to chocolate. Dry, well-decayed conifer wood turns into a soft, brownish powder that children across the continent (literally in Maine, Virginia, and British Columbia) transform into chocolate. And the availability of chocolate encourages the children to start baking, which in one Maine school led to the creation of the Chocolate River Bakery. These recurrent play motifs suggest a hidden curriculum of possibilities that savvy teachers both allow to emerge or subtly foment.

All of the educators represented in this chapter recognize what children deeply want and need and provide the scaffolding (the materials, place, generous amounts of time, and guidelines for use) that allow the playful learning to flourish.

Fortlandia: The Kingdom of Learning

by Michel Anderson

WALDORF
SCHOOL OF BALTIMORE
Baltimore, Maryland

It is no surprise that children love forts. Chances are high that anyone reading this can recall a childhood memory of building a fort. And with good reason—forts offer humans (especially small humans) a plethora of sensorial and imaginative splendor. They are special places where learning occurs on an intimate level that is often overlooked by school systems.

At the Waldorf School of Baltimore, we encourage our students to build forts in the school yard. We do this by offering them elemental loose parts—sticks, stones, string, leaves, and straw—and the modest invitation to "build something." From those humble parts and simple words, a magnificent kingdom was born. This kingdom isn't some childhood paradise—it is as complex as our adult world. Dragons, spies, and knights are everywhere—and, yes, dubious bankers exist too. Life in the kingdom gets confusing. At recess, a teacher's primary role is to ensure the physical and emotional safety of the students; the secondary role is to help them develop the mental tools needed to navigate the rich experiences they are crafting. Teachers are not there to solve their problems;

they are there to help the children learn how to solve their own problems.

At the Waldorf School of Baltimore, we understand that learning does not only occur in the classroom, and recess is not simply "taking a break." Recess is academic in its own right—it is a time of synthesis. Students are not only constructing forts; they are developing their social awareness and learning to manage the complexity of the world.

The **WALDORF SCHOOL OF BALTIMORE** is an independent, coeducational school that was established in 1971. It serves a diverse population of students from both Baltimore city and county. The school aspires to educate and inspire children to think, feel, and act with depth, imagination, and purpose. The Forest Aftercare Program provides an after-school, nature-based program for children from pre-K through eighth grade. Free play, gardening, and animal husbandry are key aspects of the program. Children and teachers are outside nearly every day—rain, snow, or shine.

Shelters

by Megan Gessler

CONNECTING INFORMATION TO ACTION

Our class had been reading books on various animal homes. They had taken several hikes looking for nests, dens, tunnels, hollowed-out logs, and beaver lodges. It seemed a natural evolution when they became inspired to try their own hands at shelter construction. There was group discussion on how to undertake such a project. They thought about where they would like to build a shelter and what they would need. Some students became the natural leaders in the group as they began to enlist workers for various tasks. They used their growing communication skills to elicit cooperation and teamwork. Some children were tasked with gathering the sticks and logs needed for construction. Others were looking for best placement of the branches to ensure full coverage and stability. To move the larger branches, the students needed to be aware of where their bodies were, where the

ends of the branches were, and where their classmates were. This took a lot of planning, spatial awareness, coordination, communication, and collaboration.

ENGINEERING

The children started out using teepee-style construction to create the shelter. Although we had not discussed this type of construction, it seemed to be innate. All of the children had an understanding of the structure as they worked, and they often paused to check out the construction to make sure that the sticks were leaning just so. If the structure was starting to lean too far in one direction, they would stop and move things around until they got the right angle.

This was STEM exploration at its finest—a completely organic learning opportunity that provided hands-on experience with engineering and construction. Through planning, building, stacking, balancing, and angling, these students were gaining a lot of experience to build upon in later learning.

KINETIC ENGAGEMENT

The physical labor of carrying several sticks at one time or carrying heavy logs as a team demanded concentration and muscle coordination. As logs were being heaved upright into place, the students relied on their budding gross-motor skills as well as the skills of their classmates. Precariously climbing the structure to place branches at the top

of the fort demanded balance and stability. The students exuded a palpable air of confidence in their teamwork and their capabilities.

RISK

Throughout the construction phase, there was a steady humming of communication. The children discussed stick placement, asked classmates for assistance, and chatted about possible shelter usage. The focused conversation was interrupted occasionally by students collectively initiating their new team chant: "Can we build it? Yes, we can!" With this team confidence and support, the students were trying out new physical feats of climbing, carrying, and balancing. They were pushing the boundaries of their physical bodies. They were taking risks. Sometimes a student would slip or lose their grip on a log, but the children never faltered. They would get back up or figure out how to work around the issue. Most of the time, things were solved through peer encouragement or assistance.

EXTENDED EXPLORATION

The construction activity did not stop after this single experiment. The students kept deconstructing this particular shelter and reimagining it whenever given the chance over the course of about three weeks. They also created several other structures in the woods that they designed for animals to take shelter in during inclement weather. They created a shelter for squirrels in an Osage orange grove that was complete with hidden hedge apples for squirrel snacks. They created a coyote den, a soft deer bed, and even a log cabin for lost hikers.

The simple introduction to animal homes through our readings led to a very in-depth look at shelter construction and usage. The cross-curricular activity that stemmed from learning about animals and their homes was astounding and yet was born from simple and organic inquiry. Allowing the students to apply their knowledge and learn from their experience provided the opportunity for growth that may not have happened inside a traditional classroom.

CONNECTIONS TO STANDARDS

ILLINOIS EARLY LEARNING STANDARDS

PHYSICAL/HEALTH

19.A.ECa Engage in active play using gross- and fine-motor skills. *(Building shelters)*
19.A.ECb Move with balance and control in a range of physical activities. *(Building shelters)*
19.A.ECc Use strength and control to accomplish tasks. *(Building shelters)*
19.B.ECa Coordinate movements to perform complex tasks. *(Building shelters)*

LANGUAGE ARTS

5C.ECa Participate in group projects or units of study designed to learn about a topic of interest. *(Building shelters)*

SOCIAL STUDIES

14.D.ECa Develop an awareness of what it means to be a leader. *(Some children naturally showed this quality while taking the lead on engineering and construction.)*

SOCIAL/EMOTIONAL

30.C.ECb Demonstrate persistence and creativity in seeking solutions to problems. *(Reworking structural issues in construction of shelters)*
30.C.ECd Demonstrate engagement and sustained attention in activities. *(Shelter building over the course of three weeks)*
31.B.ECc Engage in cooperative group play. *(Shelter building)*

NATURAL BEGINNINGS EARLY LEARNING PROGRAM is a September-to-May nature preschool program that introduces children ages three through six to the world around them by exploring various nature-based themes. We offer two-day and three-day classes for children. The Natural Beginnings Program takes place at the Hoover Forest Preserve in Yorkville, Illinois, with over 350 acres of prairie, streams, and woodlands to explore. Students are immersed in seasonal themes through nature walks, studying natural phenomenon, and engaging in activities that build physical, emotional, and academic skills.

Sit Spots: Rainbows and Puffy Little Clouds

Marion Cross School
Norwich, Vermont

by Jennifer Newberry

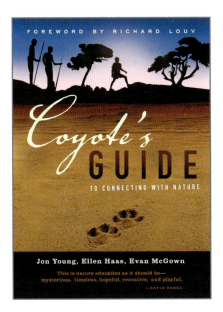

Using sit spots is one of my favorite core routines of Forest Friday. When I first read about the routine in *Coyote's Guide to Connecting with Nature* (Young, Haas, and McGown 2011), I envisioned each child leaning up against a tree beaming with joy, so silent and hypnotized by the song of birds and so focused that wildlife would appear, and we all would wonder and observe in awe. There may have even been rainbows and puffy little clouds in my image. This is our third year of introducing sit spots, and it has never been quite like my idealistic hopes, but I have seen some amazing growth in my students.

ADAPTING TO THE NEEDS AND OPPORTUNITIES OF THE MOMENT

Depending on the group, sit spots have needed to be revised or adjusted to meet the needs of the students. My colleague Ashley and I have decided to try something a little different this year because we have a large group of thirty-five kindergartners. We could not imagine thirty-five students trying to share what they noticed in their sit spots. We have grouped our students into smaller units, with each group having one or two adults. Each group has their own section within the boundaries of Forest Friday. Each group came up with a name. My group decided on Spiders and Salamanders. They are active and social, and the group is boy heavy.

CHOOSING A PLACE TO DEVELOP AWARENESS

On our first day of introducing sit spots, we encouraged students to try out different spaces, and we walked our own boundaries. The following Friday, students were tasked to find their own sit spots. It was challenging for two of my students to find their spot—one boy wanted his up in a tree. Lucas couldn't find a spot. I tried to help him. He was resistant and nothing worked. Finally I had him choose between two different spots that I picked out. I needed him to sit because others had started to replicate his behavior. Well, Lucas was quite vocal about not being content with his spot.

It was dark, boring, and there wasn't anything to look at. I wondered if it was too far away from others. He was clearly not happy and unable to move past it. Our sit spot time felt unsuccessful, and I needed to reflect and adjust to the energy and engagement of my students.

CONSIDER A CHILD'S PASSION

The next week, I chose not to have the children focus on their senses. This is what we have done in the past, and at the end of sit spot time, we share what we noticed. I felt that they needed a specific task to get them acquainted with their own spot. The task was to make a mouse house—a small structure made with natural materials, just big enough for a mouse. Lucas chose another space closer to his peers within a patch of sunshine. At the end of our sit spot time, instead of sharing what we observed, we went on a mouse house tour and got a chance to visit everyone's mouse house.

"Effective teaching is a constant process of adjustment, judgment, and responding to the energy and engagement of the students."
—*Sir Ken Robinson*

CONNECTING WITH THE NATURAL WORLD

At each sit spot time since then, the Spiders and Salamanders have added to their mouse houses, and they look to see if there have been any changes to them since we have last visited. I asked if there was any evidence of visitors to our houses. If so, who do the children think came for a visit? One student noticed some pinecone scales and reached a conclusion that a squirrel came for a visit and had some pinecone because he was getting ready for winter.

On the third Friday of sit spots, three boys were being vocal and started to become disruptive. As a distraction, I asked them in a whisper, "Do you speak forest?" One boy immediately whispered back, "No." Another boy tilted his head, perplexed, and murmured, "You mean trees talk?" and just then from about ten feet away, Lucas called out, "Did you hear that?" He very excitedly pointed up to the sky, walked on his tiptoes, and said, "It's a pileated woodpecker." All the Spiders and Salamanders gathered around Lucas and peered into the sky while Lucas described the woodpecker. "He is black with white on his wings"—Lucas flapped his arms as if he had wings—"and a red pointy head." Right then, the woodpecker flew out of the tree. After our very brief, silent moment of wonder and awe, I said, "I do believe Lucas speaks forest." The Spiders and Salamanders ran off yelling at the top of their lungs how they were going to add more rooms to their mouse houses. I chuckled and pictured my rainbow and puffy little clouds in the sky.

CONNECTIONS TO STANDARDS

VERMONT EARLY LEARNING STANDARDS

APPROACHES TO LEARNING

Children show curiosity about the world around them, take action to interact with it, and learn. *(Creating mouse houses and observing, exploring, and noticing what is different about their sit spots)*

SCIENCE

Children construct concepts about the characteristics of living organisms, their biology, and ecosystems through exploration and investigations. *(Investigating and developing a theory about the pinecone)*

MARION CROSS SCHOOL is a nurturing kindergarten-through-sixth-grade public school located in Norwich, Vermont. There are currently two full-day kindergarten classes that go out into the forest for most of the day on Fridays. The Milton Frye Nature Preserve has so much to offer, including natural streams to explore the properties of water, trails with a wide variety of trees that change with the seasons, and wildlife that depend upon both. These resources give children tangible ways of working with and in nature to increase their intimate connection to it. Some investigations might take the whole school year as we explore the changes that occur in nature over time.

The Woodland Bakery

by Harriet Hart

Dandelion and Snail Preschool
Bringing the Outdoors in:
Twinfield Union School
Plainfield, Vermont

Twinfield Union School
Plainfield, Vermont

On a cool day in early spring, I noticed some of our students deeply engaged in soup making. They had discovered a puddle in the loose parts play area, rummaged for buckets and scoops, and hunted for pinecones and grass to add as ingredients. At this moment, I deemed them ready for the return of our dramatic play bakery. Only this time the bakery wouldn't be inside the classroom: it would be out in the woods!

CREATING THE SPACE

In an ideal world, I would have created a space that had multiple levels: pans up high to reach for, the shelves of the oven down low, and in between an array of utensils on hooks and cake pans on shelves. I would have made sure that there were open spaces and closed spaces to play in. I would have created a space that encouraged and supported the children's cooking games while offering them a sense of ownership over their play.

In reality we worked with what we had. Out in our woodland play area, there is an old desk

that the children like to play around and underneath. On the day we set up the bakery, it was firmly frozen to the ground, dictating the layout. This led us to discover that while enclosed spaces are a delight to our students, laying out a boundary with logs works almost as well. We added tools for digging; a pool for collecting rainwater; utensils for stirring, scooping, and flipping; and mixing bowls, muffin trays, and cake tins. We made a recipe book, which they used to give their play authenticity.

FACILITATING PLAY

"We need customers! We need customers!" Jared shouts at the top of his lungs. He had been busy making muffins and was now drawing attention to the missing role within our bakery setup. At the sound of his voice, friends gathered outside of the bakery to purchase sweet treats without the aid of a plastic till or fake money. Watching our students explore this new area, we noticed as they drew on all of the knowledge that they had stored up over the year, from the field trip to the bakery to the gingerbread baby stories, from the indoor dramatic play area to the modeling that we had

provided outdoors. Here we found them integrating all of their experiences and becoming deeply engaged and absorbed in their culinary creations.

We limited the number of students who could play in the bakery at any one time. This improved the students' chances of successfully negotiating, sharing, collaborating, and planning, while allowing them to delve more deeply into their games with fewer interruptions.

CONNECTIONS TO STANDARDS

VERMONT EARLY LEARNING STANDARDS

Element 3: Theatre (Dramatic Play)
Goal 1: Children engage in dramatic play and theatre as a way to represent real-life experiences, communicate their ideas and feelings, learn, and use their imaginations.

Element 1: Emotions and Self-Regulation
Goal 1: Children express a range of emotions and regulate their emotional and social responses. *(Cooperative play, sharing, and collaboration within the bakery)*

Element 1: Motor Development and Coordination
Goal 2: Children develop strength, eye-hand coordination, and control of their small- or fine-motor muscles. *(Using the kitchen utensils, selecting ingredients, using the turkey basters, coordinating holding and stirring)*

Element 1: Foundational Reading Skills
Goal 1: Children develop the foundational skills needed for engaging with print, reading, and writing. *(Using the recipe book)*

DANDELION AND SNAIL PRESCHOOL is the public preschool program at Twinfield Union School in Plainfield, Vermont, serving children from ages three to five, with two half-day programs. The morning class is partnered with Head Start. Twinfield Union School provides free breakfast and lunch for all students.

Exploring Nature Themes in Dramatic Play

Dandelion and Snail Preschool
Bringing the Outdoors in:
Twinfield Union School
Plainfield, Vermont

Twinfield Union School
Plainfield, Vermont

by Harriet Hart

In January and February, northern New England can experience some very low temperatures, and this sometimes impacts our outdoor play. In our classroom this winter, we have been developing ways to continue to think about and interact with nature even when we cannot go out to play in the woods. We want to infuse our classroom with reminders of the natural world, bringing elements of the outdoors inside so that even when severe weather prevents outdoor play, our students are continuing to build their relationship and understanding of nature. Our first idea was to transform the dramatic play area into a campground.

SETTING UP CAMP

We borrowed an open-sided tent that allowed us to observe students at play. We added fake plastic food for picnics, backpacks, a saucepan, spoons, small mugs, blankets, pillows, animal puppets, and

a flashlight. Before we gave the students free rein, we modeled how to move around in the space. After a week of exploratory play in which picnics were made, monsters were warded off, bears and dolphins frolicked, and humans quietly slept in the tent, we added the means to build a fake fire. This final element created a link to our current unit of study, fires and fire making.

SUPPORTING DRAMATIC PLAY

After two weeks of observing student play, we noticed that many students had little or no experience of going camping and needed a broader frame of reference to inform their play. They needed more ideas about that theme to feed their imaginations.

In order to extend their experience and support the students in the exploration of the camping theme, we

- researched picture books that told camping stories and added them to the current library;

- used our talking stick to share ideas of what you do when you go camping;

- told stories 'round our fake fire;

- told a story about a camping trip and then took small groups into the play area to act it out; and

- turned our camping story into a picture book to add to our library.

Bringing outdoor themes and outdoor materials into the dramatic play area has given us opportunities to explore an experience that some students have not had in a space that feels safe and comfortable to them. It has forged a meaningful link between our outdoor-focused teaching philosophy and our indoor space while enabling staff and students to make cohesive connections between our outdoor play and the indoor aspects of our program.

CONNECTIONS TO STANDARDS

VERMONT EARLY LEARNING STANDARDS

CREATIVE ARTS AND EXPRESSION

Element 3: Theatre (Dramatic Play)
Goal 1: Children engage in dramatic play and theatre as a way to represent real-life experiences, communicate their ideas and feelings, learn, and use their imaginations.

APPROACHES TO LEARNING

Element 1: Play and Exploration
Goal 1: Children engage in play to understand the world around them.

LITERACY DEVELOPMENT

Element 2: Reading Element 2a: Engagement with Literature and Informational Text
Goal 1: Children develop "book language" and demonstrate comprehension.
Goal 3: Make connections between stories and real-life experiences.
Goal 4: Retell or re-enact a familiar story in the correct sequence of a familiar story's major events with prompting and support.

DANDELION AND SNAIL PRESCHOOL is the public preschool program at Twinfield Union School in Plainfield, Vermont, serving children from ages three to five, with two half-day programs. The morning class is partnered with Head Start. Twinfield Union School provides free breakfast and lunch for all students.

Feel the Rhythm: Using Real Tools

Santa Barbara, California

by Alicia Jimenez

Children feel empowered using real tools! Some of them have observed someone in their families using tools, and they are aware of the hazards of the job. Taking the risk and following safety guidelines gives excitement to our children. They will build confidence from this challenge by doing it! The strength that two small hands need to make a deep cut on a thick branch is enormous, and the self-control and engagement are greater.

Angelina mumbled, "Back and forth, back and forth." Taking pauses to breathe deeply, she exclaimed, "This is hard, teacher, but I can do it." When she noticed the small dent on the branch, she shouted excitedly, "I did it, I did it!"

THE VALUE OF TEAMWORK

During our dialogue about safety precautions using real tools, Elijah was attentive and explained to his peers, "Everybody, my daddy said that I need to be careful, because saws can make you get blood if you touch the sharp little things." Later during the week, we began to use the saw, and he supported his peers, coaching them and me. "Bottom to the top, back and forth."

The interaction that a child establishes between a tool and an object is like playing a musical instrument because it requires total concentration. Isabella, one of the older girls in the group, describes this harmony as she says to her peers, "Look, you need to listen to the sound when you are using the saw." She continues, "Put the saw in the same spot, move it, and if you hear it, you are cutting the branch."

PREP ACTIVITIES PRIOR TO USING REAL TOOLS

1. Introduce one tool at a time, describing motion (back and forth, top and bottom).

2. Use soft materials for practice, such as bar soap (potato peelers), small branches (saw), and cardboard (hammering nails).

3. Set simple safety guidelines along with children, evaluate possible hazards, and communicate needs with coteachers.

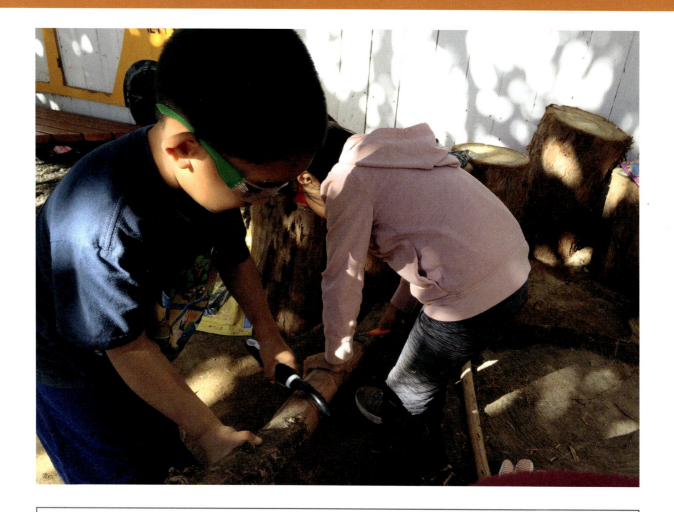

CONNECTIONS TO STANDARDS

CALIFORNIA FOUNDATIONS STANDARDS

SOCIAL-EMOTIONAL DEVELOPMENT

Social Interaction. 4.0 Cooperation and Responsibility.
(Children's cooperation with adult instructions is more reliable because of better capacities for self-control. Cooperation among peers and adults has been nurtured for this and other activities. Children are taking risks to gain other skills, such as using real tools.)

PHYSICAL DEVELOPMENT

Fundamental Movement Skills. 3.0 Manipulative Skills. Perceptual–Motor Skills and Movement Concepts 3.4 Demonstrate more precision and efficiency during two-handed fine-motor activities.
(Children show increasing fine-motor manipulative skills using hands and arms such as in-hand manipulation, hand-eye coordination during an extended time, as well as precision using real tools such as potato peelers, folding saws, and hammers.)
Health. Safety. 1.0 Injury Prevention
(Children follow safety rules more independently, though they may still need adult support and prompting. Children have a dialogue about possible hazards and participate in creating safety guidelines.)

STORYTELLER CHILDREN'S CENTER is a therapeutic preschool that provides high-quality early childhood education for homeless and at-risk children in Santa Barbara County, as well as comprehensive support services for their families. We serve eighty families each year.

Importance of Tools

by Sarah Sheldon

Socrates once said, "Wisdom begins in wonder." Tools can directly support the wonderment and awe of the natural world while developing affective and cognitive processes. Every tool has a purpose in the great outdoors (and in the classroom, too), from gardening tools to mirrors, spray bottles, mud kitchen supplies, magnifying lenses, and pinwheels. Many tools are handheld implements used to carry out a particular function. Tools can also be devices that are used to accomplish a task. Every morning after outdoor play, the children and I come together and practice a few yoga poses before heading out on the daily hike or exploration. Yoga is used to calm the body and mind and transition between outdoor play and outdoor learning.

Children are continually shaping their direct learning environment with tools and thus being shaped in return. The use of tools lays the foundation for an interconnected and experiential learning community in which children are able to move through zones of proximal development. Tools provide children the opportunity to do serious work, which shapes how they define and interact with the world. When children use tools, they build on their life experiences and grow their knowledge base. Tools as a center focus in nature-based curriculum can support the individual learner, respect the institution, and meet societal demands for "kindergarten readiness."

Cyrus and his friends were playing make-believe one morning. One was a shark, one a pirate, and one an explorer. "Let's go on a treasure hunt," I overheard one of the children say.

With the above phrase in my mind, I pulled bingo boards as a springboard tool for the daily hike. When it came time for morning yoga, we came together and practiced the tree, rock, and butterfly poses; these poses were also items listed on the bingo boards. I then introduced the bingo boards and explained to the children that we were going on a treasure hunt!

Cyrus, pointing to his board, said, "I still need bugs!" "Where could we look?" I asked. Watson said, "Bugs live in the soil." Jasper said, "Digging spoons, we need digging spoons!" But before any insects in the soil were found, Violet squealed, "Cicada shells!" Out came the magnifying lenses, small containers, and tweezers from the backpack. The children excitedly collected, counted, and examined their nature treasures.

Charlotte told her friends, "It's an exoskeleton." Kinley said, "What's an exoskeleton?" Charlotte said, "It's a bug shell!" Kinley, taking a closer look, said, "It's brown." Leon, holding the shell in his hands, said, "It sticks to my fingers!" Charlotte said, "It flew away."

Together, tools and nature have the ability to create a kind of community where every child is an active member in their own pursuit of knowledge. On any given day, you will find my backpack full of tools for the children to explore the garden.

CONNECTIONS TO STANDARDS

ILLINOIS EARLY LEARNING STANDARDS

THE ARTS

25.A.ECa,b Movement and Dance: Build awareness of and explore. Drama: Begin to appreciate and participate.
26.B.ECa Use creative arts as an avenue for self-expression.
(Dramatic play, nature yoga movement, and creative representation)

LANGUAGE ARTS

1.B.ECa,b,c Use language for a variety of purposes, participate in collaborative conversations through two or more exchanges.
(Conversing about insects and exoskeletons, dramatic play)

SCIENCE

11.A.ECa Plan and carry out simple investigations. Collect and describe observations and investigations.
12.A.ECb Show an awareness of changes that occur in the environment.
(Using bingo boards to investigate nature, collecting and describing cicada shells, beginning to describe metamorphosis)

The **CHICAGO BOTANIC GARDEN NATURE PRESCHOOL**, located in Glencoe, Illinois, is a private preschool that serves children ages three to five. Three-year-olds meet for two-and-a-half hours on Tuesdays and Thursdays, and older students meet for three hours on Mondays, Wednesdays, and Fridays. At the Garden, we cultivate the power of plants to sustain and enrich life. Within this context, the Preschool strives to create meaningful relationships with the natural world.

The Wonderful World of Brooms

CHICAGO BOTANIC GARDEN
Glencoe, Illinois

by Sarah Sheldon

The wonderful world of brooms—who knew? Brooms in the outdoor classroom have always been a popular choice for the children. But as the weather has turned cold in Chicago, with very little snow, brooms have replaced the winter tool of snow shovels. Like shovels, brooms provide the opportunity for serious work, engaging the students' minds and bodies, keeping their play active and their cores warm.

The ordinary broom transforms in the child's world of play. It provides both fantasy and authentic learning experiences. From being a simple sweeping device, to boat oars and rail wheels, to a nonscientific tool for experimentation, the broom has a bountiful array of possibilities.

Elinor said, "The tree is really tall." Violet, standing on tiptoe and bracing herself with one hand, replied, "Well, my broom is tall." Elinor said, "Yeah, but mine is the tallest." Charolette, who had been quietly observing, said, "I'll be the baby broom, okay?" The three girls giggled and agreed as they all raised their brooms in the air as high as they could.

Emily alternated between running her mittens over the various bristles and sweeping the ground. After each cycle of inquiry, she stopped to investigate how much soil remained on the

ground. She concluded that the straw broom worked best.

Meanwhile, Jasper excitedly exclaimed, "Ms. Sarah, the sand is frozen!" I wondered out loud why it was frozen. "Because it's cold," Jasper replied with glee. I cautioned Jasper that if he tried to dig in the frozen sand with his dustpan, it may break. Just then, Jasper noticed the sand on the ground! He immediately began sweeping the sand from beneath the table into his dustpan.

Then, ever so carefully, Jasper would add his dust-pan sand to the frozen sand table.

After some time, Jasper became more interested in the sand that was on the ground than the sand that was in the table. He began using a larger broom and announced, "Ooh, it makes a pattern!" "What kind of pattern?" I inquired. "A smooth one, look!" He delightedly paused to show me.

Later in the day, the students collectively built a train. "I am the conductor," chimed Hunter. With one broom in each hand, he began to move the broomsticks forward and backward, "chugging" the train along.

Bosen wailed, "Stop! The tracks are dirty!" He hopped out of the train and began sweeping. Mack said, "Let's bring the solstice tree." Bosen said, "Okay, ready!" Hunter, who had been waiting patiently, chimed in again, "All aboard the solstice train!" And away they went!

CONNECTIONS TO STANDARDS

ILLINOIS EARLY LEARNING STANDARDS

PHYSICAL HEALTH

19.A.ECa,c,d Engage in active play using gross- and fine-motor skills, use strength and control to accomplish tasks, use hand-eye coordination to perform tasks.
(Using brooms in the various fashions described, sweeping sand into dustpan and returning it to the table)

MATHEMATICS

7.A.ECb Use nonstandard units to measure attributes.
8.AECa Compare and describe objects according to characteristics.
(Measuring the tree with brooms, describing the sand)

SOCIAL/EMOTIONAL

31.A.ECb,e Recognize the feelings and perspectives of others, develop positive relationship with peers.
(Conductor Hunter waiting for his friends to complete their train tasks, developing friendships with peers)

The **CHICAGO BOTANIC GARDEN NATURE PRESCHOOL,** located in Glencoe, Illinois, is a private preschool that serves children ages three to five. Three-year-olds meet for two-and-a-half hours on Tuesdays and Thursdays, and older students meet for three hours on Mondays, Wednesdays, and Fridays. At the Garden, we cultivate the power of plants to sustain and enrich life. Within this context, the Preschool strives to create meaningful relationships with the natural world.

CHAPTER 3

Policies and Practices for Outdoor Programming

Remember when I said at the beginning of chapter 1 that taking children outdoors is full of promise *and* laden with challenges? Here's how to take on the challenges. From "How do we structure the day?" to "What about sticks?" to "What about those pesky licensing standards?" you'll find answers, or at least the beginnings of answers, to all those questions here. (Except for the question about pooping and peeing outside. Somehow none of the contributors addressed this topic, though they all deal with it. Something for the next book . . .)

SCHEDULE AND RULES

We start in the still-a-little-bit wild west with Jane Strader's documents from the Teton Community School in Victor, Idaho. Even though this school huddles in the morning shadows of the Tetons, they don't have a great woodsy area to explore near the school. So one day a week, they travel via school bus to spend their day in a corner of national forest. Jane nicely breaks down the day into consumable, understandable parts. This, along with the schedule of Wednesday in the Woods in Hartland, Vermont, in the introduction to chapter 2, provides a good prototype for how to structure your day. Jane's next document on Woods Rules lays out three simple rules and how they get children acclimated to them. The worksheets they've developed, illustrated in her article, are completed in the classroom after the rules have been discussed with the children. This process of talking about the rule and then having children draw a picture of abiding by the rule is a great way to help children internalize what they need to remember. I particularly like their big-animal drill, necessitated by the fact that they might encounter bears or moose while in the woods. One child's Woods Rules worksheet included a drawing of a child, a teacher, and . . . a unicorn! Isn't it wonderful that we work in places where encountering unicorns is still possible?

PUBLIC SCHOOL PRESCHOOL

In Vermont early childhood educators have welcomed the advent of public school preschool programs with a mixture of enthusiasm and ambivalence. On the one hand, educators are enthusiastic that public preschool affords more children, particularly those from families with limited means, access to public education at an early age. On the other hand, some educators fear that public school preschools will just mean more overly academic curriculum at a younger age. Nature-based preschool educators to the rescue! If public school preschools can adopt a nature-based approach, they hold more promise for helping children develop social-emotional readiness, early literacy and math skills, and healthy, physically active lifestyles. Harriet Hart's article describes the thinking that went into the public preschool at the Twinfield Elementary School in Plainfield, the next town over from Montpelier, the capitol in north-central Vermont. Other public nature preschools have taken root in Huntington, Norwich, and Guilford along with a grassroots movement among kindergarten teachers to have a forest day one day a week. This preschool and kindergarten movement is also exerting upward influence on teachers of the elementary grades. All elementary-age children deserve more learning and playing time in nature.

RISKY BEHAVIOR

Audrey Fergason introduces us to one of the core issues—the concern that being in the woods is risky and will encourage risky behavior in the children. To the contrary, numerous studies have shown that the frequency of injuries is higher on conventional playgrounds than equal amounts of time spent in natural settings. The problem is that parents and school leaders have forgotten how to differentiate between risks and hazards. Instead they've fallen into a risk-minimization mind-set—that is, we must act to eliminate all risk. Some adults think that if a child picks up a stick, someone might get poked in the eye; therefore, no picking up sticks. Instead, we need to adopt a risk-benefit mind-set that balances the risks of certain behaviors with an appreciation of the benefits of those behaviors. Without risk, there is no reward. And without the child's opportunity to measure risk—is this tree branch safe to put my weight on?—the child will never learn to manage risk on their own.

Adults perform risk-benefit analyses every day, oftentimes without thinking about them. Putting children in a car to take them to school is a high-risk activity. But we have decided that the benefits of using an automobile outweigh the risk of a potential accident. The same parents who ban picking up sticks might also encourage their children to play soccer because, to them, the benefits of teamwork, physical exercise, and strategic thinking outweigh the risk of a broken ankle or a concussion. We need this same risk-benefit mind-set in relationship to nature play and learning. In the face of the obesity epidemic, we should support nature-based early childhood education if only for its physical activity benefits. For example, researchers found that Ontario preschoolers spend twice as much time being active when play is outdoors versus indoors (ParticipACTION 2015). And adventure playgrounds or forested areas with loose parts (places with risky elements) lead to an increase in physical activity and a decrease in sedentary behaviors. ParticipACTION, a Canadian nonprofit, boldly stated in their 2015 report card that "access to active play in nature and outdoors—with its risks—is essential for healthy child development."

Instead of just identifying risk, we need to see that the long-term health benefits of moderately risky behavior are just as important as safety. Audrey's description of the rough-and-tumble play in her Forest Gnomes program is one example of a moderately risky behavior that has physical benefits—development of coordination, muscle tone, and aerobic capacity. This same thinking is illustrated in the following article about fire. Fire is an integral part of being outside in cold weather. Its benefits outweigh its risks, and learning fire behavior can be an integral part of your program.

In addition, I recommend that a no-picking-up-sticks policy is largely unenforceable and counterproductive. Sticks are one of your greatest resources! In fact, the National Toy Hall of Fame inducted the stick as a member in 2008 and described the stick's merits this way:

> The stick may be the world's oldest toy. Animals play with sticks, and we use them to play fetch with our dogs. Children find sticks an endless source of make-believe fun. Sticks can turn into swords, magic wands, majorette batons, fishing poles, and light sabers. When children pretend with sticks, they cultivate their creativity and develop their imaginations. Sticks are all around us; they are natural and free. . . . Sticks are not only possibly the oldest toys, they're possibly the best! (The Strong Museum of Play 2008)

When Michel Anderson found that the children at the Baltimore Waldorf School wanted to duel with bamboo stalks, he was tempted to outlaw the activity—too dangerous. Instead, he acknowledged that he loved this activity when he was a child and figured out a way to mitigate the risk while maintaining the fun and benefits. He created a set of dueling swords wrapped on the front end with foam pipe insulation. He purchased inexpensive eye guards like those used in science labs, and he designated a specific part of the playground as the fencing arena. Voilà! The risks were mitigated and the benefits of dueling—coordination, quick reflexes, self-defense, and aerobic physical activity—were preserved.

LICENSURE PROTOCOLS

Ah, the dreaded state licensure compliance officers. They strike fear into our hearts! Really, though, we just have to think about them as colleagues who want what is best for children but sometimes have a different mind-set. This finding of common ground is illustrated in Maryfaith Decker's articles. Since her preschool uses many of the 451 acres of the Lime Hollow Nature Center, the Office of Children and Family Services initially recommended placing four-foot fencing around every stream, creek, bog, and pond. That was clearly impossible. They reached a solution by creating a fenced, licensable outdoor play area next to the indoor facility and then designated any time spent outside of the play area as field trips, which have different guidelines than outside play areas. To gain approval for extensive field trips, Maryfaith then created field trip protocols for stream play, tree climbing, cold weather, and hot weather. The Office of Children and Family Services licensors now encourage other early childhood programs to use these same protocols.

This is all part of attempts to get licensing agencies to understand both that nature-based programs are good for children and that licensing guidelines need to be adapted or changed in order to provide the kind of balance between risk and safety described above. In 2017 the state of Washington commenced a five-year program to write guidelines for outdoor preschools. This is a promising development that, hopefully, will spread to other states across the country.

DOCUMENTATION

Maryfaith's last article introduces parent communication and documentation of children's activity and learning in these programs. She articulates that "our plan for documentation and parent communication is designed to address our need to have parents understand the unique opportunities for learning that nature as a classroom provides, give them the language to communicate their children's growth to friends and family members, and provide evidence-based research to share with our community of educators."

Since nature-based early childhood education looks different than its indoor counterpart to parents, administrators, policy makers, and other well-meaning adults, being able to translate what we're doing into a language they can understand is even more important. For example, nature-based programs must be able to translate an activity such as tree climbing from "Oh no—someone could get hurt!" to "This activity meets the standards for coordination, initiative, and developing physical strength."

Diverse forms of communication with parents are useful—from daily or weekly blogs to frequent parent meetings to regular emails or texts about their children to movies about the benefits of nature play. Melissa Frederick's article from her Alabama program on their student letters and student profiles provides a couple of examples of thoughtful assessment of the strengths and challenges of children in their outdoor setting. Having parents volunteer is another useful strategy for getting them on board and understanding what's going on.

If you communicate effectively with parents about what you're trying to accomplish, they can then fold your initiatives into their family culture. Here's an example of a shift in parental understanding from a mother of a child in a Forest Days program in a Vermont public school kindergarten.

I was concerned about this program because my daughter had zero interest in nature when the school year was starting. But we're Vermonters, so all we have is the outdoors—to have a kid who didn't want to go outdoors was a bummer. But now she will look at us and she'll say, "Let's go on a nature walk!" And I'm thinking, "What did you do with my child?" This happened within the first four Wednesdays! That has been awesome for our family because we thought we just had an "indoor kid."

Before this she was into nail polish and "What are you going to do for me?" and now she's out there building fairy houses and coming home with science skills and rocks in her pockets. (Minnucci and Teachout 2018)

OUTDOOR REST TIME

Scandinavian parents have been doing this forever. Walk through the streets in Stockholm on a winter day and you'll see strollers lined up outside of coffee shops. As their parents sip a latte and chat with friends, their infants are napping outside in temperatures as cold as 10 degrees Fahrenheit. Parents say that children sleep longer, and they believe that sleeping outside strengthens the immune system and therefore keeps children healthier.

In the United States, this is mostly unheard of, which makes Katie Swick's description of outdoor naptime at her AllTogetherNow! program in Montpelier provocative. It's also illustrative of how we're trying to change the whole paradigm of children's relationship with the natural world. We're not just talking about increasing outdoor play and learning for a few hours a day. To use Jane Strader's phrase, we're "turning school inside out." This means napping outside, eating outside, encouraging children and parents to walk or bike to school, having phenology-driven curriculum, and organizing parent events around the solstices and equinoxes. These all are ways that we create school policies to encourage tuning family life to the rhythm of the seasons and to the benefits of fresh air.

Days in the Teton Valley Woods

Teton Valley Community School

Victor, Idaho

by Jane Strader

"Teacher Jane, when are we going to the woods? I want to go to the woods today!" says Jack.

This is a common question and overall sentiment among the Teton Valley Community School pre-K Falcon class. A normal day in our pre-K program consists of indoor project time for half of the morning and then outdoor time in our play yard for the rest of the morning until lunch. Over the past two years, we have started to incorporate "woods days" into our program where we spend our morning exploring the national forest land that surrounds our town of Victor, Idaho. This year, we are making a large effort to bring our children to the woods once a week, if not more frequently. What does a woods day look like? How do we make the transition from school to the woods feel good to our children so we can take advantage of our day exploring? What do we do when we are in the woods? Below is our schedule for turning school inside out.

1. **Woods Ready:** When children arrive at school, they are met with a message in the mudroom that has instructions as to what they need in their packs and on their body to be "woods ready." Children get ready with their parents' help and then head out to the play yard to play until everyone has arrived.

2. **Meeting:** We have morning meeting outside once all of the students have arrived. At meeting, we discuss our three woods rules and set an intention for the day.

3. **Bus Ride:** After morning meeting, we load the bus and head to the woods!

4. **Find Base Camp:** Our first task is to find a good base camp. Our base camp setting changes to meet our needs for the day. Once we have found a suitable location, we take off our packs and have a snack.

"Base camp needs to be near a tree in a big circle where you can see everyone."
—*Grace Hatch, age four*

5. **Focused Exploration:** We split into two smaller groups for our focused exploration time. During this time, we intentionally explore the woods, expanding on our project work or uncovering new things to wonder about. We discover things on a micro and macro scale, ask questions, and put our minds and bodies to work. We encourage the children to take the lead, using the dynamic nature of the woods environment to fuel our learning wherever it may lead.

"Ready, set, go! WOOO! Let's light a fire in the fort and the bears will be our friends."

—*Jesse Sheets, age four*

6. **Free Play:** After focused exploration, we meet back at base camp and have free play for the rest of our day in the woods. During free play, children have the opportunity to freely explore, wonder, sense, and engage with one another and the environment on their own terms and in their own ways. We ask children to continue to follow the three woods rules during free play, which sets comfortable boundaries but allows the children to have a large sense of freedom.

7. **Reflection:** We take the time to reflect before leaving the woods by making a circle and sharing a special part of our day with one another.

Back at school, we make a woods day reflection page that has pictures, drawings, and quotes about our woods day and add it to our woods reflection book. Reflecting unearths experiences that have shaped us, feelings that need to be revisited or relived, questions and wonderings we would like to pursue further, and problems that we want to solve.

SEASONAL SHIFTS

Our schedule shifts during the year to build woods capacity and take account of winter weather. In the FALL, we only spend the morning in the woods, coming back to school for lunch and slowly

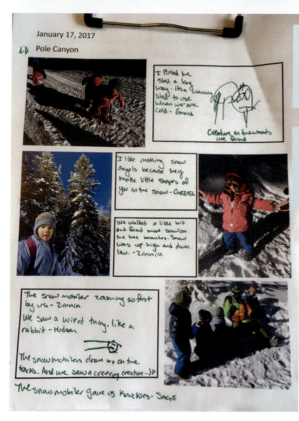

January 17, 2017

♪♪ Pole Canyon

> "I liked sitting in the tree 'cause I liked my feet not touching the ground."
>
> —*Jesse Sheets, age four*

> "We listened to a winter fluff bird. He was making 'coo-coo' noises to find his friends."
>
> —*Lila Ellis, age four*

WOODS DAY SCHEDULE

- **8–9:00** Get "woods ready" and settle in

- **9–9:30** Morning meeting and load the bus

- **9:45** Woods arrival—find base camp and have a snack

- **10:15–11:15** Small-group exploration

- **11:15** Whole class free play

- **11:45** Lunch or load bus and go back to school for lunch, rest, and reflection

- **12:15-12:45** Free play and reflection

- **12:45** Return to school for rest time and reflection journal

building resiliency and comfort in the woods. In the WINTER, we settle in inside and have both snack and lunch at school to keep hands warm and make the most of our time in the wintry weather. In the SPRING, we are finally resilient and able to spend the whole day outside, including meeting, snack, lunch, and time after lunch!

TETON VALLEY COMMUNITY SCHOOL of Teton Science Schools is a project-based, independent school located in Victor, Idaho. We aim to educate the whole child by integrating academic excellence and character development with a community focus. Students in preschool through sixth grade engage in a challenging curriculum that builds core academic knowledge.

The prekindergarten program incorporates the best practices in early childhood education as researched and outlined by the National Association for the Education of Young Children (NAEYC) and is inspired by the innovative early education centers of Reggio Emilia, Italy.

Woods Rules

Teton Valley Community School

Victor, Idaho

by Jane Strader

Teacher Erin begins our class at morning meeting in this way: "Today we are going to the woods! And you know what? It's Kyler's first day in the woods with us. So you know what our job is? We need to tell Kyler about our woods rules!"

We have been going to the woods regularly for the last six months, and since day one, we've started our woods day by repeating our three simple woods rules. By now most of the children have the rules memorized, and we are trying to enable them to hold one another accountable to the rules.

THREE WOODS RULES

Our woods rules are designed to give children as much freedom as possible while still being able to manage hazardous risks. By only having three simple rules, we hope to empower children to explore, manage risks, problem solve, and play freely and creatively. At the beginning of the year, we consistently remind children of and enforce our woods rules. When children choose to break the rules, they lose the privilege to play freely and have to be a teacher's "shadow" for a certain amount of time. After a couple of regular trips to the woods,

children remember the rules and are able to hold themselves and one another accountable. By the end of the year, teachers only remind children of the rules once before going into the woods and once while in the woods. Children enforce the rules rather than teachers, allowing children to feel empowered and free while remaining safe.

"Keep your hands to self."
—*Tess Hibbs, age five*

ANIMAL DRILLS

We share our woods with a number of large mammals that are a potential hazard to our children,

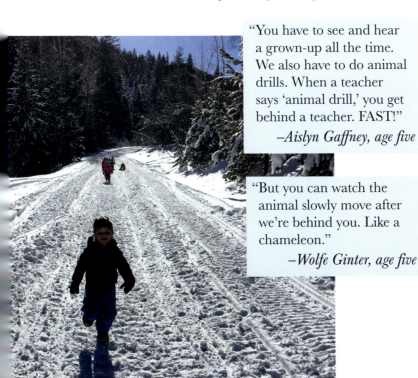

"You have to see and hear a grown-up all the time. We also have to do animal drills. When a teacher says 'animal drill,' you get behind a teacher. FAST!"
—*Aislyn Gaffney, age five*

"But you can watch the animal slowly move after we're behind you. Like a chameleon."
—*Wolfe Ginter, age five*

THREE WOODS RULES

1. **See and hear a teacher at all times**
   Children have the freedom to explore the woods without feeling constricted by physical boundaries, knowing they are safe as long as they can see and hear a teacher.

2. **Keep hands to self**
   This is language we use in our classroom that reminds children what they can do with their hands instead of giving a list of what they cannot do. If children's hands are kept to themselves, they are not pushing, punching, hitting, and so on.

3. **If a stick is bigger than you, you need a friend to help.**
   This rule is to remind children they can work together to build and play with sticks, instead of hitting one another (intentionally or unintentionally).

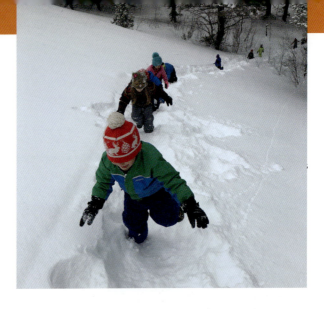

namely bears and moose. Bears and moose can be hard to see and hear and if threatened will charge. To avoid this situation, teachers survey the area before we allow children to roam freely, both teachers carry bear spray, and we have established an animal drill if there is a large-animal sighting. When we yell "animal drill," children know they are to get behind a teacher as fast as possible and stay behind the teacher. We practice animal drills often in the woods, so in the event that we do

encounter a threat, the children are well versed in what to do. Children trust in the teachers to keep them safe, knowing that bears and moose can be a threat, and practicing builds our ability to stay safe and not fear our fellow woods creatures.

> "Be helpful! And get a friend if a stick is bigger than you. Or, if a stick is bigger than you, get a friend to help you carry it."
> —*Jesse Sheets, age four*

CONNECTIONS TO STANDARDS

CREATIVE CURRICULUM STANDARDS
SOCIAL/EMOTIONAL SKILLS

Develops a sense of self. *(Knowing and enforcing these rules demonstrates developing trust in adults and rules to keep themselves safe and a developing ability to stand up for personal rights when enforcing rules on themselves or one another.)*
Develops responsibility for self and others. *(When children remember and enforce rules in the woods, they demonstrate developing abilities to take responsibility for their own safety and follow class rules.)*

COGNITIVE DEVELOPMENT

Develops problem-solving skills. *(Woods rules give children a foundation to solve problems in the woods through safe risk assessment and common language.)*

TETON VALLEY COMMUNITY SCHOOL of Teton Science Schools is a project-based, independent school located in Victor, Idaho. We aim to educate the whole child by integrating academic excellence and character development with a community focus. Students in preschool through sixth grade engage in a challenging curriculum that builds core academic knowledge.

The prekindergarten program incorporates the best practices in early childhood education as researched and outlined by the National Association for the Education of Young Children (NAEYC) and is inspired by the innovative early education centers of Reggio Emilia, Italy.

Nature Preschool in a Public School

Dandelion and Snail Preschool
Bringing the Outdoors in: *Twinfield Union School Plainfield, Vermont*

Twinfield Union School
Plainfield, Vermont

by Harriet Hart

Nature preschools come in all different shapes and sizes, from half-day programs to full day, from five days a week to one or two mornings, from those with no indoor spaces to those with indoor spaces, from those who direct and structure children's play to those who do not. The makeup of each depends upon the organization, the teachers, the climate, the space, and the children. When I first visited Twinfield Union School, I was surprised by how different this nature preschool looked compared to those I had previously seen. Having spent time with the program, I now know that many of those differences are what allow teacher Elaina Foxx to do this work in a public school.

Few public schools run preschools, and few public preschools spend the majority of their time out of doors. Dandelion and Snail Preschool is one of the few. When Elaina Foxx first arrived at Twinfield Union School in Plainfield, Vermont, she continued to work with the indoor model. By the end of that first year, however, she came to the conclusion that an outdoor program would be better able to meet the developmental needs of her students while also providing an important spiritual grounding. In that space, she would be able to honor each child's ability to be as independent as possible while also being a productive member of the classroom community. Her belief in the capabilities of her students led her to begin the process of planning and implementing an outdoor curriculum.

PROCESS AND PARENTS

Much of Elaina's preparation involved reading the literature now available on the philosophies, the benefits, and the implementation of nature-based education. She clarified her values and envisioned a program that would give back to the environment by encouraging respect, love, and connection to nature in her students. She planned meetings with her team and with her school principal to present the changes she wanted to make, and she gained their support without issue. In the days before school began, she planned responses to parent questions and prepared thoroughly to meet the potential concerns of the school community. It was a pleasant surprise when her changes and choices went unchallenged. Evidently the Twinfield school community already valued outdoor education, and many parents had experienced outdoor childhoods in the villages and on the farms in the local area.

FEATURES OF THE PROGRAM

Many Twinfield students travel on the school bus. When they arrive at school, we begin the day in the classroom with a meal. This results in quite a bit of time spent taking gear off, learning to sit and eat and converse with friends, brushing teeth, and then learning how to put outdoor gear back on with as little adult help as possible. This does take up potential outdoor playtime; however, the skills worked on in this period are essential to life. Practicing these actions, students are building resilience, perseverance, and independence in concrete ways. Dandelion and Snail Preschool also utilizes multiple areas around the school for its curriculum. This year we had a weekly schedule that the children were able to rely on. It included a day for hiking, a day for woodland play, a day for loose-parts play, and a day for exploring the playground. On two of these days, there was also time for indoor work. The variety included in the schedule attempts to capitalize on the facilities available and provide diversity within the learning environment. By providing this variety, the program attempts to engage and provide for all of its children. Public preschools are not self-selecting in the way that private preschools can be; more thought needs to be put into honoring children's preferences and providing a balanced play space.

DANDELION AND SNAIL PRESCHOOL is the public preschool program at Twinfield Union School in Plainfield, Vermont, serving children from ages three to five with two half-day programs. The morning class is partnered with Head Start. Twinfield Union School provides free breakfast and lunch for all students.

Risky Behavior in Nature Preschool Programs

Forest Gnomes Waldkindergarten
Natick, Massachusetts

by Audrey Fergason

"He hitted me in the face!" Will screamed.

Will wasn't overreacting; he had been accidentally poked in the face by a fellow forest gnome (one of our three- to six-year-old preschoolers) during an activity the children had created called the "pushing game."

In a traditional preschool classroom, the teachers would have tried to stop the boisterous pushing game before it resulted in tears. In the Forest Gnomes program, we don't stop these games but rather model for the children how to advocate for themselves and how to state their own boundaries. Most of our gnomes thrive on the opportunity to be physical with one another, to laugh and talk in an "outside voice," to shout and scream and even to push one another. The pushing game is another outlet that brings joy to the children and teaches them important lessons about communication and encourages an awareness of interpersonal interactions.

The pushing game was invented by two four-year-old gnomes in early September and was rapidly adopted by many of the gnomes. Those who don't want to participate have been vocal about their lack of interest, and their wishes have been respected. For those still playing the pushing

game in November, the frozen ground has surprised the gnomes, allowing the teachers to have conversations about the changing season and its impact on nature.

In the weeks following the game's inception, it has taken on a life of its own, shaped and directed purely by the gnomes. The gnomes advocate for themselves and have established their own set of rules and expectations for the game. A certain thicket of trees was deemed by the gnomes as "not safe" for playing the game and, as a result, has transformed into a sanctuary for those uninterested in playing.

Occasionally we have to intervene, usually by observing aloud that a gnome doesn't appear to be having fun or reminding them that they can stop the game at any time. As we go into the year, however, our reminders have been gradually replaced with self-advocacy and firm statements of personal limits.

All is not always so bucolic in the woods, however, and there are moments where behaviors or language becomes too aggressive or even disrespectful. Our policy is to continually model the behavior we want to see and to gently guide gnomes who need some extra help. Positivity

and encouragement are always the best responses to behavior challenges in young children. Our child-guidance policy is intended to be proactive rather than reactive. Children are allowed and encouraged to work out conflicts as far as they can and it is safe to; we as teachers will intervene if needed. Teachers carefully observe children's play and will move closer to situations that could be potentially problematic, to monitor though not necessarily to stop the play. We believe situations of conflict are great opportunities for learning and can have a strong impact on the development of the child, depending on how we handle them together.

Since the preschool years are so crucial for social-emotional development and since children need their parents' support as they navigate peer relationships, we work hard to inform and involve the parents in our behavioral approach. At the beginning of every year we include the following list in our Forest Gnome Parent Handbook

FOREST GNOME PARENT HANDBOOK

TEACHERS' ROLE

- Teachers will strive to use positive guidance through areas of conflict.

- Teachers will handle children's social challenges on an individual basis, usually through the use of redirection, modeling of appropriate behaviors, positive encouragement, and storytelling.

- Teachers will communicate daily with parents regarding any incidents or concerns and may work with parents to create consistency between home and school.

CONSEQUENCES FOR DISRUPTIVE OR DISRESPECTFUL BEHAVIOR

- There will be no official use of time-out. A child may be led to a quieting activity, but there will be no designated time-out space.

- If a child needs to be removed from a situation, they will shadow or sit with the teacher. Sometimes children just need to be held or cuddled for a bit until they are able to "find their warm and gentle hands."

- If the child continues to be disruptive, the teacher will direct their energy to productive or therapeutic work.

- If a child hurts another child, teachers will model how to best care for the injury, and the child will participate in caring for the child that has been hurt.

NATICK COMMUNITY ORGANIC FARM's Forest Gnomes Waldkindergarten (German for forest kindergarten) program was established in 2009. We are a nature program for preschool children in a classroom without walls, changing with the seasons. Our gnomes are outside in all weather, through the fall, winter, and spring. Grounded in the values of a traditional Waldkindergarten, our minimally structured program focuses on free play, where exploration and imagination guide our gnomes every day in our beautiful woods.

Fire: Teaching Safety, Telling Stories

Dandelion and Snail Preschool
Bringing the Outdoors in: *Twinfield Union School, Plainfield, Vermont*

Twinfield Union School
Plainfield, Vermont

by Harriet Hart

FIRE: CONNECTING THE INDOORS AND OUTDOORS ACROSS A SINGLE UNIT

Next year and in subsequent years, our students will participate in a program run by the North Branch Nature Center called Educating Children Outdoors. As part of the program, they will learn to use fires to warm themselves as they spend cold afternoons in the forest. Eventually they will learn to be fire tenders, assuming responsibility for the flame at the heart of their circle time. To begin preparing our students for this and to make connections with our camp-themed dramatic play area, we have been weaving the theme of fire throughout our days, building students' understanding of safety and benefit until we can have a fire in our woodland circle.

PREPARING FOR FIRE

Educating Children Outdoors gives each size stick a name to help students remember the components of building a successful fire. We began our study of fire by introducing these different sizes

of sticks and their names. We added them to the dramatic play area as a means to build a campfire and as a means to encourage sorting activities.

STORYTELLING BEGINNINGS

Stories are already an important part of our classroom life: we read books every morning; we take one story and carry it forward, acting it out with props; and we tell the same stories inside our classroom and outside in the woods. We began our fire unit reading the story of *Rainbow Crow* that tells of how the crow brought fire from the spirit in the sky to melt the snow that had buried the woodland animals. In our circle time in the woods, we acted out the story. A white sheet covered the children who were animals, and the "crow" had rainbow wings made of cloth.

USING PERSONAL STORIES

Studying fire has given us the opportunity to introduce a greater focus on personal storytelling. We sit around a fake fire together, practicing our safety protocol, teaching students to treat the fire with

respect. We use it indoors, in a controlled space, and we use it outdoors in our woodland space. We help students practice the routines that will come into play when the fire is real. One of the teachers offers a story that connects to our curriculum.

This story will be told and retold over the next few weeks. As we tell our stories, we explore and promote the value of personal experiences in nature. Moving towards spring, we give our students more opportunities to create and tell their own stories.

CONNECTIONS TO STANDARDS

VERMONT EARLY LEARNING STANDARDS

HEALTH AND SAFETY PRACTICES

Goal 3: Children develop the ability to identify unsafe situations and use safe practices.

ENGAGEMENT WITH LITERATURE AND INFORMATIONAL TEXT

Goal 1: Children develop "book language" and demonstrate comprehension.
Goal 4: Retell or re-enact a familiar story in the correct sequence of a familiar story's major events with prompting and support.

DANDELION AND SNAIL PRESCHOOL is the public preschool program at Twinfield Union School in Plainfield, Vermont, serving children from ages three to five with two half-day programs. The morning class is partnered with Head Start. Twinfield Union School provides free breakfast and lunch for all students.

A World of Sticks and Stones

WALDORF
SCHOOL OF BALTIMORE

Baltimore, Maryland

by Michel Anderson

Sticks and stones are amazing toys!

And not just because they are abundant and free. Sticks and stones have the historic value of being humanity's first tools for a good reason. In the hands of an imaginative child, they are infinitely resourceful. They can be employed to build forts, used to invent and play games, turned into magic wands, used in a plethora of art-and-craft activities, and when arranged properly, they can even tell time!

Each stick and stone whispers its own mysterious story; however, children need intimate time with sticks and stones in order to unravel their mystery. Adults often worry that access to these natural objects could create problems. And they can! Not only are sticks and stones easily fashioned into weapons, but the potential for accidents also increases.

Although having sticks and stones on the playground does pose risks, we must remember

stones on our playground. We believe there is no one-size-fits-all policy when it comes to stick/stone play, but we offer this four-point policy that works for us:

THE WAY OF STICKS AND STONES

1. Always play safely.

2. Play stick fighting is allowed in designated areas only. Play rock fighting is not allowed.

3. If you are upset, immediately drop the stick/stone!

4. If you purposely threaten or hurt another person with a stick/stone, you will lose your stick/stone privileges for a period of time determined by a teacher.

that one of the most important lessons of childhood is in learning how to manage one's own risk. And uncomfortable though it may be, this is the social responsibility of schools.

At the Waldorf School of Baltimore, we decided to allow the proliferation of sticks and

The **WALDORF SCHOOL OF BALTIMORE is an independent, coeducational school that was established in 1971. It serves a diverse population of students from both Baltimore city and county. The school aspires to educate and inspire children to think, feel, and act with depth, imagination, and purpose. The Forest Aftercare Program provides an after-school, nature-based program for children from pre-K through eighth grade. Free play, gardening, and animal husbandry are key aspects of the program. Children and teachers are outside nearly every day—rain, snow, or shine.**

Field Trip Protocols for Nature Preschools

Cortland, New York

by Maryfaith Decker

Lime Hollow Forest Preschool began as a partnership with Lime Hollow Nature Center. We foster deep connections to the earth by providing unstructured time in nature through all of the seasons. In order to offer a long-day program and serve working families, we decided to apply for our New York State (NYS) license. We are the first fully outdoor preschool to achieve licensing in New York State, and we are helping to craft protocols.

TIMELINE

- **April 2017:** Lime Hollow Forest Preschool submits application for licensure of an indoor classroom and 451 acres of outdoor play space.

- **June 2017:** Office of Children and Families introduces us to Alyssa's Law and recommends placing a four-foot fence around every stream, creek, bog, and pond on the nature preserve.

- **June 2017:** Through the Nature-based Early Childhood program at Antioch New England, I visit Wild Roots Nature School and notice that they have a fenced "license-able" outdoor space, and all around it are streams and ponds that are not fenced. I propose this solution to the Director of Lime Hollow Nature Center and our teaching team.

- **July 2017:** We resubmit our application with a proposed "outside play space" and decide that when we are hiking in the nature preserve, we are on a field trip.

LIME HOLLOW FOREST PRESCHOOL'S FIELD TRIP PROTOCOLS FOR STREAM PLAY

- No child shall participate in aquatic activities, including swimming. Swimming is expressly prohibited at Lime Hollow Forest Preschool.

- No child shall participate in activities at or near a body of water without a person present who is certified in cardiopulmonary resuscitation (CPR) and first aid.

- The following risk-mitigation strategies are used for stream play:

- Site assessment is performed before children are allowed to explore a stream site.

- Teacher will remove hazards such as trash or glass.

- A day is chosen when the weather is warm enough to maintain body temperature in case of wet clothing. All children will have a change of clothes within a safe distance.

- Scaffolding (building on children's knowledge) stories or activities are utilized to help children self-evaluate risk. For example, we balance on dry logs before attempting wet logs, discuss why green rocks are slippery, and engage in puddle play.

- Clear boundaries for the play area are set and maintained.

- The children are known well.

- The student-teacher ratio is six to one.

- Hand sanitizer is used after stream play.

LIME HOLLOW FOREST PRESCHOOL'S FIELD TRIP PROTOCOLS FOR TREE CLIMBING

Tree climbing is a risky play activity that can involve injury and provides many benefits. In order to mitigate that risk, Lime Hollow Forest

Preschool teachers will follow the tree-climbing protocol:

- Site assessment is performed before any child is allowed to climb. For example, dead limbs are identified and/or removed, a tree may be excluded from play due to hazardous structure or slippery weather conditions, and spiky sticks are removed from under the climbing tree.

- Tree climbing is a category under the "one teacher, one risk" rule.

- The student-teacher ratio is four to one.

- No other risky play can be happening.

- A child may not be helped up into a tree by an adult. A child can be "talked down" from a tree when necessary. A child who is worried about climbing down may be comforted by an adult who places themselves under a child.

- Scaffolding activities will be utilized to help children self-evaluate risk. Children are taught to climb only on live branches that are larger than their wrist.

LIME HOLLOW FOREST PRESCHOOL FIELD TRIP PROTOCOLS

These protocols were developed as a baseline for all field trips involving movement on the trails of the grounds of Lime Hollow Nature Center. Additional protocols may be instituted for differing types of field trips.

- Children will be counted and their names recorded on an attendance sheet prior to

leaving and before returning. The attendance sheet remains with the group at all times. Roll call is used before leaving a space and after entering a new one. Group Leaders perform the roll call. When afield, a mental roll call is performed every ten minutes. Children will always be accompanied by a staff person during the field trip; this includes the restroom and any other location for supervision.

- The group leader will verify that parents have signed the field trip permission slip.

- Field trips will be preplanned and emergency procedures prepared.

- Group leaders will notify parents of any details about any given field trip. A copy of the map indicating field trip location and departure and return times will be posted on the information board located next to the sign-in sheet.

- Group leaders will carry the "ten essentials" in their backpacks, including a fully stocked first aid kit, hand sanitizer, charged cell phone, extra charged battery, the day's attendance sheet, and the emergency contact information for every child. Medication or equipment needed to ensure the safety of a child with special medical needs (asthma, severe allergies, diabetes, and so forth) will be taken on the trip.

- Group leaders and assistant teachers will perform silent checks at intervals of less than ten minutes, or smaller intervals depending on the students in the group. These checks can include audible counts or a mental roll call. Group leaders/assistant teachers are placed at the head and foot of every hike.

- All field trips with an itinerary that includes an activity where emergency medical care is not readily available and/or an activity such as, but not limited to, wilderness hiking, rock climbing, and sledding, must be accompanied by a staff person who possesses a current first aid certificate and CPR certification.

- If off-site events are part of the program's activities, Lime Hollow Forest Preschool must develop and share with its program staff written plans that cover field trip events. The safety plan must at least include requirements set forth in 418-1.5(g), 418-1.6, and 418-1.8(o). Lime Hollow Forest Preschool does not take field trips involving bussing.

Children cannot be left without competent supervision at any time. Competent supervision includes awareness of and responsibility for the ongoing activity of each child. It requires that all children be within a teacher's range of vision and that the teacher be near enough to respond when redirection or intervention strategies are needed. Competent supervision must take into account the child's age and emotional, physical, and cognitive development. Our field trip ratio of students to teachers is six to one at all times.

CONNECTIONS TO STANDARDS

NEW YORK STATE REGULATIONS

(f) Barriers must exist to prevent children from gaining access to unsafe areas. Such areas include, but are not limited to, swimming pools, drainage ditches, wells, ponds, or other bodies of open water, holes, wood- and coal-burning stoves, fireplaces, pellet stoves, permanently installed gas space heaters, or any other unsafe area.

(g) The use of pools that have not received a Department of Health permit to operate, spa pools and all fill-and-drain wading pools are prohibited. (1) No child shall participate in aquatic activities including fishing, boating, swimming or any other activity on a body of water without a certified lifeguard present. (2) No child shall participate in activities at or near a body of water without a person who is certified.

(j) All field trips with an itinerary that includes an activity where emergency medical care is not readily available and/or an activity such as, but not limited to, wilderness hiking, rock climbing, horseback riding, and bicycling, must be accompanied by a staff who possess a current first aid certificate and cardiopulmonary resuscitation (CPR) certification.

(k) If off-site events are part of the program's activities, the childcare program must develop and share with its program staff written plans that cover field trip events. The safety plan must at least include requirements set forth in 418-1.5(g), 418-1.6, and 418-1.8(o).

4.18–1.5 Safety

(a) Suitable precautions must be taken to eliminate all conditions in areas accessible to children which pose a safety or health hazard in cardiopulmonary resuscitation and first aid present. 418-1.5(g)(4) 418-1.5(l)(5) 15

LIME HOLLOW FOREST PRESCHOOL began as a partnership with Lime Hollow Nature Center. We foster deep connections to the earth by providing unstructured time in nature, through all seasons. In order to offer a long-day program and serve working families, we decided to apply for our New York State (NYS) license. We are the first fully outdoor preschool to achieve licensing in New York State, and we are helping to craft protocols.

Field Trip Protocols: Cold- and Warm-Weather Procedures

Lime Hollow Forest Preschool

Cortland, New York

by Maryfaith Decker

Our licensor asked that we write protocols for field trips, including pond and stream play, tree climbing, and hot and cold weather, as a requirement for receiving our New York State (NYS) license for child care. The licensing agency understands that field trips are an integral part of our daily curriculum.

We were recently able to test our cold-weather protocols when a student fell into a pond on a 32-degree day. The following is an excerpt from the incident log:

A teacher was an arm's length away, heard the splash, and pulled the child out of the water. He fell into six-to-eight inches of water, face up. His face was never submerged. We had an extra staff person at the site, so one teacher could leave with the wet child. The teacher and child hiked/jogged back to the education building, taking the child's bag of extra clothes along. The pair arrived at the education building and were able to have the child in dry clothes fourteen minutes post-immersion. The child's body temperature never dropped; head, hands, and chest felt warm, feet felt cold. We dried the child's clothing and outerwear in the dryer while the child drew pictures and had a snack. We redressed and rejoined the group one hour post-immersion. I took a walk with that child at the end of the day to another pond to discuss the incident. He showed caution but not fear of the pond.

LIME HOLLOW FOREST PRESCHOOL'S FIELD TRIP PROTOCOLS FOR COLD WEATHER

Winter-weather risks are mitigated by a strong partnership with parents, well-trained staff, and strict protocols. Cold-weather injuries would represent a failing of staff procedures and protocols of which the staff is entirely responsible.

- Lime Hollow Forest Preschool children will always have a complete change of clothing available in case of wet clothing. Wet children are changed into dry layers with expediency to maintain body temperature. A note is sent to parents to replace clothing in their child's extra-clothes bag.

- In the case of a cold child who needs to be removed to a warm space (in the case of gear failure or wetness), a small group with one teacher or the entire group will move to a warm space.

- Lime Hollow Forest Preschool staff is trained in methods of keeping warm on a cold day (for example, large-muscle movement games, tea or warm snacks, timely snacks, and clothing inspections).

LIME HOLLOW FOREST PRESCHOOL'S FIELD TRIP PROTOCOLS FOR WARM WEATHER

In early fall and late spring, temperatures might reach conditions of concern for heat stress. Heat exhaustion in a child represents a failing of staff procedures and protocols.

- Lime Hollow Forest Preschool staff will work with parents to help guide proper clothing choices for the weather conditions. Clothing is

- The director holds a mandatory education meeting for parents before the beginning of the school year in which the proper techniques for dressing for our program, along with the required gear, are communicated. Parents sign a form acknowledging their commitment to, and knowledge of, the required dressing of their child.

- The teaching staff does an evaluation of each child's clothing along with the health check every day at drop-off. A staff member will work with the parents if any shortcomings are found in the child's gear. Lime Hollow Forest Preschool will maintain extra cold-weather clothing to address shortcomings.

- If no solutions are found for the child to be properly dressed, the child will not be accepted into the program for the day for reasons of safety and will be returned home with the parent.

- If during a field trip a child cannot maintain their body temperature, a check for fever will be done. The procedures for a feverish child are found in the section on the temporary exclusion of a child.

- The director will use the NOAA wind chill chart and the IOWA Weatherwatch chart as a guideline for determining wind chill and the amount of time that is safe for our children to be outside. Lime Hollow Forest Preschool will use Weather Underground apps and WSYR's live Doppler for specific local conditions.

checked at drop-off for weather appropriateness. In the case that a child comes to Lime Hollow Forest Preschool with inappropriate clothing, every attempt will be made to find suitable pieces in our extra-clothing bin. If a clothing solution is not found, a child may be excluded from our program for reasons of safety and sent home with their parent.

- Parents are expected to prepare their children for the day by applying sunscreen before the program begins. We will reapply sunscreen that the parent sends in the child's backpack.

- On a hot day, children are watched to see that they are drinking enough fluids and are not getting too much sun. Lime Hollow Forest Preschool staff can utilize shadier portions of Lime Hollow and the cooler temperatures of the forest.

- If a child shows signs of heat exhaustion, Red Cross first aid protocols are followed.

- In the case of a child who needs to be removed to a cool space, a small group with one teacher or the entire group will move to a cool space.

CONNECTIONS TO STANDARDS

NEW YORK STATE REGULATIONS

(1) The diagram must be labeled with the planned occupancy or use of all areas of the building and all outside areas to be used or occupied by the child day care center. The diagram must show: room dimensions; the age group(s) using each room; the size of the group(s) using each room; kitchens and bathrooms for children and staff; exits; alternate means of egress; plumbing fixtures such as toilets, sinks, and drinking fountains; and the outdoor play area showing its relationship to the building.
(b) Areas that will be used by the children must be well-lighted and well-ventilated. Heating, ventilation, and lighting equipment must be adequate for the protection of the health of the children.
(d) A temperature of at least 68 degrees Fahrenheit must be maintained in all rooms to be occupied by children.
(k) Daily supervised outdoor play is required for all children in care, except during inclement or extreme weather or unless otherwise ordered by a health care provider. Parents may request and programs may permit children to remain indoors during outdoor play time so long as such children will be supervised in accordance with section 418-1.8 of this Subpart.

LIME HOLLOW FOREST PRESCHOOL began as a partnership with Lime Hollow Nature Center. We foster deep connections to the earth by providing unstructured time in nature through all of the seasons. In order to offer a long-day program and serve working families, we decided to apply for our New York State (NYS) license. We are the first fully outdoor preschool to achieve licensing in New York State, and we are helping to craft protocols.

Documentation and Parent Communication for Forest Preschools

Cortland, New York

by Maryfaith Decker

Our plan for documentation and parent communication is designed to address our need to have parents understand the unique opportunities for learning that nature as a classroom provides. We want to give them the language to communicate their children's growth to friends and family members and provide evidence-based research to share with our community of educators. We planned to have a series of parent-teacher conferences, beginning with a listening conference at the beginning of the school year to find out who the children were and their parents' goals for their experience at Forest Preschool, a conference midyear to relay their strengths and challenges, and one at the end of the year to review their growth throughout the year. Budget constraints quickly edited this plan to a (less-than-ideal) questionnaire at the beginning of the year and a midyear conference. We have, however, fully instituted our evidence-gathering plan and have woven the routine of documentation into our days in the forest.

Our documentation training was offered by the Natural Start Alliance. It is similar to the documentation used at Juniper Hill School in Maine, where a teacher takes notes and dictation as children are engaged in play. We use notebooks,

GARDNER'S SEVEN DOMAINS OF EARLY CHILDHOOD LEARNING

- Gross Motor: Here children learn to use the big-muscle groups of their body. Crawling, walking, jumping, and climbing are all examples of this.

- Fine Motor: Learning hand-eye coordination is the focus here. Kids learn how to control precise muscle movement in their hands to build fine-motor skills.

- Language: This domain centers on the child's ability to speak, read, and write, involving alphabetic and phonetic learning, and learning to communicate their opinions, wants, and needs with others.

- Cognitive: Children learn cause and effect and reasoning here, as well as early math skills and counting and patterning during preschool years.

- Social/Emotional: We are all social beings, and our children are no different. Learning to play with others is a skill that is taught. Making sure a child feels safe and nurtured is part of this development, as is using manners and modeling kind behavior.

- Self-Help/Adaptive: In this domain, children begin to show a little independence and learn how to take care of themselves. Learning to dress and eat on their own, how to tie their own shoes, and how to brush their own teeth are all examples of becoming less dependent.

- Morals/Values: Knowing the difference between right and wrong is an important lesson to be learned early on. Respecting oneself includes respecting others and all that is in the world around us. The binary right and wrong expands into ever-varying shades as children grow and experience the values of different families and people they encounter.

sticker paper, or take video by cell phone and transcribe later. Then we enter the data into a binder and give each anecdote a designation that refers to Howard Gardner's seven domains of early childhood learning, or several of these domains. Within the documentation binder, each child's parent questionnaire is followed by pages of anecdotes arranged chronologically by month. Over the short time we have kept documentation, we have been able to isolate trends and track developmental growth in the children.

LIME HOLLOW FOREST PRESCHOOL/FOREST SCHOOL PARENT QUESTIONNAIRE

Child's name: _____

Events in the child's earliest years can have both subtle and profound effects on his or her later life. While some of the following questions may not seem to apply to your child's current situation, they are designed to bring parents and teachers together in forming the broadest possible picture of your child's development and daily life.

1. Tell us about your son or daughter. Please include a brief history of early childhood events, such as birth, feeding, crawling, walking, and/or any additional information you wish to share.

2. Please try to give a picture of your child: his or her interests, strengths, tendencies, outstanding characteristics, and so on.

3. What is your child's daily rhythm? (bedtime, awakening, meals, and so forth)

4. What types of activities do you enjoy doing together on a regular basis and what do you enjoy doing as a family?

5. Does your son or daughter have any dietary limitations, eating problems, or allergies?

6. Has your son or daughter ever had any serious physical condition, illness, or injuries? If so, please describe. (Please indicate the years these occurred.)

7. Please describe any circumstances in your child's life that you would like your teacher to be aware of.

8. Please describe any prior special needs of your son or daughter. For example, have there been any learning difficulties, emotional or behavioral difficulties, or previous counseling?

9. What are your hopes and expectations for your school experiences at Lime Hollow Forest Preschool/Forest School?

10. Is English your child's first language? If not, what languages are spoken at home?

Parent's Signature_____

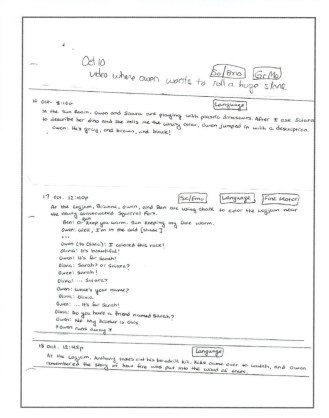

LIME HOLLOW FOREST PRESCHOOL began as a partnership with Lime Hollow Nature Center. We foster deep connections to the earth by providing unstructured time in nature through all of the seasons. In order to offer a long-day program and serve working families, we decided to apply for our New York State (NYS) license. We are the first fully outdoor preschool to achieve licensing in New York State, and we are helping to craft protocols.

Documentation: Student Story and Student Profile

Nauvoo, Alabama

by Melissa Frederick

At Magnolia Nature Preschool, we use the traditional Teaching Strategies Gold documentation, documentation panels, and floor books as ways to display student growth. In addition to primary documentation forms, we write student stories to show holistic growth both personally and academically in a format that is easy to share between parents and children.

WRITING STUDENT STORIES

We want children to connect celebrations of their growth with experiences at school. These are some practices we use to achieve this:

- We use a letter format that is addressed to each child.
- We use simple language that reinforces classroom values or curriculum goals.
- We describe both academic and personal learning.
- We use direct quotes from children or retelling of specific meaningful moments from the woods.

JACELYN'S STUDENT STORY

Dear Jacelyn,

When you first came to preschool, we thought you were a little shy. Sometimes you would hide or be very quiet. You have grown so much and made great friends! We love that you get so excited when you find a cricket or frog. You make us laugh every day when you are silly or make silly faces. You make the best birthday cakes ever. You are strong and you are tough, and when you fall down, you always get right back up. You are also smart! You know your name on your snack bag and you can write a *J*! We are so proud that you are learning how to count all the amazing things you find in nature. You find mushrooms, flowers, beautiful leaves, and tiny animals. You have so much joy inside you!

Love,

Miss Melissa

STUDENT PROFILES FOR PARENTS

Separate from the student stories, we also write student profiles to be shared with parents to document their child's growth. Below find a profile written after Timothy was in the program for only one month and then another written at the end of the year.

Timothy has spent one full year at Magnolia Nature Preschool. He began school at age three and is now four years old. His family applied to Head Start for preschool, and he was placed at Magnolia in February 2017.

TIMOTHY'S FIRST DAYS

Timothy came to school with deep interests in guns, popular superheroes, bad guys, and video games. When he first arrived at school or when he would become upset at school, he said, "I wanna go home and play my games!" He lagged behind the group during walks in the woods, sometimes lying on the ground. Timothy had at least one outburst of screaming, hitting, or fighting each day. Timothy loved sticks; he really wanted to use them as guns and was frustrated when we enforced our "No guns at school" rule. He loved water but had difficulty with boundaries around the water. He was very curious about other children but did not always know how to enter their play. Timothy's nature was very loving, and he was intelligent with letters and numbers for his age.

TIMOTHY TODAY

Timothy is still loving and smart. He shows kindness to friends more often and knows how to enter any play scenario. Timothy still loves water; he knows how to stand at the edge and throw things in it, how to only go up to his knees, and how to use water in building projects.

His interest in guns continues, but he also knows how to use a stick as a magic wand, a hammer, a saw, a fishing pole, and a horse to ride on. He still loves to "fight bad guys," but he only does so when other children wish to engage in rough play. He accepts redirection to many other activities during this time.

Timothy especially loves collecting pets from nature! He completes many cooperative projects to provide for the creatures he finds.

Timothy shows curiosity and engagement daily; he is working on regulating strong outbursts by finding new friends to play with or playing alone when he feels angry.

EMBRACING INCLUSION

Working with children in nature means risk management. Some children in the class have normal habits of small children that make an outdoor classroom more risky. In Magnolia's classroom, we have encountered children who drink water from nature and put objects in their mouths. We've had to work on special teaching strategies that sometimes make time in the classroom more challenging for teachers. All children deserve access to nature, and we must be willing to provide them with experiences that are both safe and appropriate.

MAGNOLIA NATURE PRESCHOOL is a nature-based preschool partnership between Camp McDowell and Head Start. Magnolia develops kindergarten readiness by focusing on long periods of unstructured play in nature and providing basic health, wellness, and nutrition needs for low-income families in Winston County, Alabama.

Documenting Growth

by Megan Gessler

Natural Beginnings
Early Childhood Program

Yorkville, Illinois

STEM seems to be the new buzzword in education right now. Science, technology, engineering, and math have been scholastic subjects for many years, but there is currently a new emphasis on and a demand for these subjects. At nature-based programs, we continue to observe children exploring STEM (and much, much more) in purely organic moments. While we do not separate subject matter for the children, many academic disciplines can be brought together in simple cross-curricular activities. Learning is permeable. Here is an example of a rich and powerful child-initiated experience.

At the same time on opposite sides of a [stick house], Dylan and Cordelia were using long sticks to poke at tiny icicles that were out of their reach. They desperately wanted to eat some icicles today, and they were trying hard to knock them down and catch them, but they were not having any luck with catching them before the icicles hit the ground and broke apart or became lost in the snow.

As the two started nearing each other from opposite sides, they noticed that they were each doing the same thing. I observed them huddling together to talk. When they were done conversing, I noticed that Cordelia kept the longest stick in her hand and began to gently nudge at the icicles while Dylan stationed himself below the icicles to catch them as they slid down the [house]. Dylan had to change tactics a few times for optimum efficiency until he figured out that by creating a V with his mittens, he had a better chance of catching the icicles. Once he collected two of them, they would sit down to enjoy their snack before catching some more.

These students used

- technology (tool = stick) to reach the icicle;
- engineering to achieve just the right angle and drop point;
- earth science as they observed where the icicles were forming on the house;
- math as they counted two icicles before stopping to enjoy their rewards; and
- social skills to collaborate as they took initiative in problem solving together.

This exemplifies the type of critical thinking that abounds in nature-based programs. This is cross-curricular learning at its finest. And it's completely child-led.

Recognizing and documenting the learning that is taking place is paramount to advocacy for nature-based programming. Becoming familiar with learning domains and benchmarks strengthens teacher skills in communicating the effectiveness of authentic learning experiences. You can use your state's early-learning benchmarks to document the experiences in your program. I combine photo documentation along with Dimensions' Nature Notes to detail the skills that are strengthened through such moments at my program. I send these documentations home in the students' backpacks or place them in their portfolios. Every time I document, it becomes easier for me to recognize learning as it is taking place in my program. I become much more effective at discussing the benefits of my program with potential families as well as other educators.

CONNECTIONS TO STANDARDS

ILLINOIS EARLY LEARNING STANDARDS

LANGUAGE ARTS

5.C.EC Communicate information with others. *(Brainstorming a solution to retrieve icicles)*

SOCIAL/EMOTIONAL

31.A.ECc Exhibit persistence and creativity in seeking solutions to problems. *(Problem solving icicle retrieval)*
31.A.ECe Use appropriate communication skills when expressing needs, wants, and feelings. *(Talking out the problem/solution)*
32.B.ECa Engage in cooperative play. *(Collaborating with classmate to retrieve icicles)*

SCIENCE

11.A.ECa Uses senses to explore and observe natural phenomena. *(Observing, catching, and eating icicles)*
12.A.ECb Show an awareness of changes that occur in their environment. *(Looking for icicles in winter)*

PHYSICAL DEVELOPMENT

19.B.EC Coordinate movements to perform complex tasks. *(Nudging the icicles and then catching them at just the right angle)*

NATURAL BEGINNINGS EARLY LEARNING PROGRAM is a September-to-May nature preschool program that introduces children ages three through six to the world around them by exploring various nature-based themes. We offer two-day and three-day classes for children. The Natural Beginnings Program takes place at the Hoover Forest Preserve in Yorkville, Illinois, with over 350 acres of prairie, streams, and woodlands to explore. Students are immersed in seasonal themes through nature walks, studying natural phenomenon, and engaging in activities that build physical, emotional, and academic skills.

Outdoor Rest Time

by Katie Swick

East Montpelier, Vermont

We took to the grass in the late spring when the chances of rain were finally minimal. Under the maple tree in the shade, our eldest preschoolers set up their rest mats. The children were pretty excited to be outside. Our oldest students usually have rest time in a separate room from the two- and three-year-olds and younger four-year-olds, so the move outside was an easy one.

With senses alert, one child exclaimed, "Can we go inside? It's going to rain. It is too windy out here." This surprised me. This was the child I thought would be the most happy to be outside because of his struggles to stay on his mat inside. Upon further discussion, I remembered that he had recently run outside during a particularly strong pre-rain windstorm looking for his father. Now the wind and slightly dark clouds were making him nervous. Yet he had many moments of stillness on his mat watching the wind and birds. He loved sharing what he knew about birds, too.

I modeled lying down and looking at the sky and listening to birds. "That's a chickadee!" one child exclaimed. "Chick-a-dee-dee-dee."

Another child, who usually falls asleep in the middle of her busy peers during indoor rest time, found being outside very exciting. She was full of energy and silliness most of the time outside.

Near the end, a child said, "I love this rest time. I wish we could do it all day, every day." Another child responded, "Me, too! I love it!" A third child disagreed, saying, "I thought it was too buggy out here and I wanted to go inside."

As the teacher, I felt the time outside was such a valuable time to notice, ponder, imagine,

feel, and discuss. We admired the clouds, talked about them, and used our imaginations as we watched them float by. We listened to birds. We talked about the wind and the weather. And we learned about ourselves. We have happily continued this process as long as the chance of rain looks low and the children continue to be interested.

CONNECTIONS TO STANDARDS

VERMONT EARLY LEARNING STANDARDS

Approaches to Learning: Initiative: Children show curiosity about the world around them and take action to interact with it and learn. *(Chance for children to slow down—instead of outside playing—and notice what is happening around them outside)*

Emotion and Self-Regulation: Children develop healthy positive relationships with adults and peers. *(Great time to have more complex conversations with older children)*

Health and Safety Practices: Children develop personal health and self-care habits, and become increasingly independent. *(Time to reflect, be with self)*

Language Development: Receptive Language (Listening, Expressive Language, Speaking & Listening, Social Rules of Language) *(Wonderful time for small-group discussions with children to practice language skills)*

Science: Physical Sciences and Life Sciences *(Discussions on birds, clouds, trees, weather, and whatever arises)*

ALLTOGETHERNOW! PRESCHOOL was founded in 2006 by Ellen Leonard, a music teacher. The school is located at a hilltop farmhouse surrounded by ten acres. The school recently became certified as a Vermont Act 166 Universal Pre-K partner with four local public school systems around East Montpelier, Vermont.

CHAPTER 4
Working and Celebrating with Parents

My daughter attended a Waldorf school from first through eighth grade, and one of the things I appreciate about Waldorf education is the commitment to using seasonal rituals, school trips, and volunteer activities as tools to engage parents in the culture of the school. For instance, as an alternative to trick-or-treating with its focus on sugary treats and scary and macabre experiences, my daughter's school organized a Halloween event for families. All the kindergarten through fourth-grade children and parents met at a camp in the woods and traveled a loop path around a pond at dusk in small groups. Along the way, the children encountered different characters—a fortune-teller, a story weaver, an herbalist, a puppeteer—played by a combination of teachers and parent volunteers, while the children collected nuts, dried fruit, and some chocolate. The whole event created a different kind of culture that celebrated the season rather than tiptoeing on the edge of scary dreams for young children.

Similarly, nature-based early childhood programs work to create an alternative culture that celebrates the magic of childhood, tunes family life to the circle of the seasons, and educates parents about the underlying differences between traditional preschool and the nature-based approach. The articles in this chapter portray a range of ways to work with and engage parents.

WORK DAYS, FAMILY NIGHTS

Work days are a great way to get parents into the children's space and to develop the infrastructure that staff can't create alone. Audrey Fergason's article nicely lays out how to plan a work day so that lots of parents and adults can be involved simultaneously. I like how the Forest Gnomes staff engages the children in figuring out what the program needs—strawberries in the garden and lower backpack pegs were a couple of the tasks suggested by children. This gives children a sense of ownership of the space and gives parents real projects that help them feel more connected to their children's education. And be sure to notice the unique low balance-beam matrix that a couple of parents put together—just the right task to give parents a way to be involved beyond picking up and dropping off their children. Don't you want one of these for your space?

By the way, I recommend taking the opportunity to visit the Forest Gnomes program at the Natick Organic Community Farm just so you can see the cottage nestled in the woods. (See a picture of a corner of the cottage in Audrey's Clothing article on page 9.) You'll feel like you've been teleported into a storybook. It's like the witch's cottage in *Hansel and Gretel* or the seven dwarfs' cottage in *Snow White*. There's no way to drive there; you have to walk through the pinewoods and then it appears through the mist. The cottage in the woods, or the tarp shelter or tent, helps convey to parents the security of their children cozied up in a safe place. We want children and parents to linger a bit longer in the storybook world in nature-based programs.

Melissa Frederick's and Sarah Sheldon's articles provide different examples of family meetings. The Magnolia Nature School in Alabama invites parents to a family program once a month. What could be more innovative and appropriate in the South than a reptile-themed program? Parents learn a bit of bravery from watching their children handle the nonpoisonous snakes that they're afraid to touch.

A celebratory end-of-the-year event is the focus for Sarah Sheldon's article about her program at the Chicago Botanic Garden. Getting parents and children to play together is an important aspect of these parenting events—something that's missing too much of the time in modern families. Having parents see the way you interact with children and being able to talk with parents about why you sometimes take a hands-off approach rather than always saying no is valuable, especially when trying to change a perspective on risk.

INTERGENERATIONAL JOURNEYS

Matthew Flower's article on collaborative programs for young children and senior citizens (referred to as *grandfriends* here) is a stand-alone. I know of very few examples of this kind of programming, and his description warms the cockles of my heart. Bringing young children and old folks together to sing, dance, and listen to stories makes so much sense. As Matt says, "Children gain positive feelings towards aging and show increased comfort interacting with elders in the broader community" and "grandfriends experience improved mood, memory, dexterity, and feelings of community and purpose." It's a win-win situation. I think this opportunity to befriend oldsters may help youngsters feel more comfortable with their own grandparents and great-grandparents.

FAMILY CAMP-OUT

Storyteller Children's Center in Santa Barbara, California, is an early childhood program for many homeless and at-risk, mostly Latino, children. Alicia Jimenez's work over the past five years to naturalize the Storyteller program is a great example of environmental justice—providing equal access to the natural world for low-income children and families. Though many of these families live on the nature-rich California coast, some children have never waded in streams, been to the beach, or hiked into the mountains. And many of these children and families have never camped out before.

The family camp-out is made possible through a partnership with the Wilderness Youth Project (WYP), one of the premier nature connection organizations in the country. They serve early childhood through adolescent children with a diverse array of unique programs. Their early childhood director, Kelly Villaruel, is one of the founders of the Association of California Forest Kindergarten teachers and one of the designers of this family camping program. WYP provides all the equipment and expertise so that the children, caregivers, and families can immerse themselves in the nearby natural world. There's traditional music, popcorn around the fire, herbal salve fabrication, and memories from childhood. As one parent said, "I wish from the bottom of my heart that this camp-out does not become the only one that I attend." The family camp-out experience is a potent example of helping to naturalize the culture of the family. If one of the goals of nature-based programs is to make children feel at home in the natural world, then educators need to give parents opportunities to feel at home in nature as well. We want parents to bring nature into their family lives beyond school. If your program has the capacity to organize this kind of family event, it has the potential to shape family culture and enhance your impact on children's lives.

TUNING FAMILY ENGAGEMENT TO SEASONAL CYCLES

When my children were young, we were part of a group of families with loose Buddhist leanings wanting to de-emphasize the commercialized Christian holidays. (Though it's really hard to avoid Christmas and Easter.) So we put some of our focus on celebrating the solstices (the longest and shortest days of the year), the equinoxes (the beginning of spring and the beginning of fall when day and night are equal), and the cross-quarter days (the halfway points between the solstices and equinoxes). To create events based on traditional Celtic rituals, I turned to *The Golden Bough* by Sir James George Frazer. It's an ethnography of how seasonal rituals were celebrated in diverse European cultures prior to the dominance of Christian religion. We leapt over fires on the winter solstice to encourage the fading sun to leap back into the sky, we rolled a wheel of fire downhill on the summer solstice to signify the beginning of days getting shorter. On May Day, we played rope-jumping games to encourage the newly planted seeds to jump out of the ground to become summer vegetables.

Whereas most people are aware of the solstices and equinoxes, the cross-quarter days have faded from modern consciousness, though they are the calendric underpinnings for some current minor holidays. The cross-quarter days, the halfway points between the solstices and equinoxes, have modern-day remnants. The halfway point between the winter solstice and the spring equinox is February 2, commonly known as Groundhog Day (six more weeks of winter) and traditionally known as Candlemas or Imbolc—a time to light candles to signify the beginning of the end of winter. The halfway point between the spring equinox and summer solstice is what remains as May Day or Beltane—often a time of bacchanalian celebration in medieval Europe. The cross-quarter day between the summer solstice and the fall equinox, Lammas, is largely lost and not much celebrated in North America. And the halfway point between the fall solstice and the winter equinox, commonly celebrated as Halloween, is the traditional Samhain or the Day of the Dead in Mexico—a time to celebrate the lives of those who have passed. When I visited the Storyteller program in Santa Barbara at the end of October, Alicia had the class of mostly Latino children deeply engaged in both mask making and face painting in anticipation of the celebration of the Day of the Dead. The point is to look for the culturally relevant seasonal celebrations that are appropriate for your school population.

Nature-based early childhood programs, with the goal of tuning family life to seasonal cycles, often choose to organize family celebrations around these seasonal cusps. At Wild Roots Forest School in Santa Barbara, directed by the remarkable Lia Grippo, family celebrations are scheduled for the fall equinox, the winter solstice, the spring equinox, and the spring cross-quarter day—May Day. These events are mostly outdoors and draw on some of the traditional Celtic celebration forms.

The Juniper Hill School in Alna, Maine, directed by the equally remarkable Anne Stires, has the same commitment to seasonal celebrations. In addition to these calendric events, the songs and chants in nature-based programs change every few weeks or months to signify the current phenological ephemera—the first frost, the harvest moon, when the maple sap starts to run, the big night when salamanders migrate in spring, the time when the swallows come back to Capistrano (which is right around the spring equinox), the arrival of black flies in northern New England, and so on. The goal is to live into nature rather than let nature be obliterated by the daylight-deprived digital world. (Note that the Wild Roots and Juniper Hill programs aren't represented in articles in this chapter but are great examples of seasonally attuned programs.)

Check out Katie Swick's description of Ice on Fire, a winter solstice-ish celebration of deep winter. They also conduct a similar May Day-ish celebration of spring flourishing, All Species Day. Montpelier, Vermont, really knows how to do these seasonal rituals up right. The early childhood program AllTogetherNow! is a major player in these seasonal celebrations that involve parents, numerous community organizations, and a large swath of local citizens. At Ice on Fire, there are games, storytelling, food, face painting, and a maze made of discarded Christmas trees. The preschool children participate in a production of *Yertle the Turtle*. At All Species Day in early May, the children create mammal, bird, and bug costumes and march in the parade that ends with a celebration on the State House lawn presided over by large puppets of mother earth and the stag king. Vermonters (who experience eight months of winter and four months of tough sledding) are enthusiastic about summer, so this celebration is heartfelt. Katie's article provides just enough inspiration to get you to start thinking about how you'll create your own regionally inspired seasonal celebrations for parents and community.

Celebrating seasonal changes is something families of all religious persuasions can get behind. We can all celebrate the first snowfall, the first robin in spring, the splash of fall colors, the onset of heavy rains after the dry season. Attuning family life to the seasons brings children and their families together with tangible traditions that happen year after year. And, done well, they have the potential to connect your families to the wider community.

Family Work Day

by Audrey Fergason

The Natick
Community
Organic
Farm

Forest Gnomes Waldkindergarten
Natick, Massachusetts

At Forest Gnomes, we have numerous family events over the course of the year. We offer campouts in the fall and the spring, a lantern festival at the beginning of the winter, a winter festival in February, and a parent education night in the spring. All the events are important and enable families to connect and gnomes to play together.

As a program, however, the most important event is our family work day in the spring. On our family work day, families come together and tackle projects that are desperately needed. For many of our families, it is one of the few times they can be in our program space. Siblings especially find the family work day to be exciting. It is also a time for families to bond over the shared work.

Since all of our family events are meant for the entire family, it does make planning and execution complicated because there are numerous children, both gnomes and siblings, involved. Most of the projects we tackle are big projects—our tree house, our swings, and our table and benches were all family work day projects.

We want all students and their families to feel included, but with chainsaws, circular saws, and cement being used, it can be a challenge to engage

everyone. We solve this by having the gnomes and their younger siblings work in our garden plot. A few weeks earlier, we asked all of the gnomes for their input about what plants they would like to grow. Peas, carrots, strawberries, and sunflowers were the suggestions that were agreed upon. We began seeds and then, on family work day, parents and gnomes worked together to transplant the seedlings. Not only does the garden provide a positive connection to the farm that hosts our program, it gives the gnomes something concrete and productive to do while their families tackle the construction projects.

This year our backpack rack and balance beam needed to be replaced. Our gnomes gave their wish list: a lower balance beam, lower backpack pegs, more places to balance, and so on. We took their suggestions and turned their requests over to the parents who were spearheading the individual project. The parents were able to plan,

and we repurposed scrap wood from the farm in order to keep costs down.

The end result was amazing—new structures, happy families, and a potluck supper to round out the five-hour day. A small program like ours couldn't function without parents donating their time and abilities to help us repair and update the program space. Family events like this are almost always worth the effort and coordination they require. We rely on word of mouth for enrollment, and we require a great deal of buy-in from parents when they enroll their child. By having them help us out in the woods, they feel a sense of ownership of the program and a vested interest in keeping the program running. It also helps us come together as a tighter-knit community, which is the mission of the community farm where we operate. Plus the balance beam is just fabulous, and the gnomes love it!

NATICK COMMUNITY ORGANIC FARM's Forest Gnomes Waldkindergarten (German for *forest kindergarten*) program was established in 2009. We are a nature program for preschool children in a classroom without walls, changing with the seasons. Our gnomes are outside in all weather, through the fall, winter, and spring. Grounded in the values of a traditional Waldkindergarten, our minimally structured program focuses on free play, where exploration and imagination guide our gnomes every day in our beautiful woods.

Family Free-Play Day

by Melissa Frederick

Signing a child up for a Head Start program comes with a lot of expectations and some preconceived notions about a preschool program. Most parents recognize Head Start programs with flagship components like an outside slide, an inside art table, and a fence. Nature-based preschool is an unfamiliar concept to many Head Start parents. Cultivating connections between families and Magnolia is particularly important in helping parents see the value of, feel comfort in, and understand their child's daily experience.

COME MEET OUR SNAKES!

Once a month, we invite the community to come visit Magnolia. We love sharing our outdoor spaces and allowing time to just *be* in nature together. We also get to share the teaching resources we utilize at Camp McDowell, like the teaching farm and the naturalist's reptiles. For September, our very first family free-play day, we thought it was important to show families our snakes and turtles.

Why?

- Both children and adults may feel fear even around domesticated reptiles.

- Many parents express concern that familiarity with domesticated reptiles will make children unsafe around wild reptiles.

- Adults want to share their experience and stories about reptiles and share with siblings and friends.

- Bringing nature inside can be a gentler and more accessible first Magnolia experience than a hike for some parents.

SHARING MATTERS

Both children and adults can benefit from connecting with nature. Identifying, observing, and caring for animals are valuable parts of our curriculum. It is easy for parents to value our learning tools when they get to appreciate these budding scientific skills firsthand. For October we plan on visiting the trail to experience the season changing into fall and share all the treasure we find along the way.

WHAT GUARDIANS SAY . . .

"We love snakes, we have had king snakes at home."

"Me and the snake had a special connection—did you see that?"

"We're so happy to come out to camp. Our oldest son has been asking when we get to visit Camp McDowell again!"

"I respect snakes, but I won't touch them!"

CONNECTIONS TO STANDARDS

TEACHING STRATEGIES GOLD STANDARDS

Family days promote both the parent involvement and whole-family components of Head Start education—sharing our ambassador animals helps to also address the following Teaching Strategies Gold Standards:

Objective 12: Remembers and connects experiences *(Students share recalled experiences with reptiles.)*
Objective 25: Demonstrates knowledge of the characteristics of living things *(Students discuss basic needs, niche, diet, and habits of reptiles.)*

MAGNOLIA NATURE PRESCHOOL is a nature-based preschool partnership between Camp McDowell and Head Start. Magnolia develops kindergarten readiness by focusing on long periods of unstructured play in nature and providing basic health, wellness, and nutrition needs for low-income families in Winston County, Alabama.

Fostering Family Connections

by Sarah Sheldon

The threat of rain loomed in the air and temperatures had dropped to around 40 degrees. Good thing we would be having a campfire at our Fostering Family Connections Play Night! Both parents and children alike came prepared for the weather in their gear.

The event was to be a final farewell, focusing on emergent curriculum and coming together with a campfire and s'mores. Recently the Seeds had become very interested in fox and coyote. To support and scaffold such interests, the evening's theme would focus on nocturnal animals.

Nocturnal animal masks created with reflective tape for eyes were placed along the walking route to the picnic area. As an intro to the evening, families were provided with flashlights and encouraged to meet and greet the nighttime guests. Elinor said, "Look, Mom! I think this is maybe Fox. He lives in the woodland and has whiskers like a dog." At the next nocturnal animal, an owl, Jack noticed a difference: "Look, Owl doesn't have any whiskers." Then he called out "hoo-hoo," and Elinor replied as though she were a fox, "Yip, yip, yip!"

Jack said, "Owls are really fast." Elinor replied, "Yeah, well so are foxes." The parents, knowing what was coming next, asked, "I wonder which one is faster?" The children then raced each other to the picnic area.

The Seeds had been working on their stick-safety skills all year, and our roasting sticks carried with them the same set of rules. Before the children were given their roasting sticks, they were asked, "How can you be safe with this stick?" Charlotte replied, "Stick down towards the ground." Jack said, "Walking feet only."

One simple question and a year's worth of stick play prepared the three-year-old students for roasting their own marshmallows. The children beamed with pride and exclaimed, "I did it!" as they enjoyed their special campfire treat.

Cricket was another nocturnal animal guest of the evening. Small musical insect clickers were

placed at the picnic tables with the prompt, "How can you play hide-and-seek with nocturnal friend Cricket?" At school, the children often played hide-and-seek coyote style. The hiders would howl and the seekers would find the coyotes based on their sense of hearing.

The children clicked the instruments and explained to their parents how to use their good listening ears and what number to count to. They then scurried into the surrounding pines, clicking excitedly until their parents found them. After many rounds, the game ended when the children hid under their favorite climbing tree. No longer wanting to be crickets but raccoons instead, the children asked if they could climb. It was a perfect way to conclude the evening—conversing with parents on how to support and facilitate safe climbing procedures.

CONNECTIONS TO STANDARDS

ILLINOIS EARLY LEARNING STANDARDS

SCIENCE

12.A.EC.a,b Observe, investigate, describe, and categorize living things.
(Noticing owl did not have whiskers, exploration of various nocturnal animals)

SOCIAL/EMOTIONAL

30.A.ECd,e Begin to understand and follow rules; use materials with purpose, safety, and respect.
31.B.ECa Interact verbally and nonverbally with other children, engage in cooperative group play, use socially appropriate behavior with peers and adults such as sharing and taking turns.
(Applying stick-play rules to roasting sticks; using musical clickers with purpose; creating new hide-and-seek rules; working with parents and other peers to play hide-and-seek; taking turns during this game; sharing clickers with parents)

The **CHICAGO BOTANIC GARDEN NATURE PRESCHOOL**, located in Glencoe, Illinois, is a private preschool that serves children ages three to five. Three-year-olds meet for two-and-a-half hours on Tuesdays and Thursdays, and older students meet for three hours on Mondays, Tuesdays, and Wednesdays. At the Garden, we cultivate the power of plants to sustain and enrich life. Within this context, the Preschool strives to create meaningful relationships with the natural world.

Intergenerational Journeys with Young Children and Seniors

URBAN ECOLOGY CENTER®
So much life
Preschool Environmental
Education Program
Milwaukee, Wisconsin

by Matt Flower

The Preschool Environmental Education Program (PEEP) is the Urban Ecology Center's nature-based early childhood education model for child care programs, learning centers, and preschools. Partnering with accredited, shared-site facilities that offer intergenerational programs helps to provide young children and older adults with inclusive, nature-based intergenerational experiences.

The PEEP program called Seasons Journey is designed to engage both young children and older adults (in this case from the Lutheran Home Children's Center) in mutually beneficial nature-based activities that build upon established relationships in these shared facilities and enrich the broader community.

The four seasonal programs within Seasons Journey are centered around the concepts of recurrent natural events and life cycles. Special care is taken to ensure that activities contain familiar, intuitive memories for the grandfriends and fun, movement-based learning experiences for the children. PEEP intergenerational programming has a special impact due to concepts highlighting

our common bonds. When you add fun, dynamic activities, you create a shared experience that feels good. Therein lies the magic: pairing a shared experience with a common theme in an enjoyable way produces feelings of connectedness and love, which in turn helps us grow and keeps us young!

Nature-based early childhood is completely aligned with the experiences of the grandfriends we meet; the concepts of childhood and outdoors are one and the same for them. Through this research, tangible benefits have been identified for both older adults and young children which, in turn, benefits the communities where the Urban Ecology Centers are located:

- Reciprocal relationships promote opportunities for caring, nurturing, and helping behavior for both young children and older adults.

- Children gain positive feelings towards aging and show increased comfort interacting with elders in the broader community.

- Grandfriends experience improved mood, memory, dexterity, feelings of community, and purpose.

INDOOR NATURE-BASED INTERGENERATIONAL INTERACTIONS

"Who loves stories? You do? Well, have I got a story for you! Although this story is unlike any you've ever heard. There is no book and there are no pages or pictures—just us, our puppet friends, and our imagination. So along with our friends of the field and forest, let's tell the tale of Mr. Flower coming to lead an amazing adventure on this lovely spring day!"

INTRODUCTION: SEASONS SONG

Before we start, let's warm up our voices by singing a special song about the seasons! Beginning in the current season and sung to the tune of "If You're Happy and You Know It," all participants sing, do hand movements, and make silly sound effects along with the season-themed verses.

WARM UP: SEASON'S STRETCH

Next let's warm up our bodies. Participants should be sitting comfortably and begin by leaning forward for spring (saying the season as you lean), to their right for summer, back for fall, and to their left for winter. Each time we go a little faster till we hit supersonic fast! Then we do it in super slow motion.

TALL TALES: SOUND STORIES

Now we're ready for the sound story, an interactive play where the children and grandfriends follow along a chosen thread in time, such as a full day in spring or a year in the life of a maple tree. These impromptu tales are full of movement, acting, sounds, and silliness, interspersed with fun, naturalist tidbits based on the puppets and props lined up in the space. The story begins very early in the morning. The children and grandfriends are asleep (children are lying on the floor and snoring) and are slowly woken up by the soft whisper of "sunshine." As they rise, the whisper gets louder until the sun completely peeks over the horizon with everyone giving a loud and excited, "Sunshine!" The story starts to unfold after Mr. Flower arrives to lead everyone on an outdoor adventure. On the journey, we meet birds and animals, pollinate flowers, enjoy a rainstorm and a frog chorus, say goodbye to the sun and hello to the moon, build a campfire, roast marshmallows, meet nocturnal animals, and cozy up in our sleeping bags for the night. Finally, after being woken up periodically by coyotes, owls, and Mr. Flower's snoring, we stay asleep until we're greeted by the soft, mnemonic songs of early morning birds and a crescendo of sunshine!

THE WILD LIFE: INTRODUCING LIVE ANIMALS

Finally it's time to present two live animals for everyone to see, touch, and possibly hold. A great animal to start out with is an ornate box turtle. Since box turtles are uniquely adapted for land and not water, they provide an interesting comparison to the other turtles children and grandfriends might have seen before. The second animal the children experience is a common garter snake. Small snakes are perfect animals to assist people in overcoming a perceived risk, cultivate empathy, and create a personal connection with an animal that many incorrectly consider dangerous. A shared experience helps teach children that, even though something might be different and unfamiliar, with support, we can accomplish what might seem insurmountable alone.

OUTDOOR NATURE-BASED INTERGENERATIONAL INTERACTIONS

A central goal for the Urban Ecology Center's nature-based programs is to provide participants with opportunities for authentic, direct experiences with nature in their neighborhood. Because many shared-site intergenerational programs provide skilled care, memory care, and adult day services with a wide range of mental and physical needs, outdoor exploration comes with a few challenges. Through flexible scheduling for weather issues and wheelchair-accessible green spaces, direct experience with native plantings and wild spaces right in the heart of Milwaukee is entirely possible for both young children and older adults. After observing the bookends of our human existence interacting in a world that is constantly regenerating, one can only conclude that outdoor nature-based intergenerational programming is poetic and of immense value for us all.

FIELD AND FOREST: OUTDOOR EXPLORATION

The Urban Ecology Center stewards several remarkably close, wheelchair-accessible natural play areas that are ideal for providing direct experiences in nature for participants of all ages and abilities. Whereas the range of participant abilities and interests inherently shapes the program's design, there are many open-ended activities that can be planned for and then extended indoors. Adventure Scrolls (ancient-looking scrolls usually delivered by puppets) are great ways to provide a thread to the outdoor experience while maintaining its emergent nature. Each mysterious scroll reveals a seasonal quest: birds in spring, insects in summer, seeds in fall, and tracks in winter. Nature provides us with countless experiences every season, which all but guarantees special moments for both the young and old. Discovering shapes, comparing colors, touching textures, witnessing life cycles, experiencing weather, and celebrating biodiversity can keep everyone fully engaged!

REFLECTION: DISCOVERY COLLAGE

During the outdoor portion, grandfriends can carry small collection containers so the children can bring them treasures for the collage. Cocreating a discovery collage from items gathered on the trail can be the perfect way to end an adventure.

Despite the grandfriends' inability to join in every outdoor portion, inviting children to retell quest details to the grandfriends is extremely valuable. With a large roll of butcher paper, masking and packing tape, markers, crayons, and a variety of natural items such as leaves, sticks, bark, seeds, soil, stones, and dried plants, memories can be created, saved, and added to with this simple culminating activity.

SEASON'S SNACK: THEME-RELATED TREAT

During a snack is often when you see the most natural interactions; sharing a meal is among the oldest of traditions and can be a positive bonding experience. By weaving these snacks into the seasonal activity, we can provide a great way for our generations to connect. In the winter, we enjoy cocoa, spring is perfect for pancakes with real maple syrup, summer brings cool treats with berries, and fall is a great time to make applesauce! Both children and adults can have roles in helping to create and serve these fun, edible activities.

Creating Stories on the Land

by Alicia Jimenez

Collaboration for our agency has meant the possibility of going beyond our school sites and learning in nature. The Wilderness Youth Project (WYP) staff has been inspiring our children to take risks by climbing rocks and trees, exploring creeks and meadows, and encouraging fantasy play in natural environments through storytelling. WYP mentors have worked in joyful symbiosis with Storyteller's teaching staff, and children positively perceive this camaraderie.

Thanks to this collaboration with WYP, our families have camped out at Arroyo Hondo, a local land trust preserve, for two consecutive years. Equipment, campsites, meals, and meaningful activities were offered at no cost to more than eighty people!

THE EVOLUTION OF THE FAMILY CAMPOUT

SAGE HILL 2015
On a hot and windy weekend at the end of March 2015, fifty-seven people gathered at this campsite, most of them for the first time in their lives!

ARROYO HONDO 2016
The families met on a cool and windy weekend, and many of them collaborated with food preparation under the leadership of Chef Lisa. During the night, we gathered at the kitchen, singing and eating popcorn and marshmallows. Sunday morning was full of family games, and the departure was full of words of gratitude for the organizers and the willingness to repeat the experience. Almost eighty people attended this time and enjoyed meeting the small crew of teachers from Storyteller who joined the WYP staff.

ARROYO HONDO 2017
Looking for herbs in the fields and recognizing their value got the attention of a big group of the campers. Later, we all observed the preparation of the herbal salve, took some home, and had the

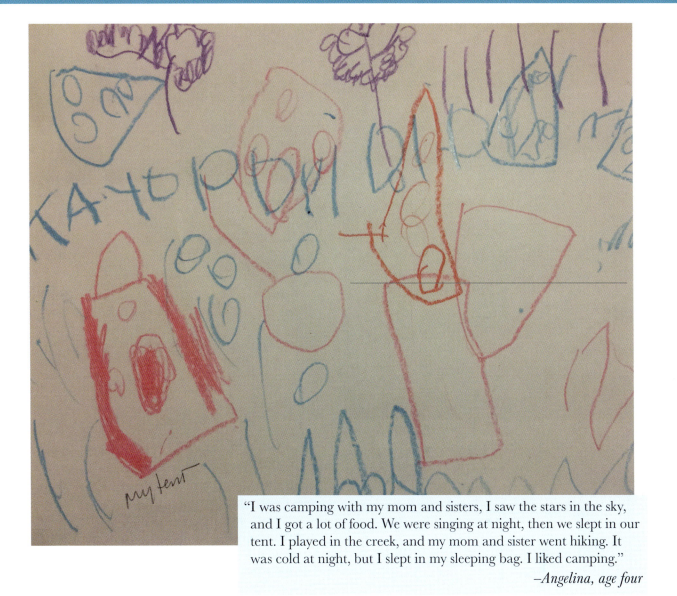

my tent

"I was camping with my mom and sisters, I saw the stars in the sky, and I got a lot of food. We were singing at night, then we slept in our tent. I played in the creek, and my mom and sister went hiking. It was cold at night, but I slept in my sleeping bag. I liked camping."
    —Angelina, age four

willingness to experiment and to know more about plants.

We came together, playing games and giving our gratitude to the land. It became an opportunity to express our feelings to be there as a community who wanted to get closer to nature.

SINGING TIME!

On Saturday night, children joined the group enthusiastically when they heard their favorite tunes. Playing instruments and dancing to the rhythm of the guitar brought many smiles!

WRITING STORIES ON THE LAND: MEMORIES OF FAMILY CAMP-OUTS

With the fresh memories of the first camp-out, parents and teachers have been writing their thoughts and words of gratitude in a journal that has been around since April 2015. Here are some examples from it:

The herbal salve included bay, horsetail, California sagebrush, black sage, plantain, and mugwort.

Black Sage

Cal-sage Brush as old man Sage

Black Sage

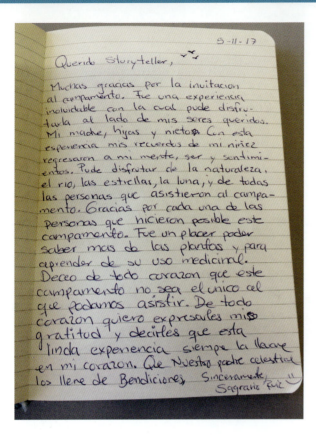

Dear Storyteller,

Thank you for the invitation to the camp-out. It was an unforgettable experience that I enjoyed with my loving family members: my mother, my daughters, and my grandson. My childhood memories and feelings came back to my mind with this experience. I could enjoy nature, the river, the stars, the moon, and all the people who attended the camp-out. Thank you to each person who made it possible. It was a pleasure to know a little bit more about plants and their medicinal uses. I wish from the bottom of my heart that this camp-out does not become the only one that I could attend. God bless you!

Sincerely, Sagrario R.

So many wonderful happenings over the camping weekend. Staff, volunteers, teachers, and families all united in the love of the children. Izzy was a whirlwind of excitement. She said afterwards, "Can we do this every day?" Thank you for giving a gift that will last a lifetime.

—Isabella and Teri

STORYTELLER CHILDREN'S CENTER AND WILDERNESS YOUTH PROJECT (WYP)

This program is one example of the collaboration between the Storyteller Center and the Wilderness Youth Project. In 2013 WYP staff came along and humbly shared their expertise with children, parents, and teachers. We became aware of the possibilities of learning and having fun in nature. In 2015 the shared vision to offer the camp-out experience to families came true. During the past three years of planning and executing this event, we have learned of the existence of different variables that impact the final attendance to the camp: late cancellations, leaving the campsite early, food planning, activities, and the culture of the stakeholders. Reflecting as a group about the positive outcomes and the growing points has been a valuable exercise for our growth as partners.

STORYTELLER CHILDREN'S CENTER helps Santa Barbara's homeless and at-risk toddlers and preschoolers achieve kindergarten readiness by providing therapeutic preschool and support services for their families. We serve eighty families each year.

Ice on Fire

COMMUNITY ARTS CENTER

East Montpelier, Vermont

by Katie Swick

This year marked Vermont's twenty-second annual Ice on Fire, a community celebration of deep winter. It was conceived by Tarin Chaplin and has since been organized and perpetuated by the community. The event consists of three hours of storytelling, song, dance, poetry, puppets, theater, games, and processions. The opening procession is a singing call-and-response dedicated to the four directions and their symbolic purposes (gathered from historic and contemporary world cultures) to nature and their connection to humans. Following the procession, a central fire is lit and the festivities begin. Guests participate in the various activities at their leisure. They may observe the performance stage, take in the storytelling stage, have their faces painted, help with the kid toss (or be tossed, if they are young enough), warm at a bonfire, navigate the tree maze, slide down the luge, imbibe some food and drinks, or simply gather with old and new friends. The closing ceremony is similar to the opening ceremony but climaxes with a mighty Christmas-tree-fueled bonfire.

COLLABORATION

Ice on Fire is a collaboration of AllTogetherNow! Community Arts Center, Kids' Fest, Montpelier's Hubbard Park's rangers, and many volunteers. The first planning meeting is held two months in advance. Planning is organized into four categories (games, performance, food, and storytelling), which are called the four "villages." Each village is named for one of the four directions, and the coleaders of each village are called "elders." The village elders manage food donations, build the physical aspects of the event, organize performers, and gather event-day volunteers. Volunteers serve food, direct traffic, paint faces, lead processions, and oversee the bonfire.

In the weeks prior, used Christmas trees are donated by people in the community and collected by Hubbard Park. Groups of Norwich University students, local K–12 students, Americorps members, and other volunteers come to build the tree maze, the igloos, the luge, the skating and hockey rinks, and the theaters. The North Branch Nature Center is the location host.

PRESCHOOL INVOLVEMENT

By participating in Ice on Fire, preschoolers use what they learn in school to become part of the larger community. Each year AllTogetherNow! Preschool students perform a small show and sing songs at the event. Adults and students performing together on stage enable the young students to feel more comfortable with an audience in front of them. Adults lead the children in song and can invite the audience to join along. Audience participation is intended to create a feeling of community between the performers and the audience.

In 2017 the performance of *Yertle the Turtle* was a joint production by the preschoolers and AllTogetherNow! Community Center's Puppet Troupe. At the end of *Yertle the Turtle*, the audience enjoyed joining in on a few well-known songs. Props and puppets are made in advance with the children. Winter weather and gear are a factor in their creation.

CONNECTIONS TO STANDARDS

VERMONT EARLY LEARNING STANDARDS

II. COMMUNICATION AND EXPRESSION: LANGUAGE DEVELOPMENT

2. Expressive Language (Speaking) 1. Young children use increasingly complex vocabulary and grammar to express their thoughts, feelings, and ideas.

II. COMMUNICATION AND EXPRESSION: CREATIVE ARTS AND EXPRESSION

Music 1. Children engage in making and listening to music as a vehicle for expression and learning.
Theatre 1. Children engage in dramatic play and theatre as a way to represent real-life experiences, communicate their ideas and feelings, learn, and use their imaginations.
Visual Arts 1. Children create art using a variety of tools and art media to express their ideas, feelings, creativity, and develop appreciation of the art created by others.

III. LEARNING ABOUT THE WORLD: SOCIAL STUDIES

2. Family and Community; Civics, Government & Society 1. Children identify themselves initially as belonging to a family, a group, and a community; eventually they develop awareness of themselves as members of increasingly wider circles of society and learn the skills needed to be a contributing member of society.

Part II
Curriculum

CHAPTER 5

Language Development and Literacy

The problem with conventional language and literacy programs for young children is that they've lost the primary connection to children's experience in the world. The language experience approach to literacy focuses on first encouraging experiences that stimulate language. Then teachers support writing that emerges out of these primary experiences, such as "I sau a skwrl 2day on ar wok."

Too often in this new world of hyperventilated academics, experience gets hopscotched over in favor of engaging with text and more text: "See Dick run. Run, Dick, run." Curriculum progressively gets pushed down into earlier and earlier grades so that preschool becomes the new kindergarten, and kindergarten is the new first grade. Didactic phonics worksheets and drill-and-kill techniques that were inappropriate in kindergarten are even less appropriate (and more damaging?) in preschool.

Somehow many curriculum designers have lost the understanding that written language, spelling, and reading need to emerge out of real experiences. Instead of decontextualized workbooks that aspire to having children learn letter names in the absence of lived experience, we need experiential approaches to language and literacy. In nature-based early childhood programs, we see children memorizing songs, having conversations about things they care about ("Let's move the woolly bears off the walkway so they don't get squished"), telling stories, acting out stories that teachers narrate, listening to storybooks under the pines, following recipes, writing and drawing about favorite trees, making letters with sticks and acorns, and drawing charcoal letters on faces. Essentially, we see diverse examples of teachers providing opportunities that bridge the vibrant experiences children are having in the natural world and progressive forms of representation of those experiences through story acting, drawing, singing, and writing.

This approach to early literacy was popular in the 1960s and 1970s and was known as the language experience approach. Building a castle on the playground led to the teacher reading a nonfiction book about castles, which led to children drawing castles and then describing their castles while the teacher wrote each child's words on the page: "The princess is trapped in the cellar of the castle." Then the child copied the teacher's words. The child's first writing, and therefore reading, was words that she had dictated herself. Incrementally, independent letter-learning, sounding out words, and writing independently emerged from this experience-to-representation progression. Instead we now have the children working on disembodied worksheets with no connection to their lived experience. And with so many reading exercises and math workbooks, there's no time for play-based learning. The princess stays trapped in the cellar because there are no children out on the playground to unlock the gate.

FIRST COMES TALKING, THEN COMES WRITING

In research we conducted at the Chippewa Nature Preschool and in the Bullock Creek elementary schools in Midland, Michigan, teachers and parents consistently reported on the increased vocabulary and the increased receptive and expressive language of children. It's widely understood that increasing a child's working vocabulary is one of the engines that leads to increased facility in reading and writing. Therefore, we started to wonder whether nature-based early childhood approaches could be contributing to more substantial language development than in comparable, high-quality traditional programs. And what might be the mechanisms for this increased language development?

We surmised that there might be three ways that nature-based approaches were impacting language development:

1. **Children are developing a large "scientific" or nature-based vocabulary**. Across the board, everyone agrees that nature-based early childhood students have a greater scientific word bank available to them. Here's a quick list of the kinds of words that parents and teachers say children were using at the Chippewa Nature Center: *hibernation, vernal pools, talons, abdomen, thorax, decomposition, carcass, exoskeleton, metamorphosis, agitating*—"just like in my washer."

And here's an example of word sophistication beyond normal expectations for children this age.

> Two bright-eyed, four-year-old girls sat patiently waiting for the speech therapist to ask her next question. The therapist's focus for the day was the *B* sound, so she placed an image of a bird on the table in front of the girls. She then pointed and asked, "What's this?" The two four-year-olds proudly answered, "Woodpecker!" They were correct. The therapist was confused—most four-year-olds would have said "bird." What the therapist had forgotten was that she wasn't working with typical four-year-olds. She was working with students in Chippewa Nature Center's Nature Preschool. (Larimore 2011)

This more substantial excitement about the content leads to vocabulary development, which then leads to greater energy for writing. The comment below from a nature-kindergarten teacher captures this sequence.

> I'm surprised at the size of their vocabulary—it's amazing—and they're just getting this at school. Bears going through torpor, frogs in brumation. Insects—it's not just a bug—they know the body parts and the functions of the body parts. Then this relates back to writing. In winter, when we're reading the *All About Book*, the children are recalling body parts, and then they don't just talk about it, they write about it. (Sobel and Larimore 2018)

2. **English Language Learners (ELL) may do better in a nature-based context.** Because of the materials-based aspect of nature learning, children who are learning English as a second language may be more successful in a nature-based rather than a traditional preschool. Simply, the word-to-referent relationship is clearer when the spoken/written word is presented in conjunction with the real thing rather than with an image of the thing. This was illustrated with the language development of a Korean child who came to the CNC program with hardly any English:

> For our English language learner, he didn't talk a lot in the beginning, but he really connected to grasshoppers and that opened the door to language and to making friends. He would collect and count dozens in a day, and making friends further helped his vocabulary. He would only say, "grasshopper," and then one day he said, "Kennedy, I have three grasshoppers." A whole sentence! Now his expressive language is exploding, because he was interested in the grasshoppers and could connect to other children through them. He felt successful and felt like he belonged. He collects a lot—now it's worms, and he wanted a zipper bag for his tadpoles. I don't think he had any experience with nature before he came here, because his family is not connected with nature. (Sobel and Larimore 2018)

3. **Language learning, beyond just science vocabulary, may be enhanced through nature.** Our speculation is that because, outdoors, social nature play is "deeper"—in other words, lasts longer and is more sustained by the children—there may be greater language expression and reception by the children. A contrary point of view is that child-initiated play is less likely to increase vocabulary because there are fewer adult-directed vocabulary lessons. We speculate that because the children encounter a greater array of natural history surprises— turkeys in the woods, birds landing on them while sitting quietly, the swarm of ants when you stumble upon an anthill, new flowers that weren't in the same place last week—there may be more triggering of questions and more receptivity to teacher language.

GRANDPA TREE SHOWS THE WAY

In this chapter, look at what contextualized language development looks like in a nature-based early childhood program. In the beginning of the year in Megan Gessler's program, the children's new relationship with Grandpa Tree sets the stage for increased language development with scaffolded dramatic play based on children's picture books. She shows us how to use books to encourage caretaking behavior in the woods. And she uses that good old early childhood technique of *animism*—giving life and personality to inanimate objects—to develop a sense of relationship between the children and nature. Then later in the year, Megan's wonderful "Digging Deep into Beaver Inquiry" article documents how many explorations of beaver activity on the banks of the Fox River in Illinois led to rich, sophisticated literacy experiences. She describes it, saying, "The children were still so completely enamored with beavers that I assigned homework by asking them to find out some information to share with the class. I left it completely open to what the children wanted to do for research or for conveying their information. The following week, some students brought in pictures, homemade books, drawings, journals, and/or dioramas to tell us what they learned about beavers. The amount of research that went into this was amazing! We learned that a single beaver can cut down two hundred trees per year. A beaver can hold its breath for up to fifteen minutes underwater. Beavers are *herbivores*—new word! We learned so much more about lodge construction, food, babies, and life-span." Keep in mind that these are four- and five-year-olds and that homework is not a normal part of preschool programs. But this homework was fueled by the children's genuine desire for knowledge.

Now also look at how these activities fully meet the Illinois Early Learning Standards as related to Language Arts.

LANGUAGE ARTS

5.A.EC Seek answers to questions through active exploration. *(Children investigated beaver sites and tried to make sense of observations.)*

5.C.EC Communicate information with others. *(Children discussed their research with classmates and gave tours to adults.)*

5. C.ECa Participate in group projects or units of study designed to learn about a topic of interest. *(The unit emerged out of serendipitously coming upon the beaver cuttings and then teacher/student investigations of the phenomena that then led to engagement with nonfiction texts.)*

This is the language experience approach to literacy education. The real experience provides the context and the glue for the engagement with text and the impulse for children's talking, drawing, and writing.

MAKING LANGUAGE COME ALIVE

Sarah Sheldon demonstrates other techniques for grounding literacy in the natural world in the next two articles. Sarah adapts a Vivian Paley technique of dictation, story narrating, and acting out in Nature's Theater. Children tell a story to Sarah during their morning exploration of the garden, and then later in the morning, she reads the story back and the children act it out. The sun and trees become embodied in the children's playacting. As Sarah describes, "Storytelling and story acting simultaneously strengthen both academics and social growth. The three-year-old Seeds must think critically, pulling various pieces of information together, to make a whole scene."

This story dictation process serves a different purpose when children encounter a headless rabbit one morning. "Who did this?" the children wonder. A shark, a fox? Some of the children begin searching for the culprit, others start to act out what might have happened. But a couple of the children are sad, and the dictation process becomes a way to process their emotions. Violet dictates, "Once upon a time, there was a bunny when it was alive. Then it broke its head off from a fox." The storytelling accomplishes two goals—a recognition of the relationship between real-world events and the written word, and the processing of difficult emotions. Sarah's commitment to Nature's Theater and dictation creates the foundations of reading and writing. And Alice Fergason's account of children discovering charcoal writing is another charming example of emergent integrated writing and art curriculum.

BUILDING A BRIDGE BETWEEN INDOORS AND OUTDOORS

Wendy Garcia's article illustrates one way to bridge indoors and outdoors. When it's just too unpleasant to have the children outdoors, Wendy shows how to create an indoor dramatic play area based on an outdoor setting. When the teachers at Cold Spring School in New Haven create an indoor campsite, making pretend fires, going fishing, and making egg salad ensue. When one child wants to find out more about a bird they saw outside and that is also represented in the indoor campsite, she pulls a book from the shelf and says, "I love reading. And I love the library." Isn't this how we want all children to feel?

ALPHABETIZING THE NATURAL WORLD

Learning the alphabet, of course, is an integral part of early literacy, and there are unique ways to accomplish this in nature-based programs. Katie Swick takes children on a letter walk—they find *V* in the ropes securing a boat tarp, *A* in the framing of a shed, *Y* in a plant stem. Letters are all around, not just on the page. Jennifer Newberry starts her kindergarten year with having each of the children create an alphabet book, with illustrations by the children based on flora and fauna found in the nature area—*F* for frog, *J* for jewelweed, *Q* for quail, and so on. This is so much better than the conventional copying of letters in the workbook.

INCLUSIVE LANGUAGE AND LANGUAGE INCLUSION

Finally, there's Brooke Larm's compelling story of Nari, who started her farm-based education program with almost no English and ended it speaking whole sentences. This article illustrates this just-being-explored territory of nature-based education—the potential of nature-based education as a context for second-language learning. Earlier in this introduction, I refer to a similar story about the effectiveness of a nature preschool in supporting second language learning at the Chippewa Nature Center. These stories crop up all the time when talking with directors whose programs serve diverse populations. Words stick when children have grasshoppers in their hands, when they're pulling carrots from the ground or milking cows. How fulfilling it must have been for Brooke when she got a note from Nari's mother saying, "The most noticeable change is that she uses English a lot more. Oftentimes she surprises us by saying whole sentences! Also, she started to ask [for] something she wants in English as well. In our perspective, it [the Farm Sprouts program] eased our concern for the language barrier."

All these stories show literacy education as it should be in the early years—speaking, drawing, dictating, letter making, nonfiction text-browsing, and second-language learning as an organic extension of children's natural-world experiences. Locavore learning leads to lissome literacy.

Grandpa Tree: Growing Connections through Personification

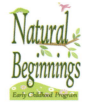

Yorkville, Illinois

by Megan Gessler

It was the beginning of the school year, and the students of Natural Beginnings Early Learning Program found themselves in the middle of a forest surrounded by unfamiliar plant species and complete strangers. For most, this is the first time away from home, and they are not sure how to act with each other or with their environment. Meet Grandpa Tree. He's a steadfast oak near the entrance to the great big forest. He is the anchor to the forest in a way. To my students, Grandpa Tree is not just an old twisted tree. He is a symbol of our connection to nature. We personify Grandpa Tree with a familiar title and explain his needs and his role in the environment we share. We quite literally hold our lessons around him. But like an acorn, as that appreciation grows, we are able to foster a greater understanding of not only this one oak but the needs of all trees and,

eventually, all the plants and animals in our forest. In Grandpa Tree, we help our children discover the symbiotic state of all living creatures.

I stopped for a while and talked about Grandpa Tree's many children and grandchildren in the forest who require a lot of his energy and focus in order to take care of them. That is such a big job. I wondered aloud if there are ways that we can help him.

SHARING A STORY WITH GRANDPA TREE

As the children learned of Grandpa Tree's role, they showed concern for him. "We can help him, Miss Megan!" "We can make sure that his family is safe." "We can water the trees." "We can keep the forest quiet so that they can rest." "We can make the forest pretty to keep them happy."

"We can sing songs." "We can read him books." "We can decorate him." These are just some of the responses that I hear. As the children learned about how to help care for Grandpa Tree, they also learned about how to care for all life. We talked about the basic needs of plants and then transitioned into the basic needs for our class-mates, hoping to elicit sympathy for living things, be they plant, animal, or human.

LITERACY BUILDING WITH GRANDPA TREE

We sat down by Grandpa Tree and read the book *Big Black Bear* by Wong Herbert Yee. At first, I showed the children the illustrations and they hypothesized the story based on the pictures. (The illustrations have fabulous facial cues.) They were learning that the illustrations reflect the words on the page, and they were sequencing the story line themselves. Then we read the book again with the written words and followed a story in which a black bear is neither nice nor polite. He barges into a little girl's home and makes a mess and demands things. Just as the bear begins to get really naughty, we find out that the bear is really only three years old. Enter momma bear. Momma comes in and talks to the little black bear about

using manners. Once he employs manners, things run smoothly.

SOCIAL-SKILL DEVELOPMENT WITH GRANDPA TREE

I ended the reading by pondering aloud, "I wonder how we should act while we are at school?" Some responses were as follows: "We should ask for things nicely." "We should not yell." "We should not act like the little black bear!"

I said, "I wonder if Grandpa Tree has any little black bears that live in this forest. . . . I wonder how they behave. . . . I wonder if he will think that we are like little black bears . . ." I like to wonder aloud and then let the children ponder the questions as we move about the forest. Oftentimes I hear their musings come out later that day, but many times I hear the topic revisited weeks, even months, later.

DRAMATIC PLAY WITH GRANDPA TREE

After continuing on with our outdoor exploration, we made our way back to the classroom, where we had set up the dramatic play area with sturdy tree branches and stuffed bears. The children organically acted out some scenes in which a naughty bear is taught to behave politely. There were also

scenes including a wise old Grandpa Tree. Some students were busy helping him care for the forest.

BRIDGING EMPATHY FROM LESSONS WITH GRANDPA TREE

After the children finished with dramatic play, they were introduced to their daily chores. Their chores center around community involvement where the children care for our classroom and the plants and animals that reside there. Children tend to the fish, turtles, bird, walking sticks, salamander, and plants just like Grandpa Tree helps care for the plants and animals in the forest. They also sweep, wipe the tables, and take out the compost. The students take great pride in caring for their environment and the inhabitants within. They show empathy towards their classroom animals through their gentle touches and their caring attitudes. Their classroom environment is a micro-environment of their 350-acre outdoor learning space. They are learning to care and build compassion for whatever environment they find themselves in—big, small, indoor, outdoor. They are finding their individual power to impact life around them.

Further evidence of empathy appeared on a subsequent hike, when the children noticed an array of woolly bear caterpillars on our paved trail. They spontaneously began to move the caterpillars off of the sidewalk to "keep them from getting squished." Again, this shows a level of sympathy extended to even the smallest of living creatures. The children acted like a cohesive unit as they carefully moved the caterpillars one at a time from the trail.

On that same hike, one of the students was accidentally hurt by another student who had pushed his way to get closer to a woolly bear caterpillar. I overheard yet another student remark, "We need to not act like Black Bear." That sparks a lively discussion about how our classmates, much like the woolly bear, need to be cared for with the same consideration. Parallels between our own needs, animal needs, and plant needs abound.

At the end of every inquiry unit, we give the students a journal prompt. For the plant life unit, we asked the children to draw a picture of their favorite plant and tell us its story. Dylan (age four) chose to dictate a story about Grandma Tree.

Grandma Tree is a faux tree in our classroom. She is made of repurposed paper end rolls. When I created the tree a couple of years ago, the students at that time decided that she was "Grandma Tree" and that she needed to be in our classroom to help us learn about the forest. The children adore her. Here is Dylan's dictation for his journal drawing of Grandma Tree: "This is Grandma Tree and she lived for a long time. She's really old. Grandma Tree loves everybody. She is the nicest plant in the world. I like to give her hugs and I like to learn from her. And don't forget about Grandpa Tree, too. Lots of people love him."

CONNECTIONS TO STANDARDS

ILLINOIS EARLY LEARNING STANDARDS

LANGUAGE ARTS

A.A.ECd Identify emotions from facial expressions and body language. (Discussions on illustrations in Big Black Bear)
1.B.ECb With teacher assistance, participate in collaborative conversations with diverse partners (for example, peers and adults in both small and large groups) about age-appropriate topics and texts. (Discussions regarding Big Black Bear)
2.A.ECa Engage in book sharing experiences with purposes and understanding. (Discussions regarding Big Black Bear)
2.D.ECa With teacher assistance, discuss illustrations in books and make personal connections to the pictures and story. (Discussions regarding illustrations in Big Black Bear)
5.A.ECa Experiment with writing tools and materials. (Journaling)
5.B.ECb With teacher assistance, use a combination of drawing, dictating, or writing. (Journaling)

SOCIAL STUDIES

14.A.ECa Recognize the reasons for rules in the home and early childhood environment. (Discussions regarding Big Black Bear)
14.D.ECb Participate in a variety of roles in the early childhood environment. (Chores)

SOCIAL/EMOTIONAL

31.A.ECa Show empathy, sympathy, and caring for others. (Caring for the woolly bears, classmates, and Grandpa Tree)
31.B.ECa Interact verbally and nonverbally with other children. (Dramatic play and group discussions)
31.B.ECb Engage in cooperative group play. (Dramatic play with the tree and bears)

NATURAL BEGINNINGS EARLY LEARNING PROGRAM is a September-to-May nature preschool program that introduces children ages three through six to the world around them by exploring various nature-based themes. We offer two-day and three-day classes for children. The Natural Beginnings Program takes place at the Hoover Forest Preserve in Yorkville, Illinois, with over 350 acres of prairie, streams, and woodlands to explore. Students are immersed in seasonal themes through nature walks, studying natural phenomenon, and engaging in activities that build physical, emotional, and academic skills.

Digging Deep into Beaver Inquiry

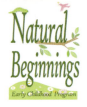

Yorkville, Illinois

by Megan Gessler

It just so happened that the students were feeling like they wanted to take a rather long hike and explore even farther than they have ever been before. About two miles into our hike along the Fox River, the students made a terrific discovery. There were about three dozen saplings that had been gnawed off about a foot and a half off the ground. The children were entranced. They quietly approached the trees and gingerly felt the fresh cuts on the stumps. They bent down and picked up wood shavings from the forest floor that they examined closely, some even holding the piece up to their nose to smell, asking, "What happened, Teacher?"

LANGUAGE ARTS

Since the initial discovery of what we now refer to as The Great Sapling Demise, the students spent a solid six weeks observing and researching beavers. They were talking about beavers nonstop. Beavers became part of their daily interactions as they playacted beaver dramas ("Beaver powers . . . activate!"), made up songs about beavers, regaled beaver facts to one another, and even made beaver jokes. This continuing child-directed dialogue kept the momentum up for maximum learning potential and for the physical commitment to continue hiking four miles to observe the daily changes at the beaver site.

CRITICAL THINKING

On our second trek out to the beaver area, the students noticed a sapling that had been cut from its trunk yet was still hanging vertically, suspended in the air just inches above where it had been cut. This piqued the students' interest. How was the sapling still hanging there? They looked all around and discovered that grapevines were in fact holding the top of the tree in the air. The vines were connected to nearby trees and attached to the top of the sapling. Those vines were holding the sapling in place even after it had been severed.

The children surmised that a beaver had recently tried to cut it down but that it did not have the strength to free the sapling from the vines. I wondered aloud how the beaver could overcome this problem. The children suggested that we help the beaver by pulling the tree down. I let them try it out. At first, just a few children tried it out. Eventually, all twelve children and two adults were holding on to the vine as if in a tug-of-war with the sapling. Despite the combined muscle power, we were not strong enough to free the tree from the grip of the vines. I wondered aloud about the use of tools. "Miss Megan, bring a saw! We can come back next time with a saw in your backpack!"

Following their idea, we returned to the site the next day and the students cut several vines that were connecting the trees. The sapling was free!

PHYSICAL DEVELOPMENT

The children then dragged the sapling to the nearby river's edge where they had noticed a beaver trail leading down into the river. In fact, the beaver had created a trench from dragging trees and branches into the water to swim the wood downstream. We left the sapling there to see what would happen.

We came back the following day to check on the sapling and, much to the children's pleasure, it was gone! The children began hypothesizing about where the beaver took the sapling and what he did with it. We hiked a little farther upstream and found a much larger tree that was in the process of being gnawed down. The children tried to imagine cutting down a tree that size with their own teeth.

They used their hands to feel the deep grooves that the beaver had left behind.

The children were so amazed at their findings that they wanted to continue hiking even farther. Their efforts paid off as they found about forty more trees that had been felled or were in the process of being cut down by beavers. One tree in particular was just barely defying gravity as the beavers had gnawed it down to two balancing pencil points.

We followed another beaver trail to the river's edge and found perfect beaver tracks! Those can be hard to find, as the beaver's tail or the tree branches will often wipe out the tracks. We all whooped for joy when we found them. The children's momentum carried them all the way back to the classroom, which was about a half-hour hike back up from the river in the icy snow.

BACK TO LANGUAGE ARTS

The children were still so completely enamored with beavers that I assigned homework by asking them to find out some information to share with the class. I left it completely open to what the children wanted to do for research or for conveying their information.

The following week, some students brought in pictures, homemade books, drawings, journals, and/or dioramas to tell us what they learned about beavers. They shared their expertise during circle time. We learned that a single beaver can cut down two hundred trees per year. A beaver can hold its breath for up to fifteen minutes underwater. Beavers are *herbivores*—new word! We learned so much more about lodge construction, food, babies, life-span, and so on.

During subsequent hikes, we checked on the beaver progress. The large tree that had been gnawed to a pencil point had been felled and was lying near the river, ready for transport. We watched the progress for three weeks as the beaver methodically cut branches from the tree to transport first, then came back to cut up the trunk into smaller pieces to haul away.

To culminate our beaver study, the Blue Jay class had a special day for our families to come and see the beaver area. The children gave their families a tour and regaled them with beaver facts.

CONNECTIONS TO STANDARDS

ILLINOIS EARLY LEARNING STANDARDS

LANGUAGE ARTS

5.A.EC Seek answers to questions through active exploration.
5.C.EC Communicate information with others. *(Talking with classmates about research and giving tours to adults)*
5C.ECa Participate in group projects or units of study designed to learn about a topic of interest.

SOCIAL/EMOTIONAL

30.C.ECd Demonstrate engagement and sustained attention in activities. *(Six weeks of beaver interest and activities)*

SCIENCE

11.A.ECa Uses senses to explore and observe materials and natural phenomena. *(Touching beaver teeth tracks)*
11.A.ECb Collect, describe, and record information. *(Researching beaver facts)*

PHYSICAL DEVELOPMENT

20.B.EC Exhibit increased endurance. *(Hiking four miles)*

NATURAL BEGINNINGS EARLY LEARNING PROGRAM is a September-to-May nature preschool program that introduces children ages three through six to the world around them by exploring various nature-based themes. We offer two-day and three-day classes for children. The Natural Beginnings Program takes place at the Hoover Forest Preserve in Yorkville, Illinois, with over 350 acres of prairie, streams, and woodlands to explore. Students are immersed in seasonal themes through nature walks, studying natural phenomenon, and engaging in activities that build physical, emotional, and academic skills.

Nature's Theater

CHICAGO BOTANIC GARDEN
Glencoe, Illinois

by Sarah Sheldon

I melodically called to the children, "It's time to act our stories, our stories . . . so join us at the theater, at the theater!" The children eagerly came running, ready to assume the role of story actors and audience members. There was no "me, me, me" called out, because every child understood they would have a turn in both roles.

I assumed my role of stage director, saying, "Ladies and gentlemen, boys and girls, welcome to Nature's Theater." The children stilled their bodies and quieted their voices; their disposition told me that they were indeed ready to begin!

Perhaps you are wondering, "Where might this theater be?" Nature's Theater can transpire anywhere in the Botanic Garden based on the location of our daily adventure. At the pond, the children may choose to construct a stage out of old willow branches; in the growing garden, our take-along tarp does the trick.

When dictating the children's stories during morning play, I always begin the same way: "Your story can be about anything and as long as you'd like, but it can't go past the period." I then place a period at the end of the page as a stopping point. The children have figured out that the longer their story is and the more characters they include, the more friends will be invited onstage. The students are actively practicing kindness and inclusion in their storytelling and acting.

Jasper created the following story that was dictated and acted out at the pond: "Once upon a time, there was Sunny-Go! He is a sun. He shines on us. Then it is his birthday! He has a party. He gets a lot of presents. Then all his friends give presents to him. Mom and Dad gave him presents, too. Then they eat cake. Then a tree knocked over Sunny-Go. Then some workers pushed it back up.

The tree, that tree, a pine tree [pointing to the large pine right behind us]. The end."

At Nature's Theater, the children came onto the stage, one by one, giving Sunny-Go presents. Jack, pictured on page 117, brought with him a real stick as a gift. But when we came to the end of the story, there were no more friends to become the workers. I asked Jasper, "What could we do?" Jasper replied, "Our friends could become the workers!" Everyone agreed and shifted roles so that they could help push Sunny-Go back up.

Storytelling and story acting simultaneously strengthen both academics and social growth. The three-year-old Seeds must think critically, pulling various pieces of information together to make a whole scene. Furthermore, the stories told often reflect the collective location, bringing another element to the storytelling framework.

Onstage, acting becomes a communal effort. The children must follow directions, work cooperatively with one another, and transform the abstract into the concrete. Individual actors must move abstract ideas into concrete representations. Interpersonal growth becomes visible as the actors must work collaboratively to put on a production in real time. Story acting has created a learning environment full of caring and inclusive members both on- and offstage.

CONNECTIONS TO STANDARDS

ILLINOIS EARLY LEARNING STANDARDS

LANGUAGE ARTS

1.A.ECa Follow simple one-, two-, and three-step directions.

PHYSICAL/HEALTH

19.B.ECa Coordinate movements to perform complex tasks. Demonstrate body awareness when moving in different spaces.
21.A.ECa Demonstrate ability to cooperate with others during group physical activity.

THE ARTS

25.A.ECb Drama: Begin to appreciate and participate in dramatic activities.

SOCIAL/EMOTIONAL

30.C.ECb,d Demonstrate persistence and creativity in seeking solutions to problems, demonstrate engagement and sustained attention in activities.

THE CHICAGO BOTANIC GARDEN NATURE PRESCHOOL, located in Glencoe, Illinois, is a private preschool that serves children ages three to five. Three-year-olds meet for two-and-a-half hours on Tuesdays and Thursdays, and older students meet for three hours on Mondays, Wednesdays, and Fridays. At the Garden, we cultivate the power of plants to sustain and enrich life. Within this context, the Preschool strives to create meaningful relationships with the natural world.

Death and Dictation in the Great Outdoors

by Sarah Sheldon

CHICAGO BOTANIC GARDEN

Glencoe, Illinois

An age-old question in the field of early childhood education is "How does one best support and explore death in relation to a child's level of cognition?"

As we headed into the woodland for a day of exploration, the three-year-old Seeds stumbled upon a deceased and decapitated rabbit.

Bosen asked, "Is it dead?"

David, keeping his distance, said, "It has no head."

Connor pondered, "Maybe something ate it."

Leon said, "Maybe it was a shark."

Malone replied, "Sharks live in the ocean. Maybe it was a fox that ate it?"

Leon said, "Where's its head?"

Bosen said, "Come on, let's find it!"

The small group began searching for other animal evidence but came up empty-handed. Then they shifted their focus and began acting out the scene from above. Bosen and David became the rabbits while Connor, Leon, and Malone became the hungry foxes tracking their prey.

In the meantime, a few others stayed back, examining the bunny and their feelings.

Violet said, "Ms. Sarah, I feel sad for the bunny."

Elinor added, "Me too."

So I asked the girls, "But what about the predator? Does anyone feel happy for the fox? After all, everyone needs to eat." I continued on, "Maybe you'd like to tell me a story about the rabbit and its predator."

Vivian Paley's style of dictation and storytelling has been utilized in our classroom as a springboard for learning, building on literacy and using make-believe as a learning tool. The boys needed no direction in acting out their own version of predator/prey. But Violet and Elinor, on the other hand, used dictation to explore the scene that lay before them.

Violet's story: "Once upon a time, there was a bunny when it was alive. Then it broke its head off from a fox. And then it was bleeding. A big predator ate it. Then the family came to see the dead bunny. Then they took the bunny to the hospital. The doctor came and fixed it. Then it was all better but it was still hurting. So the doctor gave it a big Band-Aid and made it feel better. Then the bunny was better. The bunny went home and took a nap. The end."

When we returned to the woodland a few weeks later, the children went to check on the rabbit. Much to their disappointment, the rabbit was gone, but the theme of predator and prey remained. The boys began to play their game of fox and rabbit, adding in an element of hide-and-seek behind the trees. Elinor played a few rounds and then asked if she could tell me a story.

Elinor's story: "It's about the woodland. Once upon a time, there was a squirrel. Then the squirrel climbed up a tree. The coyote was going to eat the squirrel, but then coyote gave up."

I interjected, "Why did the coyote give up?" Elinor continued on, "Because coyote predators cannot climb trees. They don't have sticky paws. The squirrel went up the tree even higher to get an acorn. Then he came back down with the acorn to play with the other squirrels."

Elinor, pointing to the period I pre-placed at the end of the page, said, "Look, Ms. Sarah, it's almost time." She continued on with her story, "Then the squirrel went back to his house with his family of squirrels. That's the end." Elinor proudly pointed to the period again and then went on her way.

CONNECTIONS TO STANDARDS

ILLINOIS EARLY LEARNING STANDARDS

LANGUAGE ARTS

1.C.ECa Describe familiar people, places, things, and events, and with teacher assistance provide additional detail.
1.E.ECa,d,e Begin to use increasingly complex sentences, exhibit curiosity and interest in learning to use new words acquired through conversations.
4.A.ECb,c,d Begin to follow words from left to right, top to bottom, recognize the one-to-one relationship between spoken words and written words, understand that words are separated by spaces in print.
5.C.ECb With teacher assistance, recall factual information and share that information through drawing, dictation or writing.

THE CHICAGO BOTANIC GARDEN NATURE PRESCHOOL, located in Glencoe, Illinois, is a private preschool that serves children ages three to five. Three-year-olds meet for two-and-a-half hours on Tuesdays and Thursdays, and older students meet for three hours on Mondays, Wednesdays, and Fridays. At the Garden, we cultivate the power of plants to sustain and enrich life. Within this context, the Preschool strives to create meaningful relationships with the natural world.

Indoor Campsite and Literacy

Cold Spring School

New Haven, Connecticut

by Wendy Garcia

Indoor campsite: bringing the outdoors inside to encourage literacy while connecting with nature in an urban setting in a joyful and meaningful way

Our thematic study for this year continues to be the natural world. At the beginning of the year, we talked with the children about what kind of space they would like to create in the dramatic play area for the year. Some of them remembered that it had been a rainforest, and that prompted conversations about the different kinds of forests there are. The children related camping to the forests that we find in Connecticut, and we decided as a class that this year our dramatic play area would be a campsite.

There is a hawk in the Pear Tree Yard that has inspired conversations and questions about birds. This led to the children researching different kinds of eggs and the birds that lay them, and the students made bird's nests and eggs of their choice

in Tinkering. (Tinkering is a space and time of day when children get to tinker with loose parts and art materials.) A parent created a related field guide and a papier-mâché tree for the children to display their birds, eggs, and nests.

"I'm putting the light on the rocks and logs in here because it looks like fire," said Ariosa. "Two matches in the wood—now the fire is lit! Elton, will you go fishing with me?"

Elton explained that the fish are in the pond and you have to hook them.

"I love reading," said Ariosa. "And I love the library," she continued as she pulled an alphabet book on birds from the book basket in the campsite.

Elton explained, "I'm going to try and make egg salad" as he collected goods for the task. "That's the wrong basket for eggs. Here they are. We're going to need a lot of eggs for egg salad. This will help with the salad—trees." Tossing the trees into the pot, he said, "One of the trees fell

into the fire. I see it! I can't get it. Let's say it just fell in. Egg salad's ready!"

The children collected leaves from the park across the street and studied them, writing down their observations. They created artwork and found similarities and differences between leaves and conducted research to find out which leaves came from which trees.

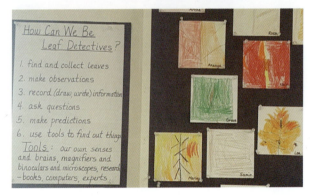

CONNECTIONS TO STANDARDS

CONNECTICUT EARLY LEARNING STANDARDS

W.K.7 Participate in shared research (*Researching, pairing, and making birds and their eggs, resulting in a collaborative art project*)

SL.K.1 Participate in collaborative conversations with peers and adults (*Deciding as a group what the dramatic play area would be*)

SL.K.6 Speak audibly and express thoughts, feelings, and ideas clearly (*Elton making egg salad at the campsite, Ariosa "lighting" the campfire and inviting Elton to go fishing*)

CT AINQ.4 Read, write, listen, and speak about observations of the natural world (*Collecting and identifying leaves, documenting questions and observations, sharing what they've found with others at school*)

COLD SPRING SCHOOL is a progressive, independent school in New Haven, Connecticut, that welcomes children from diverse backgrounds in multi-grade classrooms from preschool to sixth grade. Small by design, Cold Spring serves about 145 students. Children's voices are heard and are integral in the process of learning, and a balance of collaboration and independence is intentionally fostered. Teachers create vibrant learning environments where discovery, engagement, and kindness are valued.

Outdoor Letter Search

COMMUNITY ARTS CENTER

East Montpelier, Vermont

by Katie Swick

"Hey, look I made my letter *T*, " said one of our three-year-olds as he picked up two sticks and put one stick horizontally on top of the other vertical stick.

"Me too!" said another three-year-old, as he tried to hold three sticks horizontally onto a vertical stick to make an *E*. I helped him place the sticks on the ground to form the *E*.

Before going on a letter-search walk, we read *Alfred's Alphabet Walk* by Victoria Chess. This is the story of a boy that goes on a walk to learn his letters by looking for animals that start with each letter of the alphabet. This story focuses on first-letter sounds and on creating an association of a beginning letter to objects and words the children know. We changed the rules for our walk to match our students' readiness for letter concepts. We looked for letters we could see. The walk took place around the school campus, which included human structures and nature.

As we walked by the boat with a tarp tied down by multiple ropes, one child said, "Look, I see a *V*," while another exclaimed, "I see a letter *M*." The teacher asked, "What is the other letter we can see?" When she had the children trace the rope with their fingers, a few children responded, "*W*!"

The walk helped the children become aware that they can recognize letters in human-made and natural places outside of the classroom. Whether the letters were identified in human-made objects—such as the letter *A* on the side of a building or the letters *W*, *V*, *M*, and *N* seen in the ropes on a sailboat—or the letter *Y* in a plant stem, the children's increased awareness and excitement revealed the creation of early literacy learners.

INSIDE NATURE, ART, AND LITERACY

Many of our three-to-five-year-olds are still learning all the letters in their names. Instead of just having the children practice writing their names on the chalkboard or paper, another approach we took was to have the children first paint on and around their prewritten letters, with one letter per page. This enabled them to trace over their letters with brushes and also add their own artistic flair to their letters.

While outside in the field, we collected pieces of dried plant matter such as plant stalks and grasses. Back inside, the children glued the plant matter to the painting to create their letters. Other days, we used seeds to create letters. As the season progressed, we added fresh plant materials. Eventually the children created their names with

nature, and we hung their creations for all to see. It was great way to learn one another's names, too!

POETRY RAIN WALK

As with most projects in nature, you can never quite predict the weather. With a plan to purposely walk in the rain, we dressed in our rain gear and carried buckets to collect rainwater. The rain did not show up. Luckily, it had rained plenty the night before, which allowed for a consolation walk in soggy grass. On our walk, we looked for signs that it had rained. We found stripes in the gravel driveway where rain had created little streams. We discussed how water wants to go downhill. "Can we run down the hill?" asked the children. So down the hill we went too. Along the way, we only found one little puddle. But at the bottom of a large grassy hill, we found something to work with: splashy, splashy, grassy puddles. The children were delighted to stomp around, discovering the depths of puddles while trying to scoop up water in their buckets. Many enjoyed the puddles with the kind of enthusiasm of experiencing something new. After the sloshing fun, we set a plastic tarp down on the ground to sit on and listen to poems about rain. Two poems were written by Shel Silverstein, and one was by Nicola Davies from the book *Outside Your Window*.

CONNECTIONS TO STANDARDS

VERMONT EARLY LEARNING STANDARDS

GROWING, MOVING, AND BEING HEALTHY

Gross- and Fine-Motor Development and Coordination *(Letter walk and rain adventure: running in field, splashing in puddles, getting stuck in mud; practice writing letters, painting, gluing different types of natural materials)*
Health and Safety Practices *(Letter walk and poetry adventure: learning safe navigation around school's community)*

LANGUAGE DEVELOPMENT

Receptive Language (Listening) and Expressive Language (Speaking) Social Rules of Language *(Listening to teacher and other children identify and describe letters found in nature and human structures; listening to poetry; discussions about rain, rain flow, puddles, collecting rain water, and wetlands)*

LITERACY DEVELOPMENT

Foundational Reading Skills *(Reading poetry; reading Alfred's Alphabet Walk; finding letters in nature and in human-created structures; discussions of letters, sounds, and words while letter searching; rhyming)*
Engagement with Literature and Informational Text *(Reading Alfred's Alphabet Walk and going for a letter walk; reading poetry about rain when experiencing rain and aftermath of rain in nature)*
Writing Goal *(Learning, writing, and engaging in letters of their own names)*

CREATIVE ARTS AND EXPRESSION

Visual Art *(Creating letters with paint and gluing natural material in shape of letter)*

ALLTOGETHERNOW! PRESCHOOL was founded in 2006 by Ellen Leonard, a music teacher. The school is located at a hilltop farmhouse, surrounded by ten acres. The school recently became certified as a Vermont Act 166 Universal Pre-K partner with four local public school systems around East Montpelier, Vermont.

E Is for Evergreen: A Vermont Forest Alphabet Book

The Natick Community Organic Farm

Forest Gnomes Waldkindergarten
Natick, Massachusetts

by Jennifer Newberry

The ABCs are the building blocks of language. Children need to recognize the letter symbol–letter sound relationship, both in and out of the alphabet order. This is the heart of early literacy.

I use a couple of different resources as inspiration for a Vermont Forest Alphabet Book. Using animals and plants from the surrounding landscape will allow for meaningful learning and enhance the development of a sense of place.

One resource is from the Vermont woodcut printmaker Mary Azarian, a Caldecott Medalist. She has illustrated over fifty books, my favorite being *A Farmer's Alphabet*. The woodcut prints are elegant and beautiful and capture farm life in Vermont. This book is used as inspiration and is read before we start our own alphabet book.

The second resource is *ABC Animals* from TLC lessons created by Kaye Espinosa. This directed art-lesson book gives step-by-step illustrations on how each art lesson is done. This is helpful getting started with an alphabet book.

Each letter lesson is an extension of the phonics program we use. We learn two to three letters in a week. It usually takes about twelve weeks to complete all the pages. After all the pages are done, the children bind them into a book. The art lesson can be done in whole or small groups in a literacy station. It helps to hand out materials on

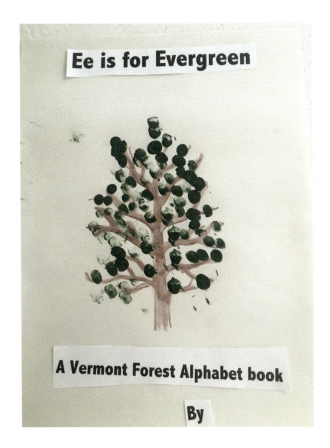

FOREST ALPHABET BOOK

A—apple tree	N—newt
B—beaver	O—owl
C—coyote	P—pinecone
D—deer	Q—quail
E—evergreen	R—rabbit
F—frog	S—snowflake
G—garter snake	T—turtle
H—hawk	U—underground
I—inch worm	V—Vermont
J—jewelweed	W—woodchuck
K—kestrel	X—fox
L—leaf	Y—yellow jacket
M—moose	Z—zigzag

a tray. Each child has everything they need on the tray.

Each page is a 9-by-12-inch piece of construction paper. The capital letter and lowercase letter is glued in the upper right-hand corner, and a typed interesting fact about the plant or animal is glued on the bottom of the page.

All of the children begin with the same materials and follow the same directions, but the results are individual and no two creations will look alike. The books become a wonderful gift during the holiday season.

Frogs drink water through their skin by sitting in the water. A frog's favorite food is flies.

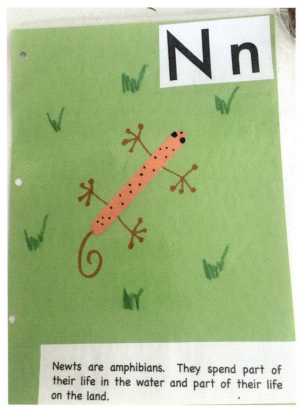

Newts are amphibians. They spend part of their life in the water and part of their life on the land.

CONNECTIONS TO STANDARDS

COMMON CORE KINDERGARTEN STANDARDS

PRINT CONCEPTS

CCSS.ELA-LITERACY.RF.K.1
Demonstrate understanding of the organization and basic features of print.
CCSS.ELA-LITERACY.RF.K.1.A
Follow words from left to right, top to bottom, and page by page.
CCSS.ELA-LITERACY.RF.K.1.B
Recognize that spoken words are represented in written language by specific sequences of letters.
CCSS.ELA-LITERACY.RF.K.1.C
Understand that words are separated by spaces in print.
CCSS.ELA-LITERACY.L.K.5.C
Identify real-life connections between words and their use (for example, note places at school that are colorful).

MARION CROSS SCHOOL is a nurturing kindergarten-through-sixth-grade public school located in Norwich, Vermont. There are currently two full-day kindergarten classes that go out into the forest for most of the day on Fridays. The Milton Frye Nature Preserve has so much to offer, including natural streams to explore the properties of water, trails with a wide variety of trees that change with the seasons, and wildlife that depend upon both. These resources give children tangible ways of working with and in nature to increase their intimate connection to it. Some investigations might take the whole school year as we explore the changes that occur in nature over time.

Inclusive Language and Language Inclusion

MICHIGAN STATE UNIVERSITY | Extension

Tollgate Farm and Education Center
Novi, Michigan

by Brooke Larm

"We are all a part of the farm community" becomes a statement we repeat often, beginning the first day of the program and continuing through to the end of the season. Creating a sense of community in which each child feels included and empowered to learn and contribute is an important component of our program. All children benefit from being involved in authentic learning experiences. For our children with limited English proficiency, this sense of belonging and involvement is especially important to their engagement and growth, particularly in terms of both their language and social-emotional development.

Nari arrived in our program from a home in which Korean is the predominately spoken language. She had attended a parent-and-child library program in English one hour per week prior to joining us. Farm Sprouts was her first independent experience apart from a parent. Nari's parents' concerns included her social development and the language barrier, which could certainly be a contributing impediment to her social integration into a new learning community.

To ensure that our nonnative speakers, including Nari, felt connected to the group, we strove to embrace language diversity. To introduce this concept, we stated, "We speak many languages at the farm." "Not me," said one child, "I speak kid!" To develop a global perspective of

languages in a developmentally appropriate way, opening children's minds to the fact that more languages exist than the one that they speak, we chose to connect language diversity to our farm animals. We asked, "What language do cows speak?" The children responded among giggles, "Moo!" We worked to learn and practice the languages being spoken within our farm community, such as by greeting each other in Korean with "Annyeong-haseyo" or the cows with "Moo!" Soon, hearing languages that may not be understood by a child became normal and even celebrated.

How could we then support language learning? By developing a strong learning community, combined with repeating targeted vocabulary in multiple contexts, we created an environment in which Nari felt she could experiment with speaking a nonnative language. She heard vocabulary focusing on common themes by engaging in authentic tasks, such as brushing a horse or milking a goat. She also heard targeted vocabulary through the use of puppets, children's literature,

games, music and movement, nature journaling, and discussions. We used gestures and other visual cues, such as photos, to aid understanding. Nari was given the opportunity to hear and use English in a social setting through guided and free play.

Nari not only developed confidence in speaking English but with handling the animals as well. Her mom writes, "She used to [be a] little bit afraid of touching animals, but it seems she feels more comfortable getting closer to these animal friends." At home Nari's parents followed our program through a blog, and her dad supported her English learning through conversation. As the program continued, she verbalized words like *raspberry*, *moo*, *bee*, *apple*, and *horse* as we interacted with these plants and animals. By the end of the program, her familiarity with English had grown and we began to hear sentences consisting of two to three words, such as, "I'm done" at the end of snack. Nari's mom shared, "The most noticeable change is that she uses English a lot more. Often-times, she surprises us by saying whole sentences! We believe this is great since she can be social-ized well. We saw she speaks, says hello, giggles with friends in English more. Also, she started to ask [for] something she wants in English as well. In our perspective, it eased our concern for the

language barrier." Most importantly for Nari, her first independent experience was one that was filled with joy, as evidenced by the many wide smiles and laughter we observed and overheard from the moment we stepped outdoors.

CONNECTIONS TO STANDARDS

MICHIGAN DEPT. OF EDUCATION EARLY CHILDHOOD STANDARDS OF QUALITY EARLY LEARNING EXPECTATIONS

EXPRESSIVE ENGLISH LANGUAGE SKILLS

Children demonstrate an increasing ability to speak or use English at an appropriate developmental level. *(Celebrating diversity in languages through the development of a strong learning community)*

OBSERVATION AND INQUIRY

Children develop positive attitudes and gain knowledge about science through observation and active play. *(Authentic and varied learning experiences to support social interaction and learning through play)*

Our early childhood education (ECE) programs at **MSU TOLLGATE FARM AND EDUCATION CENTER** focus on an inquiry-based project approach to learning. We provide young children with opportunities to explore local food and our Michigan natural resources to meet the increasing need within our community for learning experiences in the outdoors. We aim to develop a growing understanding of food, community, and ecosystems in order to support a healthy and sustainable future. Children ages three to five years old attend our program one day per week over the course of four to eight weeks during the winter, spring, and fall seasons. Many of our children participate in the program for two to three years.

CHAPTER 6

Math Learning and Numeracy

As with literacy, so with numeracy. How have we managed to lose the connection between number systems and quantifying the real world in early childhood development? Numerical systems emerged in human culture to order, make sense of, and keep track of everyday things. How many roots do we need to dig up for dinner, how far to the waterhole, how many days till the solstice? Numbers need to stay rooted in things for a long time in early childhood. Children count on their fingers, or count out loud, for as long as they need to. Once it's no longer necessary for the child, these concretizations fall away. We should support these supportive thinking techniques rather than discourage them.

And learning numbers should be fun, not dry and drained of color. In keeping with our Antioch New England core conviction that we should practice what we preach in teacher education, here's a scavenger hunt for the articles in this chapter. As you read these articles, see if you can find the reference (one is pictorial) to all these quantifications of things:

- one ladybug
- a two-year-old child
- three robins in my yard
- four maple leaves
- five tally marks
- six sunflower seeds
- seven shells
- eight deer (maybe tomorrow)
- nine acorns
- ten hoses (or ten inches of rain!—no climate change editorializing allowed)
- eleven people (nine children plus two adults)
- twelve trees
- thirteen? (No can find. Related to why there's no thirteenth floor in hotels?)
- fourteen dewy spider webs

Math can also be incorporated into scavenger hunts, treasure hunts, and math puzzles: How many children will we have in our group if Susan and Jamal leave? How many cups do we need for juice? Is that branch as long as you are tall? Math should be embedded in every activity possible without becoming tedious.

The articles in this chapter fall into three natural categories with lots of overlap: 1) number learning and keeping count, 2) early computation, and 3) patterns in nature.

NUMBER LEARNING AND KEEPING COUNT

Maria Montessori, Friedrich Froebel, John Dewey, and Marilyn Burns all had the right idea when they advocated for concrete math materials. Look at the Montessori materials—they're beautiful and polished but somewhat characterless. Why not use real things to learn counting—leaves, acorns, dandelion heads? Sticks and stones can math skills hone. Lauren Skilling's number line activity is the most straightforward of all the articles in this chapter. Instead of the prefab number line charts on the classroom wall, Lauren's kindergartners make their own number line with objects collected in their forest classroom.

Then Jane Strader, Melissa Frederick, and Wendy Robins (great geographical spread here from Idaho to Alabama to California) show how collecting leads to counting leads to data collection. Jane Strader's keeping-count activity is an example of the fusion between Reggio Emilia approaches to curriculum documentation and the nature-based education approach. This fusion is showing up around the country and the world, and it's a match made in curricular heaven—both approaches bring out something new in the other. Reggio approaches make what's happening out there in the woods more understandable to parents. Nature-based approaches take Reggio out of the plaza and into the woods, fields, and gardens. Finally, in Wendy Robins's article, it's interesting to see how the garden treasure hunt on a cool, overcast day turned up hardly any lizards and butterflies, leading to a bit of science trundling in on the heels of this math activity. The realization was this: weather affects how animals behave!

EARLY COMPUTATION

In 2017 we produced a film titled *The Best Day Ever: Forest Days in Vermont Kindergartens* to document the grassroots movement among kindergarten teachers to take their classes into the woods for one day a week. (There's a companion book called *A Forest Days Handbook: Program Design for School Days Outside* by Eliza Minnucci and Meghan Teachout [2018] that resonates nicely with this book.) One of my favorite scenes in the movie flies by quickly, making it hard to see what's happening. The teachers at Hartland Elementary School (Lauren Skilling and Amanda Soule) have created a set of oak cookies for creating math equations. There are cookies for the numerals 1–20, cookies with the three operations signs (+, −, x) on individual cookies, and an equal-sign (=). Teachers and students make number sentences with the cookies to challenge each other. There are also blank cookies for when children want to create something more challenging. The number sentence in the movie is $6000 - 0 = 6000$, indicating that the child understands that any number minus zero equals the same number. This is not normally part of the kindergarten curriculum that is usually limited to addition and subtraction up to twenty. It may be hard to attribute this sophisticated math problem to doing math in the forest. But at least it suggests that math is an integral part of working with children outside.

Wendy Garcia's articles from the Cold Spring School in New Haven, Connecticut, show early computation activities with sunflower seeds and stories. After planting the sunflowers, watching them grow, and then harvesting them, the children do math problems with the seeds. She also describes having children trace their feet and then measuring objects in the schoolyard using their "foot"-length measure. Why is Lexi's measurement of the bench different from Juan's?

The charming-est article in this section, included because the children are using a pluviometer (new vocabulary) to measure rainfall, comes from normally dry Santa Barbara, California. The charming aspect doesn't have much to do with math, but what a great idea! In anticipation of the coming rain, Alicia Jimenez showed the children excerpts from the movie *Singin' in the Rain*, and the children and teachers identified different activities that Gene Kelly did in the rain. Then, dressed in raincoats and equipped with umbrellas, the children ventured out into the downpour. Raindrops were falling on their heads and the water gushed from gutters onto their umbrellas. When it rains lemons, make lemonade.

PATTERNS IN NATURE

Early math shouldn't just be about numbers and counting; it should also focus on seeing and replicating patterns. The natural world is rife with opportunities to support this kind of early geometry. The article by Katie Swick captures some of the intriguingly different ways we can engage children in understanding patterns—both out in the natural world and with natural materials back in the classroom. Katie describes making mandalas from nature as a paired activity. The emphasis is on understanding symmetry. There's a basket with many of the same things—acorns, fern fronds, twigs of the same length, pinecones, and so on. Each child has their own circular piece of paper, and they face each other across a stick boundary. One child chooses an item and places it on her circle. Then the mirror child picks up a similar object and places it in the parallel location on her own paper. This is early geometry at its innovative best. And there's collaboration, planning behavior, and self-regulation all being developed in this activity.

Could many of these activities occur completely inside using plastic materials? Probably yes. But then you lose out on the gross-motor development of walking to collect the materials, the fine-motor development of picking up sticks, the tactile and olfactory stimulation of pine needles and violets. Embodying math leads to both healthier physical development and stronger numeracy understanding.

Nature Number Line

Hartland Elementary School
Hartland, Vermont

by Lauren Skilling

A nice way to seamlessly connect math learning from within the classroom to learning in the woods is to have students work together to gather materials to create a number line. This learning activity promotes students' understanding of the relationship between numbers and quantities, as they gather a defined number of natural objects found in the woods. It also allows for students to explore painting with watercolors and introduces them to the word *perimeter*.

I have done this activity several times over the years and have found that students are always engaged in the lesson. They love being outdoors, exploring and finding "cool stuff." They also love the artistic element of the lesson. Once displayed in the classroom, the number line becomes a go-to tool for many students. And honestly, the number

line itself is a work of art that everyone enjoys viewing!

MATERIALS NEEDED

- bags numbered 1 to 10
- paper
- watercolor paints and paintbrushes
- cups for water
- markers
- clipboards
- hot glue (to be used when the class is back indoors)

THE PROCESS

Students are given a bag with a number written on it. This defines the number of objects that the

student needs to find. The set should be of like items, for example, nine acorns or nine sticks or nine stones. (Note: Some students find it can be challenging to narrow down their selection to just one type of item. There's so much to find in the woods!)

Once students understand their objective and know their boundaries, they can be released to explore and find objects of interest. When students have gathered their objects, they return to the teacher and show what they have found. As they do this, they demonstrate their ability to count with one-to-one correspondence, as well as to quantify the set. Once they have conferred with the teacher, students may then begin to prepare their papers that will display their findings.

They are given two pieces of paper: one will display their objects and the other will display the written numeral for their set. Students are asked to paint a frame around the perimeter of the paper.

After the frames have dried, students write their assigned number inside their frame. Upon returning to their classroom, students can arrange their sets and the teacher can use hot glue to secure the pieces to the second paper that features the watercolor frame. Regular school glue could also be used, but hot glue tends to hold the items better.

When all students have completed their portion of the number line, they can work together to place the numbers in order. The teacher can then display them in the classroom as a number line for students to use as a reference, or in the hallway as a beautiful display of kindergarten learning.

Note:

- This lesson has typically been completed with numbers one to ten but could easily be modified and completed with larger numbers.

- Number words can also be added so that the word, the set, and the written numeral are displayed together.

- It should also be noted that the size of the bag given to the students will determine the size of the objects that the students can gather. Brown paper lunch bags or plastic sandwich bags work well.

- When counting objects, say the number names in the standard order, pairing each object with one and only one number name and each number name with one and only one object.

CONNECTIONS TO STANDARDS

COMMON CORE STATE STANDARDS

CCSS.MATH.CONTENT.K.CC.B.4.B Understand that the last number name said tells the number of objects counted. The number of objects is the same regardless of their arrangement or the order in which they were counted.

HARTLAND ELEMENTARY SCHOOL is a K–8 public school serving approximately three hundred children in the town of Hartland, Vermont. We believe that every child can succeed, and we are committed to fostering a love of learning and a spirit of inquiry in our students. The sign at the front of the school says, "Whole Child. Whole School. Whole Community." Hartland Elementary School is located on a wooded campus, and kindergarten students participate weekly in a forest program, referred to as Wednesday in the Woods.

Keeping Count, Collecting Data

Teton Valley Community School

Victor, Idaho

by Jane Strader

"Ooh, we're going to the woods tomorrow! I wonder what we're going to find there. Can we go to the big hill where we find shells? I wonder how many we can find!" wonders Jack (four years old). "I saw three robins in my yard this morning. I wonder how many we can find or hear singing in the woods," ponders Harriet (three years old). "Remember when we saw five deer? Maybe there will be more like six or eight tomorrow," adds Grace (four years old).

It is springtime and the frozen world of Teton Valley is slowly thawing and coming back to life. Snow is melting, revealing mud and dry ground; seasonal birds are migrating back, singing us their songs; color is returning to the forest; and the children have a case of spring fever. It is tempting to simply let the children run free and play all day in the woods to get their energy and excitement out, and we will certainly create plenty of time and space for unstructured play. But springtime is a beautiful time to challenge what the children have learned all year and continue to fuel their natural wonderings and desires to track, count, and collect data that will help them recognize their own observations and questions about seasonal change in the natural world.

Hearing the children's wonderings and observations before going to the woods helps us plan what data we will collect when we arrive. This day, the children are interested in collecting shells, identifying birds, and tracking deer. We bring a clipboard with us to keep track of our data, and as we explore in small groups, children are encouraged to count what they find. As children find shells, look and listen for birds, and follow tracks in the snow and dirt, they keep track and report back to me, giving me an exact number, a descriptive quantity, or a verbal description of what they have collected or encountered. I write down their data, which we can later compare with other children's findings or data from past or future days in the woods. Writing down and acknowledging children's observations and collections shows children that their work is useful and beneficial to our growing knowledge about the world around us. Data collection also gives

children words and numbers to share with friends and family about their work in the woods.

Children have a natural tendency to make observations and ask questions about those observations. As teachers, we can guide children through the data-collection process by recording their numbers and descriptions, comparing these to past observations, and asking probing questions. Collecting data is a simple way to engage children in using numbers and math vocabulary that is self-initiated and important to the child, helping children draw conclusions and make more observations about their ever-changing world.

> "I had four shells and then I found three more so now I have seven shells. I think I found the most!"
>
> —*Carter, age four*

Logical-thinking skills: These are precursors to math skills and include recognizing and repeating patterns, arranging objects into series, measuring, and using numbers to count. The outdoor environment provides countless materials

to engage children's minds into developing their logical-thinking skills.

Pattern problems: Children are asked to look for objects with hidden patterns and identify the pattern or find materials to make a beautiful pattern of their own.

Building, predicting, and testing: Children use natural materials to build and construct objects, predict their project's outcome, and test their predictions. These projects ask children to measure, count, compare, and naturally go through the steps of the scientific method.

CONNECTIONS TO STANDARDS

NATIONAL ASSOCIATION FOR THE EDUCATION OF YOUNG CHILDREN STANDARDS

LOGICAL THINKING/COGNITIVE DEVELOPMENT

Classifies objects *(Identify animals, plants, and rocks by color, shape, size, and characteristics)*
Compares/measures *(Compare and measure size of tracks and scat to identify tracks)*
Recognizes and creates patterns *(Find natural object that reflects patterns, such as leaves, colors, size)*
Uses numbers and counting *(Count the number of identified objects to keep track of how many they find each woods day; for example, number of birds, shells, tracks, and so on)*

TETON VALLEY COMMUNITY SCHOOL of Teton Science Schools is a project-based, independent school located in Victor, Idaho. We aim to educate the whole child by integrating academic excellence and character development with a community focus. Students in preschool through sixth grade engage in a challenging curriculum that builds core academic knowledge. The pre-kindergarten program incorporates the best practices in early childhood education as researched and outlined by the National Association for the Education of Young Children (NAEYC) and is inspired by the innovative early education centers of Reggio Emilia, Italy.

Inside Look: What Happens on the Trail?

Magnolia
NATURE SCHOOL
At Camp McDowell
creating good stewards of God's earth

Nauvoo, Alabama

by Melissa Frederick

The year is just beginning, and Magnolia Nature Preschool is heavily focused on building the community and stamina necessary to visit our outdoor play spaces. We enter a wide trail with the intention of building observation skills, woods awareness, leg strength, and routine. I read a short passage from *Naturally Curious* by Mary Holland about the first day of September—spiders are laying eggs! I hope to spark student interest in spider webs; maybe we can find some and investigate them! A sense of calm spreads over the children, replacing the restless energy we felt all morning. Their brains are busy, and the feelings of hurry and stress lift as the woods fully take over as teacher. "Look," I shout to the group of children walking between Teacher Annie and me, "a spider web!"

FROM SPIDER WEBS TO ACORNS

"This is gonna be so COOL," Sarah Ann yells. She completely disregards my spider web intention and picks up a green acorn next to the web. We gently introduce and model the word *acorn* (the children call them "nuts"). We are interested in collecting acorns, and *collection* joins our vocabulary. Before I have time to think about how best to use this loose part/math manipulative, I am frantically scribbling observations as the children take ownership of their lesson plan.

INGENUITY

Kaydence looks down at her full hands and must problem solve. She forms a pouch in her shirt and gleefully yells, "Another one! Another one!" Sarah Ann's shirt is tight, so she teams up with Kaydence, who acts as verbal director while Sarah Ann picks up acorns and places them into the shirt pouch.

COLLABORATION

Brodie, Tripp, and Timothy use teamwork to make a collection in their world of play. "I think there are loads more somewhere around here hiding!" Brodie says suspiciously, "I don't know who has all of them, but we can find them!" They begin to pile acorns on the trail, Brodie and Timothy trekking through dangerous, prickly

greenbrier territory while Tripp guards the acorn tower. Timothy goes to grab a huge handful from Thomas's carefully constructed pile of "green and sparkly" and "shiny and wet" acorns. Before I can mediate, Timothy murmurs, "I'm sorry," and Thomas already self-soothes, proclaiming, "I can build it back up! I have a plan."

CURIOSITY

I must bite my tongue from mechanically prompting, "Why don't we count the acorns?" Instead I wait until I hear "One, two, three, four . . ." Timothy is counting out big clumps of acorns from where he has stored them in his backpack. I make a note, wondering if he is misunderstanding how to count the number of acorns or if he wants to know the number of clumps.

VALUES

At the end of our lesson, we must decide what to do with our acorns. Thomas decides to count out four acorns, and one more for a friend for a total of five. "The rest are for the squirrels!" Sarah Ann decides to keep a heavy backpack full of acorns, claiming that she does not intend to share. Acorn exploration is now a captivating part of our curriculum.

CONNECTIONS TO STANDARDS

TEACHING STRATEGIES GOLD STANDARDS

Objective 3: Participates cooperatively and constructively in group situations
(Students used teamwork, small-group participation, cooperative play, and social problem solving.)
Objective 20: Uses number concepts and operations
(Students compared, counted, gauged sizes, and even added numbers of acorns in piles.)
Objective 24: Uses scientific inquiry skills
(Students observed, wondered where acorns came from, asked questions, and investigated trees and ground for possible answers.)

MAGNOLIA NATURE PRESCHOOL is a nature-based preschool partnership between Camp McDowell and Head Start. Magnolia develops kindergarten readiness by focusing on long periods of unstructured play in nature and providing basic health, wellness, and nutrition needs for low-income families in Winston County, Alabama.

Garden Inventory: Tally Mark Counting in the Garden

Santa Barbara, California

by Wendy Robins

Scavenger hunts of any kind are always fun in the garden. Searching for items encourages the children to slow down and see the garden through a different lens. A hunt can be tailored to what is being studied in the classroom, for example, insects or colors. Hunts are a way for exploration to happen but with intention. The children can look for an endless number of things: animals, textures, shapes, living/nonliving things, and so on. For this hunt, we searched for just seven items, but instead of simply checking each item off, we kept a count of how many of each item we found. We counted using tally marks, a method that was being used in the classroom to count other variables but could be introduced in the garden. Before we began, we did a quick review of counting by fives using tally marks. We also went over the items we were looking for to ensure everyone understood the worksheet.

I created the worksheet using simple drawings with space for tally marks. The goal for this activity is continued exploration of the garden and to practice counting objects. An accurate inventory of the garden is not the objective, although for older students, this could indeed be a useful tool. I'm certain the younger children counted the pair of western scrub jays every time they flew by. Some worksheets came back completely filled in, as if the student saw fifteen (or forty-five, if their tally marks were small) of everything. The worksheet below was done by a student who focused on one item at a time and didn't quite get the tally marks right; however, every time he saw a tree, he cheered, "TREE!"

The day we did this particular count, it was cool and overcast; butterflies, lizards, and ladybugs were not easily seen. Upon finally finding a ladybug, Sebastian called out to everyone, "Okay, everybody, write *one* ladybug!" Angela was amazed at how many hoses she found in the garden. "Ten hoses?!" she exclaimed incredulously. At the end of our garden time, we gathered to review what we found and didn't find. We talked about why there weren't many lizards or butterflies because of the weather, incorporating science into our math activity in the garden. We also did some

totaling to see how many items we recorded and if those numbers were realistic.

In the following weeks, the children asked to have clipboards, paper, and pencils so they could create their own counting worksheets. On one particularly foggy morning, Jimmy and Sloane searched for dewy spider webs. I kept hearing shouts of "I found another one! That's fourteen now!"

EXPLORE ECOLOGY is a nonprofit organization that oversees a garden-based education program in over twenty elementary schools in Santa Barbara County. I work at two schools, seeing children in grades TK–8 in the garden once each week for thirty to sixty minutes. Sometimes we have a structured lesson, sometimes we perform garden work, and always we explore our beautiful gardens.

Math with Seeds

Cold Spring School

New Haven, Connecticut

by Wendy Garcia

The preschool and kindergarten/first-grade students use sunflower seeds harvested from the previous summer's flowers to hone their math skills.

Students plant sunflowers each year in the Pear Tree Yard, and when they harvest the seeds, they save them. When it's too early to plant, the preschoolers use them for math in the classroom. Once the planting season is upon them, the kindergarten/first-grade students take the math lessons outside.

The kindergarten/first-grade students grouped more than two hundred sunflower seeds saved from the previous year, sorting them into

groups of ten. They measured the length along the fence in the Pear Tree Yard using rulers, yardsticks, and tape measures. They dug two-inch holes every six inches to plant the seeds, using sticks with yarn to help protect the seedlings.

Teacher: Can you give half of your garden to your bear friend?

Ian: I gave four to my bear and I have four left.

Teacher: Good. So, four plus four equals . . .?

Ian: Four plus four equals eight!

Teacher: Good. How many do you have, L?

Lila: I have nine. My bear has three.

Teacher: So, you have twelve seeds. How many are you going to take? Maybe we can do this one together?

Lila: Yeah.

Teacher: Let's put all your seeds right here. If we split them in half, that means every time you give one to the bear, you get one too. Let's give one to the bear and take one for you. Now give one to the bear. One for you. Keep going. [A little later] Is that all of them?

Lila: Yes.

Teacher: How many does the bear have?

Lila: Six.

Teacher: Six. She gave away half of her twelve seeds, and now they each have six.

Lila: Yes. Six plus six equals twelve!

Ian pulls a number three from the bag.

Teacher: How many seeds do you need for your garden?

Ian: Three.

Teacher: Good. Now take another number.

Ian pulls the number two from the bag.

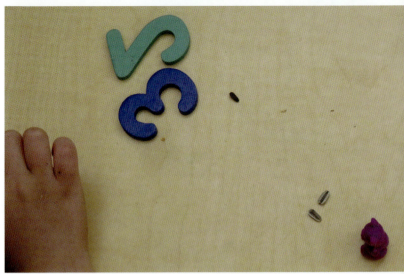

Teacher: How many seeds does baby bear eat?

Ian: Two.

Teacher: So how many seeds do you have left for your garden?

Ian: One.

Teacher: Hai, your turn. How many seeds will be in your garden?

Hai rolls the dice: Two and . . . two is . . . four.

Teacher: Good. Count out your four seeds.

Hai: One, two, three, four.

CONNECTIONS TO STANDARDS

CONNECTICUT EARLY LEARNING STANDARDS

C.48.4 & C.60.5 Engage in and complete learning activities with peers and plan and complete learning activity with a peer. *(Preschoolers doing math activity with a teacher and kindergarten students working together to count seeds and measure out for planting)*
M.60.2 Count up to ten objects using a one-to-one correspondence, using the number name of the last object counted to represent the total number of objects in a set. *(Kindergarten students counting out seeds in groups of ten)*
M.48.7 Understand that adding (or taking away) one or more objects from a group will increase or decrease the objects in the group. *(Preschoolers playing a game in which baby bear eats some of their seeds for their garden and needing to figure out how many they have left to plant)*

COLD SPRING SCHOOL is a progressive, independent school in New Haven, Connecticut, that welcomes children from diverse backgrounds in multi-grade classrooms from preschool to sixth grade. Small by design, Cold Spring serves about 145 students. Children's voices are heard and are integral in the process of learning, and a balance of collaboration and independence is intentionally fostered. Teachers create vibrant learning environments where discovery, engagement, and kindness are valued.

Measuring by the Kindergarten Foot

by Wendy Garcia

Measuring objects with tracings of kindergarten students' feet redefines what a foot is.

The kindergarten/first-grade class has been taking more of their math lessons outside to the Pear Tree Yard, and most recently the kindergartners decided to measure different objects—with their feet! We traced their feet and they cut them out, and that made it easier for them to see that some of their feet were bigger or smaller than their friends' feet.

We gathered in the Pear Tree Yard to talk about what we thought we might discover when each of us measured objects and what it might mean:

Teacher: If your foot is smaller, will it take more or less feet to measure something?

Raquel: More.

Teacher: Why?

Raquel: Because of how much space the foot takes up.

This lesson began indoors as the children started measuring things before they got outside and started realizing how having a different-size measuring tool made a difference in the answer you got. The information was documented so they

could see how many of each of their feet it took to get the lengths. By seeing that it took more of some children's feet than others, they came to the conclusion that those friends had smaller feet.

OBJECTS OF MEASUREMENT

The children took turns measuring various items outside, including a bench, a flowerpot, the raised garden bed, a railing, and a stump.

Some students found a broken tree branch and decided to measure it against their own heights to see who was taller than the branch and who fit beneath it.

Teacher: How many of us are there?

Sophie: Nine.

Teacher: Add me.

Sophie: Ten.

Teacher: Add Wendy.

Sophie: Eleven.

Teacher: How would you write that?

Students demonstrating that the equal sign is two lines parallel to one another, as opposed to perpendicular.

Sophie: Nine plus one plus one, or nine plus two, equals eleven. Or nine kids and two grown-ups is eleven people.

CONNECTIONS TO STANDARDS

CONNECTICUT EARLY LEARNING STANDARDS

K.OA.A1 Represent addition and subtraction with . . . equations. *(Sophie reframing the total number of people in the group with the equation 9+2=11)*
K.CC.B.4 Understand the relationship between numbers and quantities; connect counting to cardinality. *(Counting the number of traced feet an object measures and knowing that the last number is the length of the object, or the total number of traced feet of the object, and that it may be different for each child)*
K.MD.A.2 Directly compare two objects with a measurable attribute in common to see which object has "more of/less of" the attribute, and describe the difference. *(The children measuring themselves against a branch and comparing who was shorter or taller than the stick to determine who was shorter or taller than one another)*

COLD SPRING SCHOOL is a progressive, independent school in New Haven, Connecticut, that welcomes children from diverse backgrounds in multi-grade classrooms from preschool to sixth grade. Small by design, Cold Spring serves about 145 students. Children's voices are heard and are integral in the process of learning, and a balance of collaboration and independence is intentionally fostered. Teachers create vibrant learning environments where discovery, engagement, and kindness are valued.

We Are Singing, Feeling, and Learning in the Rain

by Alicia Jimenez

Santa Barbara, California

Rain has become an exciting event in our normally dry region; it is a necessity and a memorable sensory experience. Jumping in the puddles, seeing and hearing a creek with running water, and wondering about the destiny of the stream have become exciting for our children. They were measuring how much rain we could catch, and they even enjoyed tasting the rain! These have been some of the fun and sensory activities that our children have been enjoying these days. Our children watched a video clip of Gene Kelly dancing and singing in the rain. They were joyfully inspired; they emulated his umbrella's movements and stood under the rain gutter. Raindrops were falling on top of their heads; the children were holding the water in their hands and splashing in the puddles with their feet.

The Oak Park Creek offers our children a place to climb on rocks and boulders during most of the year. While watching the dark running water, numerous questions were asked by the group. "Why does the water look dirty? Look, it is making bubbles!" A child asked, "Where is this water coming from, Teacher?" "From the mountains," somebody answered. "It is a lot of water and my mom said that it is going to rain more; she looked on her phone. We need rainy boots."

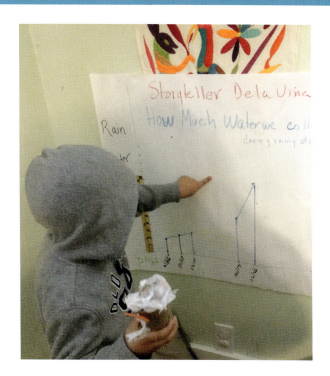

I ask the group, "Where is this water traveling to?" Juliana answered confidently, "To the ocean; all the water goes there."

RAIN MEASURING CHART

We collected rainwater in the pluviometer for five days. Every morning, we checked the amounts on the ruler. Our children were amazed when they saw how much the water level had increased each time: two inches, two-and-a-half, four. . . . Then the big storm arrived! The pluviometer could not handle that amount of water, and it overflowed. It reached more than ten inches!

During the second trip to the Oak Park Creek, the children had an idea that they might find fish swimming happily. They recalled what they saw on the information display board in the park, which included a picture of the living organisms at Oak Park. Holding and scooping nets

in the water, they found leaves, pebbles, and little sticks. A boy asked, "Where are the fishes? I do not see any. What about sharks?" A peer answered quickly, "Sharks live in the ocean, not here!"

Feeling the cold water with our feet was the best part of the rainy season. The children's ability to walk barefoot (or with rain boots) in the creek allowed them to have a unique sensory experience of the rain.

CONNECTIONS TO STANDARDS

PRESCHOOL FOUNDATIONS STANDARDS

MATHEMATHICS.MEASUREMENT

1.0 Children begin to compare and order objects.
(Children showed interest in measuring how much rainwater they collected, and in comparing the difference between dates of water collection and quantity and communicating their findings.)

HISTORY-SOCIAL SCIENCE

Sense of Place. 2.0 Caring for the Natural World
(Children showed an interest in nature [including animals, plants, and the weather] especially as they experienced it directly when they spotted and observed running water [after or during rainy days] at different points in the Mission Creek.)

SCIENCE

Scientific Inquiry. 1.3 Begin to identify and use, with adult support, some observation and measurement tools.
1.5 Make predictions and check them, with adult support, through concrete experiences.
(Children are developing the ability to use language and specific terms to describe their observations and communicate findings, explanations, and ideas to others during these activities related to the rainy season.)

STORYTELLER CHILDREN'S CENTER helps Santa Barbara's homeless and at-risk toddlers and preschoolers achieve kindergarten readiness by providing therapeutic preschool and support services for their families. We serve eighty families each year.

Collection of Natural Objects

by Katie Swick

With baskets in hand, we set out to collect a variety of natural materials on a field and forest walk-through. The intention of the walk was to pick two samples of any object and put it in your basket. We gathered flowers, rocks, sticks, cones, plants, pine needles, and bark to bring back to school for later. "Look at this shiny rock," said one girl, "but I can't find another one. But I got lots of sticky pinecones!"

"Hey guys, look at all these little flowers!" one girl called to the group. They all came over to see. Another responds, "So tiny!"

Not only did we find materials to bring back, but also we found many other interesting objects that stayed in the forest that were great for a discussion along the way.

OBJECTIVE

This is a mirror game of natural materials to develop math, language, social, science, and creativity skills for all ages.

MATERIALS

- baskets for collecting
- sticks for creating a "mirror"
- circles for the base of the mandalas—paper or cloth or wood cookies
- two of each of a variety of natural objects

- space for the game: blanket, tables, or raised wide logs next to each other
- optional: pictures of mandalas or pictures of arrangements of natural objects
- optional: mirrors to compare or explore with

NATURAL MATH MANDALAS

That afternoon we were stuck inside because of a thunderstorm. Instead of sitting on a blanket outside, we paired the children up at opposite sides of the table: a two- or three-year-old with a four- or five-year-old. The kids had previously been introduced to the mirror game with a variety of small loose parts from the classroom. To reintroduce the game, I modeled with one of the older children. To start, on one side of the table sat the "mirrors," which were the older children. On the other side of the table sat the "children." First, the "child" chooses an object from the basket and places it somewhere on their paper circle or mandala. Then the "child" hands the basket to the "mirror."

The "mirror" finds the matching object and places it on their mandala, with the goal of placing it in the same mirror location as their partner. From here they take turns, back and forth, creating their mirror mandalas. When finished, we take pictures and the children trade roles. Usually the two-year-olds were unable to be the mirrors, so we traded partners or some of the older child helped the two-year-olds be mirrors.

Depending on the developmental age of the child, the children mirror the mandala, or they may just place objects how they see them while looking at their partner's mandala (for example, the stick at top of the child's mandala becomes the stick at bottom of the mirror's mandala). Previous play with mirrors and introductions to art with mandalas help to scaffold this game.

This is a great activity for symmetry, geometry, leadership, spatial awareness, executive functioning, language development, and social development. On this one day, the activity encouraged some great partner conversation. "I got three sticky pinecones. You need one more," said one child to their mirror partner. Another child in conversation with their mirror said, "I made lines." "I can too," replied their partner.

POSSIBLE EXTENSIONS

- Notice how the objects change through the seasons. You could glue the mandalas to save them and compare seasonal differences, or you could take and print pictures.

- Focus on symmetry or fractions (halves or quarters or thirds). Encourage children to create symmetry in the circle, then mirror it. Collect objects in multiples to use for fractions.

- Model language of plant identification or geometry or adjectives in game conversation.

CONNECTIONS TO STANDARDS

VERMONT EARLY LEARNING STANDARDS

SOCIAL AND EMOTIONAL LEARNING AND DEVELOPMENT

Emotion and Self-Regulation 1. Children express a range of emotions and regulate their emotional and social responses. *(Taking turns with basket of objects and taking turns being "mirror" and "child"/"follower" and "leader.")*

GROWING, MOVING, AND BEING HEALTHY

Motor Development and Coordination. Children develop strength, coordination, and control of their large muscles and small or fine-motor muscles. *(A walk in a field and/or the woods to find materials and picking objects)*

LANGUAGE DEVELOPMENT

Speaking and Listening. Children demonstrate an increasing ability to comprehend and participate in collaborative conversations. *(Children discussing with each other how objects do or do not match, descriptions of objects and placements of objects)*

MATHEMATICS

Measurement, Classification, and Data Goal. Children develop awareness of the differences of the objects and learn to sort, compare, and classify objects by their attributes and properties. *(Comparing and classifying different types of natural objects)*
Geometry and Spatial Reasoning and Spatial Sense Goal. Children increasingly recognize two- and three-dimensional objects and use spatial reasoning. *(Symmetry, mirroring of objects on circle mandalas uses spatial reasoning)*
Number Relationships and Operations Goal. Children increasingly use numbers to describe relationships and to solve mathematical problems. *(Counting by twos and matching objects)*

ALLTOGETHERNOW! PRESCHOOL was founded in 2006 by Ellen Leonard, a music teacher. The school is located at a hilltop farmhouse, surrounded by ten acres. The school recently became certified as a Vermont Act 166 Universal Pre-K partner with four local public school systems around East Montpelier.

CHAPTER 7

Science, Technology, Engineering, and Math (STEM) Learning

First let me get a few things off my chest. The emergent emphasis on STEM learning is a good thing in schools. And the evolution of STEAM, with the *A* standing for *arts*, tends to round out the approach even more. But really, if the school is emphasizing science, technology, engineering, arts, and math—and, of course, everyone does literacy—doesn't STEAM mean everything but social studies? And why should social studies be the neglected stepchild of the curriculum? Couldn't the focus of schools be on good old-fashioned integrated curriculum without having to single out some higher- and lower-value subjects?

Second, technology education should not be equated with computer education. Teaching programming in first grade may be a good thing (though I'm not convinced yet), but I do know that technology education should be about making things. About inventing see-saws, adjusting the location of the water bottle on the gerbil cage, figuring out how to fix flashlights, and designing boats that will make it through the rapids in the little stream on the edge of the playground. The maker movement is a great counterpoint to too-early computerization of children's lives.

The teachers at a professional development workshop in Lyndonville, Vermont, recently told me that when they asked their students what they wanted more of, the most common response was, "We want to make things!" And by "things," they didn't mean computer images. They meant mittens, fires, spoons, lanterns, forts, bracelets, and fruit leather. And so the articles in this chapter are, for the most part, about making things and solving real problems.

Hannah Lindner-Finlay's articles are the core of this chapter, with Megan Gessler's brilliant piece on pirate play leading off and Lauren Skilling's marble run batting cleanup. When Hannah was a kindergarten teacher at The Gordon School in Providence, Rhode Island, the school adopted a STEAM Lab program that involved three-week sessions focused on different topics. Hannah's self-imposed challenge was, "How can I take all the same concepts and teach them outside?"

Linder-Finlay's articles insightfully illustrate that all the STEAM topics were nicely addressed in the outdoors, using the relatively limited outdoor space at this urban school. Let's look at the collection of articles here to illustrate the virtues of taking STEM or STEAM outside.

EMERGENT CURRICULUM

One of the core principles of nature-based early childhood teaching is the balance between teacher-scaffolded and child-directed learning. Megan Gessler's "Pirate Play" article is one of the finest examples of emergent curriculum, with a developmentally appropriate STEM twist, that I've seen in years. When Megan's preschoolers came upon a geocache box filled with simulated gold coins, they were convinced that this was pirate treasure and that there must be more treasure on the other side of the little creek—a place where they'd never been. We have to cross the creek to find more treasure! The creek was more than boot high and it was winter, so Megan asked, "How will we make it across without our feet getting icy cold and wet?" This was the perfectly inserted question at just the right time to stimulate creative thinking and problem-solving. As Megan says, "It was almost as if I could see their minds whirring with activity."

It would have been easy to squelch this activity at this point. She could have said, "It'll be too hard to cross the creek. Let's look for more pirate treasure on this side." Another option could have been, "Pirates wouldn't spread their treasure around. I don't think we'll find any more pirate treasure over there"—which is probably true since it's unlikely there are more geocache boxes—"so I don't think it's worth the bother." Or she could have provided a prefab solution and said, "Let's find three or four fallen-down trees, drag them to the stream, and make a bridge." Instead she challenged the children to solve the problem. She trusted the process.

What follows is the perfect cycle of inquiry. They tried gluing sticks together. That didn't work. They brainstormed other solutions. What about a raft? Perhaps we could bang the sticks together with hammer and nails, or maybe weave them with bandages? Megan stepped up, and the next morning, she had hammer, nails, string, rope, fabric scraps, and bandages ready to go—the perfect set of loose parts. Remarkably, they fashioned a raft, but it was big and awkward to carry. Getting it to the stream, a long ways away, was another problem to solve. And they figured that out too. All the while Megan watched, encouraged, asked the right questions, taught weaving techniques when necessary, and didn't take over. And amazingly, when they got the raft to the creek, it worked! It was less like a raft and more like a bridge, but it allowed access to the other side.

Of course, then there was the next problem for Megan. She was pretty sure they wouldn't find more geocache boxes. How would she deal with the great disappointment of not finding any more pirate treasure? Well, laddies and lassies, you'll just hafta read her darn good yarn to find out where the treasure be.

Keep in mind that searching for pirate treasure, or raft building, or creek crossing, are not part of any specified early childhood curriculum. But the Illinois Early Learning Standards encourage teachers to have children use measuring tools, express wonder and curiosity by asking questions, solve problems, and design things and engage in engineering investigations. This is so completely what happened here. And it happened because Megan realized the genuine thrill of the children wanting to find more treasure and cross that stream and went for it, *not knowing what would happen.* Emergent curriculum at its bloomin' best.

APPLYING THE CHILDHOOD AND NATURE DESIGN PRINCIPLES

In *Childhood and Nature: Design Principles for Educators* (Sobel 2008), I describe seven different play motifs, things all children like to do in nature all around the world. Some of these are making special places, constructing small worlds, going on adventures, and enacting fantasies. I contend that you can translate these play motifs into design principles to help create activities that will have implicit appeal for children. Hannah Lindner-Finlay's STEAM outdoor activities manifest these design principles, and that's part of what makes them successful. To be clear, she didn't set out to create these activities with the design principles in mind. Instead, like many good early childhood teachers, she has an intuitive sense of how to use play and children's fascinations as the engine for learning. Therefore she uses children's fascination with fairy houses (small worlds and fantasy) to teach about the principle of stability, sledding (adventure) to teach about friction, and damming little streams (small worlds and adventure) to teach about how water moves.

Let's look at the stability example. Prior to going outside, children did indoor activities and she introduced some of the vocabulary of the unit. Outside, she challenged children to make sticks stand upright and not fall over—that is, to make them stable. Then she challenged them to make stable fairy houses. As Hannah says, "The fairy houses were much more exciting than the idea of stability," but by harnessing the fairy house idea, she could rope the children into investigations of stability—using the design principle to engage the children in learning. Moreover, this led to one of her most productive writing workshops to date during that year. (Another plug for integrated curriculum!)

A couple of years later, Hannah was working at the Putney Central School in Putney, Vermont, with second and third graders, where she recruited the same interest in fairy houses and small worlds in the service of STEM Learning. (This example is not described in this chapter, but it illustrates the design principles idea.) These are the Next Generation Science Standards she targeted:

- Develop a simple model to represent a proposed object or tool.
- Make a claim about the merit of a design solution that reduces the impacts of a weather-related hazard.
- Analyze data from tests of an object to determine if it works as intended.

The unit was called Meeting NGSS Standards by Constructing Mini-Forts That Can Withstand Wind, Rain, and Falling Acorns. *Mini-forts* is a slightly more developmentally appealing way for older children to refer to miniature structures than *fairy houses*. They drew simple designs in the classroom, built miniature structures in the woods, and then tested them by pouring water, dropping acorns, and blowing on them. (The perfect tool for this activity could be one of those backpack leaf blowers for simulating hurricane-force winds.) Then the children had to analyze the data from their tests and determine if their structures worked. One child wrote, "I first did the acorn test and it [the mini-fort] did not stay up. I changed it by adding more bark and adding more support to the bottom. But it still wobbled. Then I found out the problem was there was nothing to keep the bark stable, so I put sticks on top and it worked!"

When another child still had a problem after six testing trials, Hannah translated this back into STEM language by saying, "This is something that engineers do all the time. When they have a problem, they look at other people's work and ask for new ideas. Does anyone have any ideas or suggestions for materials that Allen could use next time?" One of the students suggested, "Well, I think you should use birch bark. You should add a lot of it as a topcoat because it seems to work well with water and the water just slides off. Plus I think you should get slanted pieces because on my fort, I used a slanted piece of bark on the bottom of the base. That way, the water just kind of goes off the slant."

Children care about their mini-forts, fairy houses, and chipmunk homes, and therefore they get invested in the engineering challenges of making the structures waterproof and sturdy. And this is just the right scale, with easily available natural materials, to engage in engineering discourse at their level. These two activities designed by Hannah illustrate how to use the same design principle at slightly different developmental levels to engage children in scientific thinking.

CAN YOU TEACH EXPERIMENTAL DESIGN TO FIVE-YEAR-OLDS? LEARNING TO SPEAK STANDARDESE

Science education often falls prey to the too-cognitive, too-early problem of curriculum design. This is encouraged, in my analysis, by the fact that most curriculum design is about two years more sophisticated than it should be. In other words, curriculum guidelines for second graders are more like what we should be doing with fourth graders. You'll see this in science curriculum all the time. One example is trying to teach experimental design to first graders. First you create a question, then you create a hypothesis, then you design an experiment to test the hypothesis. In the experiment, you collect data, then you analyze the data to determine whether it supports your hypothesis, then you redesign the experiment with better control of the variables . . . are you lost yet? Then you feel just like the young children being asked to wrap their heads around all this.

However, free of all this terminology, and out in the woods with lots of moveable parts, you can actually get kindergarten students engaged in this process, especially in regard to engineering challenges. More simplified, the process is wonder, design, test, observe, redesign, and retest, over and over again until a solution is found.

Recently when someone asked me to recall an experience from childhood when I got dirt under my fingernails, I remembered making tennis ball runs on the beach. We lived near a strand of shore with a relatively steep-sloped beach, so tennis balls placed at the top of the beach gained a reasonable amount of steam as they rolled down the slope. I loved the challenge of figuring out all the things I could make the tennis ball do on its downward trajectory:

- Could I make a tennis ball track that curved around and tunneled under itself without the ball getting stuck or grinding to a halt?
- Could I make the tennis ball go over a jump and land in the track a foot farther down the beach?
- Could I make a really long tunnel, without the tunnel collapsing, so the ball was out of sight for a long time?

I spent many happy hours trying to solve these problems by myself or with my brother or friends. I repeated the wonder-design-test cycle over and over again without really realizing that I was involved in solving a STEM engineering problem.

This is exactly what Lauren Skilling's students are doing in the hillside marble-run activity. They create practice courses indoors on tabletops with paper towel rolls, cardboard, and tape and then try the same thing on a steep slope in the woods. The object is to have the ball follow a zigzag path, maybe go over a jump, and end up in a designated corral or hole at the bottom of the hill. They go through the same cycle as I did.

The teacher asks if students can make the tennis ball do x, y, and z, and then she stands back and asks appropriate questions. Do you think this corner is too sharp? How could you keep the ball from hopping over this barricade? Skilling cautions teachers to stand back when children are having trouble. "Don't jump in too soon. You should allow them to work on problem solving independently if possible." They'll do the wonder-design-test-observe cycle over and over again, learning the basic dispositions that eventually lead to good scientific and engineering thinking.

The challenge for you as teacher is to turn students' learning into standardese (speaking the standards language) for children, parents, and administrators. It would be easy for parents to complain that the children are just out there playing in the woods and getting dirty. Your job is to show them how hillside marble runs are helping them meet the Motion and Stability: Forces and Interactions standards:

- K-PS2-1. Plan and conduct an investigation to compare the effects of different strengths or different directions of pushes and pulls on the motion of an object.
- K-PS2-2. Analyze data to determine if a design solution works as intended to change the speed or direction of an object with a push or a pull.

Building the track and running the tennis ball down it is "conducting an investigation." Building up the wall in the corner where the ball is hopping out is "analyzing data to determine if a design solution is working." Your communication to parents makes it clear that the children's work in the woods is preparing them to be good scientific thinkers.

The through line in all of the articles in this chapter is that STEM-worthy design challenges are waiting out there on the playground and in the woods and fields. Provide the children with interesting, kid-level challenges, add in the appropriate science terminology, provide materials, and ask good questions. The result will be, as Lauren Skilling describes, "gleeful cheers when their balls successfully navigate the course and stop at the bottom. The cheers alone signify success!"

Connecting Pirate Play to STEM

by Megan Gessler

Ahoy, mateys! Batten down the hatches and prepare to set sail on a swashbuckling pirate adventure like no other! Follow a magical journey of inquiry-based education complete with hidden treasure, diamonds, and rainbows. And now, the story . . .

The pastoral images of rural cornfields and prairies speckled here and there with patches of deciduous forest that denote the land-locked state of Illinois do not usually conjure up images of plundering pirates depositing buried treasure. However, my nature preschool class recently stumbled upon a hidden geocache treasure chest, and they have been obsessed with buried treasure and pirate play ever since. Each one came up with a pirate name, and they have been using pirate speak in their daily conversations. They assume that there must be dozens of buried treasures within our 350-acre forest preserve, and they are bound and determined to find each one.

Shortly after stumbling upon the cache, we were hiking on the far eastern side of the preserve when the students noted that they would like to cross the creek to go explore an area where we had not yet been. They posited that pirate treasure was likely buried on the far shore just out of their reach.

I wondered aloud how we could possibly get to the other side of the creek when the water level was higher than our boots, which meant that walking across the creek would surely cause the icy-cold water to flow into our boots and result in very cold feet. So they thought about it for a second and then one student suggested creating a raft to get us across the creek. Great idea! I wondered aloud how we could do that. "Sticks, Miss Megan! We could put sticks in the water and float across just like a pirate ship!" I wondered about what that would look like. They threw out a few ideas and tried out some different things but discovered through the process of trial and error that none of their ideas worked especially well. Then one of them exclaimed, "Miss Megan, we need glue!" Oh. I asked if anyone brought glue. "No, but we could take some sticks back to the classroom and glue them!" Okay. They brought back some sticks to glue together.

At the start of our next class, students checked on their sticks and observed that the glue did not successfully hold the sticks together. So we hiked to a closer and more familiar creek to

think through some more engineering possibilities. We talked about the size of the raft needed and the scale of the sticks that could hold them. How many students would be on the raft at once? How far would the raft need to travel? What size logs? How many? Where would we find them? What would hold them together?

The children were abuzz with ideas. It was almost as if I could see their minds whirring with activity. They could hardly keep from shouting their excited ideas at one another. One child thought that bandages could hold the sticks together. She also thought maybe a bridge would be easier than a raft and that we could saw down some big trees for the bridge. Another child thought that the sticks that we had collected into a pile at their favorite fort-building area would be the right size, but the children weren't sure how to drag those all the way to the creek. One student suggested that we "bang" the sticks together with a hammer and nails. And one child remembered a story that we had recently read, *The Mitten* by Jan Brett, in which Baba knitted a really strong mitten for her grandson. She thought that maybe we could knit the logs together to hold them tight. They conferred with each other and all were in agreement that the sticks should be about the same height—as tall as themselves. They also decided that they should be as wide around as a fist. They thought that the raft should only hold about one or two children at a time and that they could use a stick to shove the raft across the creek and then they could use a rope to pull it back to the other side for more passengers.

TECHNOLOGY (TOOLS) AND MATH

When the students arrived in class the next morning, I had a hammer, nails, string, rope, fabric scraps, and bandages ready to go. They grabbed the logs they had been collecting for their raft and began measuring and lining up the similarly sized logs and lashing them together. Some tried to nail down boards on top so that when the first layer of logs sank into the water they would have a dry and flat surface left to stand on. They were concerned that the water would come through the cracks and get their feet wet. The round surface of the sticks combined with how thick the boards were proved to be too much of a challenge for the students. They decided that they could just lay a thin board on top of the raft once we carried it down to the creek. After they finished weaving and knotting the scraps of fabric and bandages to hold the wood together, they noted that the raft did not transport well due to it folding in upon itself.

One student mentioned that we should create an X on the back of the raft to hold it together, so we lashed on some crossbeams for stability.

Then came the issue of getting the raft to the creek. The nearest creek is about three-quarters of a mile away from our classroom. And the terrain is mostly off trail, log strewn, and steep. Students tried to use the wagon, but the raft was too long to fit. So they used the teacher's heavy backpacks to weigh down the front of the raft on the bottom of the wagon while the students who walked behind the wagon held up the other end. Through trial and error and good team communication, they ended up placing scouts in front of the wagon to pick up any logs that would be in the way of the wagon's wheels. Once they got to the creek, they placed the raft across it at a narrow point where it became more like a bridge due to the low water level.

Success! It worked! Students beamed with delight at their own triumph! When the children got to the other side, I was worried that they would expect to find another geocache right away because all they had been talking about for the last few weeks was finding buried treasure. No need to worry; they found their treasure! About fifteen feet away, they discovered an area that had recently

been underwater when the creek level was higher. As the creek thawed and receded, it had left behind dozens of huge ice chunks that remained frozen even now with our warmer weather.

The children gasped at the sight of the treasure. Those magical ice chunks glittered and sparkled in the sunlight just like diamonds! Ahoy pirates, we had found our jewels! There be pirate treasure in Illinois after all!

SCIENCE

What does one do with all that pirate treasure? Well, the students know that they are allowed to bring back natural items to observe in the classroom, so they began to carry the heavy ice chunks back across our raft/bridge and proceeded to dump them into the wagon for easier transportation. Upon return to the classroom, we placed some ice into our sensory bins for observation. We added some food coloring and eyedroppers along with small bowls of salt. The children became fully engaged and engrossed in their work. They noticed how the salt melted little tracks in the ice, and they began to fill up those holes with food coloring. One group even created a rainbow.

Sometimes I have to pinch myself when an inquiry cycle is just so perfect. Our pirate adventure was truly magical. All I needed was faith, trust, and a little bit of pirate dust to aid them on their journey. As teachers at a nature-based program, we follow child inquiry. We provide the provocation, observe where the interest lies, look at possible lines of development, provide more provocation, and watch where it takes them. By supplying the proper environment, tools, and dialogue, these children were able to follow their self-created pirate adventure. For science the pirates found their treasure, brought it back to study, and explored the properties of water/ice. They utilized technology through the use of tools such as a hammer, nails, glue, and fabric. They honed their engineering skills while creating and recreating the raft. And they developed math skills when they learned how to compare and measure the size of sticks.

But this pirate adventure didn't only touch on STEM. The students also gained experience with critical-thinking skills when they figured out how to get the raft all the way to the creek. And they developed social skills by communicating with each other and problem solving together until they found successful solutions to each obstacle along their journey. We created and sang pirate songs and learned and utilized pirate terminology as they worked on language development. They even encountered art through the process of color mixing. I'm sure that I could not have come up with a prepackaged curriculum that would have been half as good as what we all came up with together. This is the amazing benefit of following child inquiry.

CONNECTIONS TO STANDARDS

ILLINOIS EARLY LEARNING STANDARDS

MATH

7.A.ECb Use nonstandard units to measure attributes such as length and capacity.
7.A.ECc Use vocabulary that describes and compares length, height, weight, capacity, and size.
7.C.ECa With teacher assistance, explore use of measuring tools that use standard units to measure objects and quantities that are meaningful to the child.

SCIENCE

11.A.ECa Express wonder and curiosity about their world by asking questions, solving problems, and designing things.
11.A.ECf Make meaning from experience and information by describing, talking, and thinking about what happened during an investigation.
11.A.ECg Generate explanations and communicate ideas and/or conclusions about their investigations.
13.A.ECa Begin to understand basic safety practices one must follow when exploring and engaging in science and engineering investigations.

NATURAL BEGINNINGS EARLY LEARNING PROGRAM is a September-to-May nature preschool program that introduces children ages three through six to the world around them by exploring various nature-based themes. We offer two-day and three-day classes for children. The Natural Beginnings Program takes place at the Hoover Forest Preserve in Yorkville, Illinois, with over 350 acres of prairie, streams, and woodlands to explore. Students are immersed in seasonal themes through nature walks, studying natural phenomenon, and engaging in activities that build physical, emotional, and academic skills.

STEAM in Nature: Stability

GORDON SCHOOL
East Providence, Rhode Island

by Hannah Lindner-Finlay

The purpose of STEAM in Nature is to provide children and teachers with the opportunity to relate each STEAM Lab topic to direct experiences in nature. This will encourage children to transfer and reassess their knowledge in a new setting and will provide them with the opportunity to learn science concepts through the lens of natural intelligence.

My kindergarten class started exploring stability indoors. Children know so much about this concept from their early explorations that they quickly brainstormed a list of related words. I separated the students into teams, gave each team a different material, and asked them to build something stable. When the buildings were complete, each child had a chance to share with the group why an aspect of their building was stable or unstable.

To introduce stability in nature, I brought the children to the small woods on our playground. We sat together in a circle on the ground, considering the rocks, pinecones, and sticks that we had gathered for a counting lesson the day before. I asked, "How can I make a stick stable?"

As the children shared ideas in the circle, I asked them to explain why they thought the stick was stable.

A child held a stick upright and surrounded the stick with rocks that held it in place. She explained, "Rocks are more stable than sticks by themselves because they have flat bottoms, and they can balance."

A child dug a stick deep into the dirt and explained, "The top is more stable because the bottom is stable."

From our circle, I sent students out in pairs to build stable fairy houses. The fairy houses were much more exciting than the idea of stability. The children were putting all these wonderful details into their buildings, such as fires made from yellow leaves and collections of berries to store over the winter. I found myself asking about stability and

getting thoughtful responses, but I could tell it wasn't the children's main interest. If you try this lesson, I would recommend slowing down the pace. After exploring how to make a stick stable in a group setting, I would give each child three sticks and ask them to make them stable. Then I would have them turn and talk with a buddy about the stability of their sticks. On another day, I would bring the children out and have them explore ways to make walls and a roof stable using natural materials. After exploring that concept for a while, I would introduce the fairy houses.

Student: This part's not so stable . . . because it has little sticks.

Me: Why aren't the sticks stable?

Student: Because they are not so heavy.

Student: The feather is stable because I poked it into the ground.

Me: Why is your building stable?

Student: Because I put it on the bottom. It's not so rough.

Me: So you made the bottom flat by moving the wood chips?

Despite moving too fast, the fairy house lesson has generated a lot of excitement about playing in the little woods on the playground, a space rarely used in the past. The day after this lesson, children started their day by telling me that they couldn't wait to go build more fairy houses during recess. That day we found a woodpile and collected logs for the little woods. I introduced a whole new stability conversation about weight and shape. The other day, I heard a child exclaim, "This is so stable I can sit on it!" When I asked him why, he explained that he had used heavy logs. I now hear children explaining how they could make something more stable as they negotiate with each other during the fairy house building process. I also hear children asking each other for ideas about how to make their buildings more stable.

The children were so excited about the details of their fairy houses that I took photos and had them label their work during writer's workshop. This was the most engaged and productive writing time to date because the children had such a strong investment in sharing their ideas.

CONNECTIONS TO STANDARDS

NEXT GENERATION SCIENCE STANDARDS (NGSS)

Make observations (firsthand or from media) to collect data that can be used to make comparisons. *("Rocks are more stable than sticks by themselves because they have flat bottoms and they can balance.")*
Children communicate information. *(See fairy house labels made by children.)*
Patterns in the natural and human designed world can be observed and used as evidence to describe phenomena. *("The feather is stable because I poked it into the ground.")*
Directly compare two objects with a measurable attribute in common, see which object has more or less of the attribute, and describe the difference. *(Children repeatedly observed that heavier things tend to be more stable than lighter things.)*
Construct an argument, with evidence, to support a claim. *("This is so stable I can sit on it!")*

The **GORDON SCHOOL** is a racially diverse nursery-through-eighth-grade coeducational independent school in East Providence, Rhode Island. In 2016 Gordon opened an Early Childhood STEAM Lab. Every three weeks, the students explore a new scientific domain through explorations that integrate science with technology, engineering, art, and math.

STEAM in Nature: Observing and Experimenting with Shadows

GORDON SCHOOL

East Providence, Rhode Island

by Hannah Lindner-Finlay

Later in the day, when we returned to our original shadow tracings, the school building had cast a shadow over some of the students' traced silhouettes. We noticed that the children in these spots no longer had shadows and wondered why. All of the other children's shadows had shifted to the right. For some children, this meant that their shadows appeared vertically on a rock wall, which was surprising.

That afternoon, we discussed questions like, what is a shadow? Why did our shadows change direction this afternoon? Why did some of the shadows disappear today? What were some of the important strategies you discovered in shadow tag? Why did they work? The children suggested that the shadows moved because "the wind blowed them" and because "the sun changed where it was." They also explained that "if a cloud comes and then it blocks the sun, it can't be a shadow." These were some ideas we decided to test in the following days.

OBSERVING SHADOWS OUTSIDE

To introduce the study of shadows, I finished morning meeting with a partner activity outside. Each child was given a piece of chalk and was tasked with tracing their partner's shadow on the cement. I explained that we would be watching our shadows throughout the day and asked children, "Do you think your shadow will change?"

After the tracing activity, I introduced shadow tag. The tagger tried to step on the other children's shadows. When a child had been shadow tagged, they became a tagger too. The children quickly noticed that when they hid in the shadows of the school building, their shadows disappeared and they could not be tagged. They also noticed that their shadows were sometimes behind them and sometimes in front of them as they ran. One child explained, "When it's behind, then you really have to run fast. If you run the other way than where your shadow is, you have to make sure that no one is coming that direction."

INVESTIGATING CHANGES IN SHADOWS

The next day, it was overcast. At morning meeting, we remembered what we had noticed about our shadows the day before and wondered if our shadows would be different or the same that day. The children went to their drawn silhouettes and discovered that each of their shadows had disappeared! We then looked for other kinds of shadows on the playground and discovered that some of the big things, like the slide, had very light shadows on the ground. We also discovered that our hands made light shadows when we held them close to the walls of the school. Some students wondered why the shadows were lighter and smaller today. We remembered the prediction about clouds the day before and decided that the clouds did block the sun and keep the shadows from being strong.

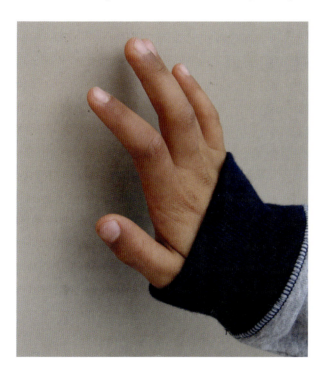

A few days later, it was windy and sunny. We went outside and traced our shadows in the morning again. While we were tracing our shadows, we drew a chalk arrow pointing to the sun. Then I gave children strips of plastic flagging to hold in their hands to see if their shadows were pointing in the same direction that the wind was blowing. We discovered that while the wind changed directions frequently, our shadows remained in place. This discovery ruled out the idea that the wind blows shadows. In the afternoon, we drew another arrow to the sun and discovered that when the sun moved, then our shadows moved in line with it!

The **GORDON SCHOOL** is a racially diverse nursery-through-eighth-grade coeducational independent school in East Providence, Rhode Island. In 2016 Gordon opened an Early Childhood STEAM Lab. Every three weeks, the students explore a new scientific domain through explorations that integrate science with technology, engineering, art, and math.

STEAM in Nature: Force, Weight, Friction, and Slope

by Hannah Lindner-Finlay

GORDON SCHOOL

East Providence, Rhode Island

PREVIEWING CONCEPTS INSIDE

Before going outside, we used large, wedge-shaped blocks, cloth of varying textures, and marbles of different sizes to explore the following question: How does force, weight, friction, and slope impact the speed at which an object travels and the distance an object covers when rolling down an inclined plane? We defined each of these words and then used them while experimenting with the materials at hand.

DISCOVERING FRICTION WHILE SLEDDING

I paired students up and asked one child to lie down in the snow while the other child pulled on their partner's feet. After they took turns doing this, the children tried the same thing with sleds. The class discovered that it was easier to move their friends when they were on a sled. We decided that sleds have less friction than bodies do!

Students also noticed that their sleds moved faster on packed tracks than in fresh snow.

Student: It's slower over here.

Teacher: Why is it slower that way?

Student: Because it's more softer.

Teacher: Does that mean there is more or less friction?

Student: More friction.

Teacher: And what is the friction doing?

Student: Stopping us. In front of us, it's going like this.

EXPERIMENTING WITH WEIGHT AND STABILITY

At the big sledding hill, we raced down the hill, comparing speeds and distance traveled for one child versus an empty sled, one smaller child versus one larger child, and one child versus two children.

Teacher: When there were two people versus one person, sometimes the one person went faster.

Student: Because two people make it fall down and the one person doesn't make it fall down.

Student: Two people tip and the other people stay.

Teacher: But when it was just one person versus another person, or one person versus no one, which went faster, the heavier sled or the lighter sled?

Students: Heavier!

EXPERIENCING SLOPES AND FORCE

We visited many hills on campus to experience different kinds of slopes. Some hills were steep and tall, while others were short and shallow.

Student: The sled is light. But we're heavy. But the sled is bigger than you. It carries you down. On a steeper hill you can go faster, and on a little hill you go a little bit less.

Student: The force of the sled! So when there is a steeper hill, the force is way faster. The steepness of the hill! So when we were going down, it was difficult to go on a flat surface. When we were at the top [of the hill] we had to hold on [to the sled] so it wouldn't race down.

Teacher: What force is pulling it down?

Students: Gravity!

CONNECTIONS TO STANDARDS

NEXT GENERATION SCIENCE STANDARDS (NGSS)

Use observations to describe patterns in the natural world in order to answer scientific questions.
(Student: I noticed that when I went on [the snow], it sunk. When I went on the sled, it just stayed up. But when I don't go on the sled, I just sink into the snow. Maybe because the sled is holding us up. And the sled just takes apart all of our weight. And it's just the sled, so we can just feel the sled. But when we take the sled away, then we don't have the sled. Then we sink in.)
Construct an argument, with evidence, to support a claim.
(Student: Only if you have snowshoes on you cannot sink into the snow. But if you have snow boots, you are so heavy! [Snowshoes don't sink] because they are wider than our feet!)
Analyze and interpret data.
(Student: I know why we don't sink on the sled: because it's wider!)

The **GORDON SCHOOL** is a racially diverse nursery-through-eighth-grade coeducational independent school in East Providence, Rhode Island. In 2016 Gordon opened an Early Childhood STEAM Lab. Every three weeks, the students explore a new scientific domain through explorations that integrate science with technology, engineering, art, and math.

STEAM in Nature: Catching the Wind

by Hannah Lindner-Finlay

GORDON SCHOOL

East Providence, Rhode Island

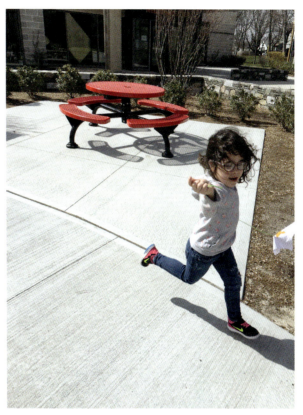

STOPPING EVERYTHING TO MAKE KITES

The weather was unusual. It was bright, sunny, and warm outside, but the wind was whipping wildly through the trees. My students had spent the last few months exploring pushes and pulls. It seemed like the perfect opportunity for learning about the forces of nature. I canceled our math lesson for the afternoon and gathered materials for kite making. We brought tape, paper, markers, scissors, and string outside, as well as some rocks to hold down our papers as we worked. There were some great problem-solving moments as children struggled to complete their kites without losing them in the wind.

EXPERIMENTING WITH KITES

After building their kites, the children were on a mission to catch the wind. They tried standing in place, running around the playground, and climbing to high heights. One student observed, "When I was up high, it was kind of flapping around me. But when I ran, it sometimes did that, but it mostly went behind me. When I went on the structure, it went up, down, up, down, and would spin in a circle."

Another student attached his kite to a pinwheel. He used the pinwheel to find the direction of the wind so that he could make his kite fly high. "[The pinwheel] was helping us change which way [the kite] was going to fly. So we tried that way, and then we tried that way, and then we tried that

way. When the windmill stopped or moved, that meant the kite could flap."

EXPERIMENTING WITH CUPS

Another student asked if he could bring a plastic cup outside. He wanted to know which way the wind was blowing, so he designed an experiment. He threw his cup as high as he could into the air and then watched where it went. He also tried holding the cup above his head and letting it go without throwing it at all. "[I was] throwing [the cup] in the air and then seeing which way the wind would go, and it seemed to be changing every second. I was throwing it up a lot, and it would just change. When it got up in the air, it would choose its own direction. Sometimes I would throw it up and it would go behind me."

This student also tried placing the cup at the bottom of the slide. He gathered a large audience of peers when he discovered that the wind blew the cup up the slide! "I was experimenting. I saw that I put [the cup] right down on the slide and it went right up to the middle and I saw it jumped over to the other side and back up and it went up to the top of the structure."

CONNECTIONS TO STANDARDS

NEXT GENERATION SCIENCE STANDARDS (NGSS)

Use tools and materials provided to design and build a device that solves a specific problem or a solution to a specific problem. *("When the windmill stopped or moved, that meant the kite could flap.")*
Analyze data from tests of an object or tool to determine if it works as intended. *("[The pinwheel] was helping us change which way [the kite] was going to fly.")*
Apply an understanding of the effects of different strengths or different directions of pushes and pulls on the motion of an object. *("[I was] throwing [the cup] in the air and then seeing which way the wind would go, and it seemed to be changing every second. I was throwing it up a lot, and it would just change. When it got up in the air, it would choose its own direction.")*
Pushing or pulling on an object can change the speed or direction of its motion and can start or stop it. *("When I was up high, it was kind of flapping around me. But when I ran, it sometimes did that, but it mostly went behind me. When I went on the structure, it went up, down, up, down, and would spin in a circle.")*

The **GORDON SCHOOL** is a racially diverse nursery-through-eighth-grade coeducational independent school in East Providence, Rhode Island. In 2016 Gordon opened an Early Childhood STEAM Lab. Every three weeks, the students explore a new scientific domain through explorations that integrate science with technology, engineering, art, and math.

STEAM in Nature: Learning with Water

GORDON SCHOOL
East Providence, Rhode Island

by Hannah Lindner-Finlay

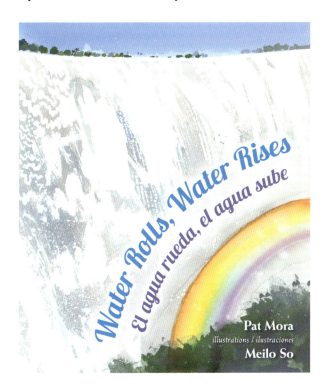

HOW DOES WATER MOVE?

I read *Water Rolls, Water Rises* by Pat Mora to my students on the first day of their water explorations. It was one of those spontaneous moments in teaching when the students come fully alive to the story. As I read about waves crashing, fog weaving, and rivers winding, the children tumbled, tiptoed, and lay down to make a long curving river with their bodies. The language in this book made sense to them, bringing forth past experiences with water and showing me just how much they already knew about how water behaves.

In the STEAM Lab, we explored the question, "How can you make water move?" Students experimented with clear tubing and funnels at the water table, used eyedroppers to spread colored water on coffee filters, and rearranged bottles on the water wall. Then we took our exploration outside. We walked the length of the stream searching for water in motion. Students said the following:

"Some waterfalls were fast and some waterfalls were slow. I noticed they made sounds. Splash, splash, splash! And also some like plip, plip, plip, plip!"

"Every waterfall, they bubbled down and up. And then they exploded everywhere! When the bubbles cleared away, the water made ripples."

"When there is a waterfall, it makes it go fast because it's coming from a really high height!"

"There are bubbles on top and they are sort of floating [downstream] . . . because the water is pushing them!"

BUILDING DAMS

Several days of free play at the stream evolved into a whole-group focus on dam building. The students soon discovered that they had to keep modifying their plans to keep up with the insistent push of the water: "It's stopping! It's pushing through! It's pushing everywhere!" There were several groups of students working on different dams, but they shared new discoveries as they went along. One child explained, "If you put the rock here, it just flows right over there. But if you put another rock in front of that, it just stops and stops." Another child shouted, "We need sand! We need sand . . . because the sand sticks the rocks together." As they worked, students used their hands and then their arms to measure changes in water depth.

Student: It's getting higher! It's getting higher!

Teacher: How can you tell it's getting higher?

Student: Because look! [Child plunges arm into stream.]

Some students also began to design experiments.

Teacher: What if we take the muck away?

Student: Water will flow!

Teacher: Oh look! What's happening?

Student: It's going down.

When our time at the stream came to a close, we took our dams apart. I explained to the students that we wanted to share the water with all the creatures we had found downstream on other visits.

CONNECTIONS TO STANDARDS

NEXT GENERATION SCIENCE STANDARDS (NGSS)

Students are able to apply an understanding of the effects of different strengths or directions of pushes and pulls on the motion of an object. *("The water is getting fast because the water is shooting down, and then it is going up . . . it is hitting the rock and going back.")*

Before beginning to design a solution, it is important to understand the problem. *("It was trying to get higher, but then we blocked it.")*

Analyze data from tests of an object or tool to determine if it words as intended. *("It's getting higher! So we stopped it!")*

Because there is always more than one possible solution, it is useful to compare and test designs. *("If you put the rock here, it just flows right over there. But if you put another rock in front of that, it just stops and stops.")*

The **GORDON SCHOOL** is a racially diverse nursery-through-eighth-grade coeducational independent school in East Providence, Rhode Island. In 2016 Gordon opened an Early Childhood STEAM Lab. Every three weeks, the students explore a new scientific domain through explorations that integrate science with technology, engineering, art, and math.

Hillside Marble Run

Hartland Elementary School
Hartland, Vermont

by Lauren Skilling, Shannon Cramer,
and Amanda Hull

One area that kindergarten science focuses on is forces and interactions. In our science classroom, this had us playing with marble runs—building marble-run courses and testing them and then modifying as needed. After a few days of exploration with these toys, students were challenged to use toilet paper rolls and paper towel rolls to create their own marble runs. They were also given old textbooks and large boards to create ramps and further experiment with rolling balls. As an extension and culminating activity for this experimentation, we had students create "marble runs" in the woods. This lesson proved to not only assess their understanding of rolling balls but also their ability to cooperate and establish a group plan. Had there been a microphone recording their conversations, you would have heard a bit of arguing, some bossing, a lot of kindergarten brainstorming, and gleeful cheers when their balls successfully navigated the course and stopped at the bottom. The cheers alone signify success!

MATERIALS

- tennis balls (one per group)
- sticks (hopefully found all around your outdoor learning space)
- a rake (we did this in the fall and found it necessary to clear a path)
- a hillside location

THE PROCESS

You will need to find a hill where students can safely work to build their ball runs. We went out the day prior to clear the paths and make sure that the space would work as we intended.

On the day of the investigation, assess students' prior knowledge about their marble run and ramp investigations in the classroom and explain that they will be applying what they have learned to a new challenge. Next present them with the challenge: create a run that will allow a tennis ball to follow a zigzag path down a hill and stop at the bottom of the course. When the buzz of excitement subsides, gather students in small groups (we had thirty-two students and five teachers, so about

six to seven children per group) and bring them to their site. Explain to them that, like they had used paper towel rolls in the classroom, they will use sticks to make the course for the ball.

As the teacher, your role in this lesson should be as an observer. There will be lots of trial and

error, but the students will work their way through the process, and they will develop their own course. There will likely be a need for you to also work as a mediator to assist them in navigating the social aspects of working cooperatively. However, don't jump in too soon. You should allow them to work on problem solving independently for as long as possible.

As the students build and test their runs, you can pose questions to promote further experimentation. For example, as my students were building their courses, they often encountered the problem of the ball picking up speed and rolling right over one of the stick walls. Simply asking, "How can you prevent the ball from rolling out?" prompted them to change the structure of their course (adding more sticks or building up dirt piles).

Since the hillside we were working on was quite long, students also had to come up with a

Once all of the groups had designed a run that allowed for a ball to successfully navigate the course and stop at the bottom, we took "a tour" and visited each site. The kids enjoyed seeing the different designs and were very complimentary of each group's work and effort. As the teacher, it was interesting to see how different the course designs were and to see the additional elements that some groups added (like bark tunnels).

A FEW NOTES

Remember, the pitch of the hill will impact the speed of the ball. The lesson could be continued by having students find other hills within your learning space and making runs on them. A follow-up discussion about what they noticed about the different hills and the way the ball moved would be a rich conversation.

We chose to rake paths; however, it may be interesting not to do so and to see if the students would notice that the leaves are a factor influencing the motion of their ball.

Our students loved their ball runs and continued to work on their courses week after week. They extended the courses, and we presented them with additional challenges, such as making the courses go around a tree.

way to stop the ball once it had run the course. This again was an amazing opportunity for discussion and trials. It was also really interesting to see how each group ended their run. Some gathered lots of sticks and made a wall, one group made a leaf pile, and another group dug a hole.

CONNECTIONS TO STANDARDS

NEXT GENERATION SCIENCE STANDARDS (NGSS)

MOTION AND STABILITY: FORCES AND INTERACTIONS

K-PS2-1 Plan and conduct an investigation to compare the effects of different strengths or different directions of pushes and pulls on the motion of an object.
K-PS2-2 Analyze data to determine if a design solution works as intended to change the speed or direction of an object with a push or a pull.

HARTLAND ELEMENTARY SCHOOL is a K–8 public school serving approximately three hundred children in the town of Hartland, Vermont. We believe that every child can succeed, and we are committed to fostering a love of learning and a spirit of inquiry in our students. The sign at the front of the school says, "Whole Child. Whole School. Whole Community." Hartland Elementary School is located on a wooded campus, and kindergarten students participate weekly in a forest program referred to as Wednesday in the Woods.

CHAPTER 8

Natural Science

THE BIRD IN THE WINDOW

David Hawkins was one of the leaders in the constructivist science education movement in the 1960s and 1970s. He helped to create the Elementary School Science (ESS) materials that have served as the jumping-off point for much of the science curriculum of the last fifty years. One of my favorite essays of his is "The Bird in the Window" (Hawkins [1969] 2007), in which he explores the relationship between the ordained curriculum, as manifest in the textbook, and the spontaneous curriculum. Especially in the upper grades, the textbook-driven curriculum dominates. In the lower grades and in early childhood settings, there's more opportunity for balance, for spontaneity. One of the problems, of course, has been the increasing rigidification of the early years curriculum. The workbook has become the big bully that has pushed play into the dusty corners of the classroom.

Much of the time, Hawkins describes, you're on the curriculum train going where the text and worksheets tell you to go. But once in a while, a bird shows up in the window, and it's appropriate to get off the curriculum train and spend some time with the bird. Why is it here? What kind of bird is it? Is it hurt? Can we take care of it? What kind of food does it eat? Being open to these serendipitous moments often leads to some of the most fruitful curricular pursuits. Especially in early childhood, there needs to be a balance between your intended curriculum and the curriculum that just emerges. Of course, this is why "emergent curriculum" is one of the core principles of nature-based early childhood approaches.

Audrey Fergason's owl observation article is one of the purest examples of the "bird in the window" curricular endeavors I've encountered in the past decade. In this case, it's the "owls in the pine tree." Interesting to note that this parallels Megan Gessler's pirate play article in the previous chapter, where it was the "treasure in the tree" that was the serendipitous nudge that started the exploration. In that case, an engineering endeavor emerged; in this case, a natural science exploration unfolds. When a pair of great horned owls takes up residence in an abandoned squirrel's nest, a month of remarkable observations and science emerges. From a developmental perspective, I wouldn't imagine that four-year-olds would have the cognitive ability to dissect owl pellets and make sense of the morass of bones and fur. Audrey's article convinces me otherwise. As she says, "This is one of those educational experiences that cannot be replicated." But what can be replicated is the openness to the bird in the window when it shows up.

Alicia Jimenez's children develop a similar relationship with the scrub jay that shows up on their playground. The interesting problem that sparked their interest was noticing that the scrub jay was stealing food from the garbage bins, and the children learned that this wasn't what scrub jays were supposed to eat. The solution was to coat pinecones with peanut butter and sunflower seeds to attract the jays away from the garbage bins. This led to the making of signs to redirect the jay's attention to the appropriate food source, and, by golly, their efforts were successful. "It is working, Teacher. He found the seeds!" The children's drawings and sculptures are a testament to their affinity with the scrub jay. The owls in the pine tree, the scrub jay in the garbage bin—there's an emerging pattern here.

BECOMING ANIMALS

It's somewhat self-indulgent to quote yourself, but it's appropriate here. In *Childhood and Nature: Design Principles for Educators* (2008), I describe that one of the recurrent nature-play themes for children is animal allies: "If we aspire to developmentally appropriate science education, then the first task is to become the animals, to understand them from the inside out, before asking children to study or save them" (29). Young children feel an implicit sense of empathy, of oneness with the flora and fauna of the world, and the instinctive response is to become those creatures. In early childhood, we should allow children to become animals, to play at what they look like and how they behave, to nibble on the things they eat, so they can develop a deep sense of compassion and care for them.

In Walt Whitman's well-known poem "There Was a Child Went Forth," he wrote:

There was a child went forth every day,

And the first object he look'd upon and received with wonder or pity or love or dread, that object he became,

And that object became part of him for the day or a certain part of the day . . . . or for many years or stretching cycles of years.

The early lilacs became part of this child,

And grass, and white and red morning glories, and white and red clover, and the song of the phoebe-bird,

And the March-born lambs, and the sow's pink-faint litter, and the mare's foal, and the cow's calf, and the noisy brood of the barnyard or by the mire of the pond-side . . . . all became part of him.

If the morning glories, the phoebe-bird, and the March-born lambs all become a part of the child, they will grow up wanting to care for, protect, and advocate for them.

This is exactly what Megan Gessler describes in her "Mammal Play" article. Baby opossums make a visit to their classroom and then, prior to a walk to look for signs of opossums, each child gets an art smock with a pouch where they carry thirteen kidney beans, the beans representing the number and approximate size of a newborn opossum litter. It was their responsibility to make sure they didn't lose any of their precious little ones on the walk. On another occasion, the children become foxes and skunks. No spoiler here. You have to see what happens.

Jennifer Newberry is one of the early initiators of the one day a week in the woods in Vermont kindergartens, and she's the associate producer of *The Best Day Ever* film. Her "Poop Is Not Food" article is a good example of designing curriculum that takes advantage of the "becoming animals" precept. To bring the kindergartners deeper into understanding the lives of deer, one of the winter forest days' activities is for each child to collect the kind of food a deer would eat. Each child gets a paper bag to represent the deer's stomach and a not-sharp plastic knife. They can use the plastic knife to clamp twigs against their thumbs and pull to represent the way deer use their bottom-only incisors clamped against their upper gums to pull off twigs. They fill their bags with buds and grass and then weigh it to see if they've "eaten" enough to fulfill a deer's metabolic requirements. It's a hands-on way for children to understand the dietary preferences and needs of local wildlife.

At the risk of being redundant, let me point out that though all these four previous articles are "science" activities, there's literacy (writing signs for the scrub jay), math (counting out thirteen opossum babies), reading (consulting field guides to identify owl pellet bones), and physical development (fox and skunk play). This is why I get frustrated when elementary school principals say, "We don't have enough time for science because we have to focus on developing children's literacy and math skills." This is why we have to learn to speak standardese to show how the bird in the window leads to increased reading and math test scores.

AFFORDANCES

Psychologist James Gibson (1979) coined the term *affordances* to refer to the features of the physical environment that encourage or support specific interactions. For an adult, a chair affords sitting, but for a crawling infant, a chair might afford hiding underneath or something to hold onto to get yourself erect. In play landscapes, sandboxes afford small-world play and grassy slopes afford rolling. Nature-based early childhood educators are learning to look at the nearby landscapes to assess what opportunities they afford for play or learning for their children. And it's important to recognize the dynamic relationship between the developmental stage of the individual and the same landscape features. For the three-year-old, the eighteen-inch-high stump might afford an exciting platform to jump off of. For the six-year-old, it might afford getting up high enough so you can grab a limb and climb that tree.

When I was doing ethnographic research on children's geography and play on the isolated island of Carriacou in the Caribbean, I wound up going on a lot of hunting and gathering outings with elementary-aged children. I "embedded" with groups of boys going out to hunt birds and iguana lizards. Boys cut small saplings to both make bows and arrows and to make traps. In other words, sticks afforded tool-making for hunting. To hunt iguanas, boys treed iguanas and then pelted them with stones until they fell out of the tree, and then delivered the final blow with a branch. Stones and sticks were the tools, the affordances, that allowed them to catch the food that supplemented their diets. These experiences helped me understand why boys are always pelting things with stones and whomping them with sticks. Sticks and stones afford hunting, a genetic impulse deep in our constitution.

The last two articles in this chapter describe how to use different affordances in the landscape. Whereas animate objects like animals and birds afford observation and imitation, inanimate objects, being less dynamically interesting, afford manipulation, doing, and playing with.

Trees: Matt Flower's inner-city adventures with children are less about learning about trees and more about doing things with trees. His article is about the activities that trees afford. Look at his Gifts of Trees list on the last page. Matt and the children play tag in between trees, they throw leaves into the air, they drum with sticks, they roll tree cookies on the playground, they throw maple samaras into the air and watch them twirl. Trees afford a diversity of physical development opportunities.

Acorns, Shells, and Pine Needles: When it's too cold to be outside, it's good to bring the outside in. Harriet Hart's article describes a wonderful fine-motor activity of sorting pasta and acorns into different bowls for children and squirrels using tweezers. The slippery acorns afford an interesting fine-motor challenge. And the ingenious pattern-making activity she describes with bins of spruce cones, pebbles, and shells will make even the most critical math curriculum coordinator happy.

One fall I visited Aimee Ostensen's second-grade class at the Manhattan Country School, located on the Upper East Side just a block from Central Park. One of Aimee's goals for the year was to utilize all the rich affordances for playing and learning in the park. One afternoon I observed a group of second graders playing on a large outcropping of pudding stone. They leaped across a cleft in the rock, then climbed with rope support up the sides, made small worlds in the puddles, constructed forts by leaning sticks up against the rock, and piled up leaves in a rock hollow, and jumped in. In other words, the rock afforded a diversity of natural-play activities. The last child to leave realized he had left his hat on the rock. Unaware of my presence, he came back, scooped up his hat, looked around and said, "Thank you, rock."

When we allow children to freely follow their instincts and playfully respond to the affordances of the landscape, they develop empathy, appreciation, and respect for the natural world.

Owl Observation in Nature Preschool

by Audrey Fergason

Forest Gnomes Waldkindergarten
Natick, Massachusetts

"I think it's a mouth bone!" Linnie declares.

Midway through the month of March, the Forest Gnomes had a wonderful surprise. We spotted a pair of owls flying next to our program space, hunting. The rest of the day was spent in very active inquiry, leafing through field guides until we had identified the owls as great horned owls. The next day brought an even bigger surprise: the mated pair had taken up residence in an abandoned squirrel nest in a tall pine tree, right in the middle of our program space. The rest of the week was spent watching the owls and discovering owl pellets.

Though our program is firmly rooted in child-led, child-directed free play, we took advantage of this opportunity presented by the owls living in our midst. We, the teachers, became armchair owl experts, and our daily routine now involved checking on our owls. Every day our gnomes who were interested would examine the tree with the nest and poke around in the pine

needles for owl pellets. We found numerous owl pellets as well as a rat head, a duck wing, and two chicken heads. There was a lot of discussion of life and death, hunting, and vegetarianism. We wrote emails home to the families every day, and our entire extended farm community became very invested in the owls. We invited a naturalist from Mass Audubon to come out, and they confirmed that our owls were, in fact, great horned owls, that it was a mated pair, and that there were three owl chicks in the nest. Three chicks living to adulthood is very uncommon, and we were cautioned that one of the chicks might be pushed out of the nest.

The first week of May, a teacher discovered one of the owl chicks lying by the door to our structure. We were worried that the chick was injured, and carefully we wrapped it in a blanket and brought it to the Farm. We put a call in to Mass Audubon and a volunteer came out. The owl, we were told, was perfectly fine. The gnomes, who had been very worried about the owl chick being injured and not able to return to the nest, were excited that the owl was healthy. We, the teachers, were less thrilled when we were informed that great horned owls learn to fly and to hunt on the forest floor, supervised by watchful parents. We did not look forward to weeks of monitoring the crawl spaces and cozy nooks of our

space for owl chicks and keeping our gnomes away from them. Fortunately, the owls decided to learn to hunt and fly away from our clearing where we hold our program.

By mid-May all but one of the owl chicks was grown enough to leave the nest, and the gnomes noted this in the decrease in owl pellets. We have several bags of bones, collected, cleaned, and labeled by the gnomes during the month. Though this was not something we could have ever planned, the month of observing the owls reinforced how important it is to be immersed in nature. Our gnomes had the privilege to observe and document the growth of an owl family. They were able to see what owls ate, to understand more about digestion and the subsequent regurgitation of the fur and bones. They became adept at

identifying owl pellets, finding the smallest clump of fur and bones. They experimented with binoculars and a telescope, used tweezers to clean the bones, and compared and guessed as to which bones belonged where and what the bones did.

Having the owls nest in the gnome woods was a happy accident, but nature is about observing and being immersed in your surroundings. It is an amazing example of how allowing young children to be outdoors can produce educational experiences that cannot be replicated. Our gnomes might not remember what the great horned owl call sounds like or what their feathers looked like, but I believe that all of our gnomes have been greatly impacted by learning to share space with wild animals and to observe their surroundings.

NATICK COMMUNITY ORGANIC FARM's Forest Gnomes Waldkindergarten program was established in 2009. We are a nature program for preschool children in a classroom without walls, changing with the seasons. Our gnomes are outside in all weather, through the fall, winter, and spring. Grounded in the values of a traditional Waldkindergarten, our minimally structured program focuses on free play, where exploration and imagination guide our gnomes every day in our beautiful woods.

Good Morning, Dear Jay

Santa Barbara, California

by Alicia Jimenez

The mornings at Storyteller are filled with the blue and rambunctious scrub jay flying around, announcing his presence. Our children receive him with a good-morning song. They have observed with surprise his quick movement in and out of the food bin. We know that this is not appropriate food for the jay, so we are discussing solutions to this problem.

"Good morning, dear jay. Sorry that you ate our food. Your seeds are there!"

SOLVING THE SCRUB JAY PROBLEM

Bird feeders prepared with pinecones, peanut butter, and black sunflower seeds were one of the solutions to the problem. We also created written signs to guide the scrub jays to find their seeds. When the scrub jays perched on the square food box where the pinecones were located, we all celebrated the accomplishment. One day Isabella, who wrote a message to the scrub jay, commented

enthusiastically, "It is working, Teacher. He found the seeds!"

RESEARCHING THE BIRDS

Our children had a long-term relationship with some of the specimens from the lending library of the Santa Barbara Museum of Natural History. Walking around and looking at the different exhibits, it resembled a visit to a friend's house. When they entered the Birds exhibit, our children exclaimed assertively, "hummingbird," "crow," "owl," "woodpecker," and the most celebrated, "scrub jay!"

The western scrub jay became an inspiration to our children. This was expressed in their drawings and modeling sculptures. A constant dialogue flowed back and forth among them and with the teachers. They asked, for example, "Who is the daddy scrub jay? Where do they sleep during the night at school? Do they have a tummy ache when they eat our food? Why are we not finding acorns

for them at the park? Do they like us? Do they like our song? Why didn't they come, because it is raining? Where is their nest? They traveled all the way from Oak Park to our school?" Children have access to field guides and read informative facts about the scrub jay. The whole class also has composed their own book.

Angelina proudly holds the sculpture that took her a week to finish. She modeled it, put back some fallen-off pieces, painted it, and then had to wait for it to dry.

Observing the body shape and colors to create their own version of the scrub jay involved several sessions of working diligently and overcoming frustration in the process.

CONNECTIONS TO STANDARDS

CALIFORNIA PRESCHOOL FOUNDATIONS STANDARDS

LIFE SCIENCE

1.0 Properties and Characteristics of Living Things
1.3 Identify the habitats of people and familiar animals and plants in the environment and begin to realize that living things have habitats in different environments.

VISUAL AND PERFORMING ARTS

3.0 Create, invent, and express through visual art.
3.2 Draw more detailed figures or objects with more control of line and shape.

LANGUAGE AND LITERACY

1.4 Use language to construct short narratives that are real or fictional.
4.2 Demonstrate knowledge from informational text through labeling, describing, playing, or creating artwork.

STORYTELLER CHILDREN'S CENTER helps Santa Barbara's homeless and at-risk toddlers and preschoolers achieve kindergarten readiness by providing therapeutic preschool and support services for their families.

Mammal Play: A Socio-Dramatic Experience

by Megan Gessler

Natural Beginnings
Early Childhood Program

Yorkville, Illinois

ESTABLISHING AN INFORMATION BASE

Fur, teeth, feet, movement, babies . . . these are just some of the things that my students wanted to know about regarding mammals. Their curiosity ushered in a good three weeks of mammal exploration. In that time, we read several books about mammals, went on mammal observation hikes, and even met mammals up close inside and outside of the classroom.

We talked about how the differences in certain mammals' physical characteristics and movements helped them to survive. The children were smitten with some specific mammals. They found opossums very interesting, and one day we filled our art smock pockets with thirteen kidney beans (which are roughly the size of a newborn opossum), and we took a long hike in the woods to look for signs of opossums. Each student took great ownership in making sure that all thirteen "babies" were still in their pouch throughout the day.

BUILDING SYMPATHY THROUGH PERSONAL INTERACTIONS

When we returned to the classroom, the children had a surprise visit from two baby opossums. They got to touch and feed the babies. Those kidney beans began to take on an even bigger meaning to the children as they cooed over the opossums. The connection was made and the children were hooked. Over the course of three weeks, the students also enjoyed visits from rabbits, raccoons, and squirrels. Then we spent some time learning about mammals that are pets and the work that is involved in taking care of those pets. At the end of their study, the children took therapy dogs for a walk through the forest.

The children still showed an immense interest in mammals, and that became even more apparent as they began to devote their outdoor free time to socio-dramatic play centered on mammal life. Their dialogue and actions demonstrated a grasp of the material covered through our readings and discussions.

LEARNING THROUGH DRAMATIC PLAY

During an unseasonably nice late-fall day, the students spent a large chunk of time at a place that the children have named the Underground Forest. This is an area populated by evergreens that grow close enough together that in winter, when the branches become snow-laden, they block out the sunlight and it looks like a secret underground world. The students chose this special destination, and they led the way there. Once the children had made their way inside the group of evergreens to a small clearing, they organically began playacting. There was a group of "foxes" that got busy making a den in a fallen tree.

On the other side of the clearing was a group of three boys who had become skunks. They made a soft bed out of pine needles at the base of a tree. Once the skunks noticed their fox friends at the other end, they huddled together to discuss

a skunk attack. Having learned about mammal movements, they got on all fours and waddled over to the fox den.

The other group noticed them coming, and they had a moment to discuss a strategy. They sent two foxes to the front of the den to snarl and

bare their teeth at the intruders. The rest of the foxes hid in the den and filled the air with quite a snarling ruckus and exhibited clawing motions. This did nothing to intimidate the determined skunks. They simply turned tail one at a time and sprayed the foxes as they slowly but confidently waddled away.

The skunks taking turns spraying their fox victims before waddling back to their home

---

CONNECTIONS TO STANDARDS

ILLINOIS EARLY LEARNING STANDARDS

LANGUAGE

1.B.ECa Participate in collaborative conversations with diverse partners about age-appropriate topics and texts. *(Discussing mammal habitats and defense strategies during dramatic play)*

SCIENCE

11.A.ECa Express wonder and curiosity about their world by asking questions, solving problems, and designing things. *(Child-led inquiry into certain mammals and their attributes; designing mammal habitats)*
12.B.ECb Show respect for living things. *(Taking care of the mammal visitors)*

MATHEMATICS

6.A.ECa Count with understanding and recognize "how many" in small sets. *(Repeatedly counting the beans in their pouches during opossum simulation)*

THE ARTS

25.A.ECb Drama: Begin to appreciate and participate in dramatic activities. *(Fox and skunk dramatic play)*

SOCIAL/EMOTIONAL

31.B.ECb Engage in cooperative group play. *(Fox and skunk dramatic play)*

NATURAL BEGINNINGS EARLY LEARNING PROGRAM is a September-to-May nature preschool program that introduces children ages three through six to the world around them by exploring various nature-based themes. We offer two-day and three-day classes for children. The Natural Beginnings Program takes place at the Hoover Forest Preserve in Yorkville, Illinois, with over 350 acres of prairie, streams, and woodlands to explore. Students are immersed in seasonal themes through nature walks, studying natural phenomenon, and engaging in activities that build physical, emotional, and academic skills.

Poop Is Not Food: An Authentic Learning Experience in Kindergarten

Marion Cross School
Norwich, Vermont

by Jennifer Newberry

One of the great joys of teaching at Marion Cross School (MCS) is that collaboration is embedded in the culture of the school. It was a mild January day, and the MCS kindergarten students were learning that deer only have bottom incisors. Lindsay Putnam, our Learning about the Environment Experiential Education Program (LEEEP) coordinator, and I collaborated on a lesson about deer in winter.

That day our goal was to reinforce foundational skills through authentic learning. Authentic learning engages all the senses, allowing students to create a meaningful shared outcome. This task was designed so that the students had the opportunity to connect directly with the real world.

Lindsay brought in a skull to spark interest, and she demonstrated how deer eat. The wide-eyed, captivated audience was curious about the white-tailed deer skull. "Where did it come from?" asked Dora. "My dad has a skull like that. He likes to hunt," added Page. Lindsay quickly added, "This came from the woods behind my house. I found it on a nature walk." There was a sigh of relief.

Our task was to collect food as if we were white-tailed deer. The knives represented the deer's incisors; they only have bottom incisors, unlike us. Deer bite against their upper gum rather than against another set of incisors. The upper

gum was represented by the thumb of the person using the knife. We had to break off the woody material rather than cut it off cleanly.

We decided to go by the apple trees in the meadow. The children were used to using the marked trail, but that day it was too slick with ice. Lindsay asked us to follow her on the soft snow away from the trail. A few students were having a hard time resisting the urge to navigate the ice. "Which path do you think a deer would take, the slippery ice or the soft snow?" Lindsay asked. Kallie chimed in, "Deer have hooves and would want to walk on soft snow."

We browsed for five minutes, putting twigs or grass into the bag "stomach." The students took turns using the plastic knife and holding the "deer stomach," the paper bag. They were looking for evidence that real animals had been browsing in the area. If a twig had been snipped off cleanly, it was probably done by a rabbit or hare because they have both upper and lower incisors. If it looked ripped or torn, it was probably done by a deer or moose. Spencer exclaimed, "Look, deer poop—let's grab some poop." Kallie smoothly

redirected her pal and interjected, "Poop is not food. Look, here are some buds."

We returned to the school, weighed the bags, and added the total. In early winter, a doe needs fifteen pounds of food but only eats around six pounds. The kindergarten students understood that six is less than fifteen. We discovered that deer are hungry in the winter.

CONNECTIONS TO STANDARDS

NEXT GENERATION SCIENCE STANDARDS (NGSS)

INTERDEPENDENT RELATIONSHIPS IN ECOSYSTEMS: ANIMALS, PLANTS, AND THEIR ENVIRONMENT

Use observations to describe patterns of what plants and animals need to survive. *(Deer need fifteen pounds of food to survive in the winter.)*
Construct an argument supported by evidence for plants and animals changing the environment to meet their needs. *(Students noticing that deer dig at the snow to find grass and snag off twigs and buds)*
Use a model to represent the relationship between the needs of different plants and animals and the places they live. *(Deer eat buds, grasses, and leaves and therefore usually live in forested areas. The students used the paper bags as a model of the deer stomach. They simulated deer teeth with the plastic knife and their thumb.)*
The students demonstrate understanding of more and less. *(Recognizing deer are hungry in winter)*

MARION CROSS SCHOOL is a nurturing kindergarten-through-sixth-grade public school located in Norwich, Vermont. There are currently two full-day kindergarten classes that go out into the forest for most of the day on Fridays. The Milton Frye Nature Preserve has so much to offer, including natural streams to explore the properties of water, trails with a wide variety of trees that change with the seasons, and wildlife that depend upon both. These resources give children tangible ways of working with and in nature to increase their intimate connection to it. Some investigations might take the whole school year as we explore the changes that occur in nature over time. The **LEEEP** program is currently in its fifteenth year at Marion Cross School. This enrichment component of the life sciences program seeks to engage children in appreciation, understanding, and inquiry about their local natural world and our collective responsibility towards it. The coordinator, Lindsay Putnam, directs these environmental science inquiry studies and assists classroom teachers with related curriculum development.

Exploration in Urban School Yards

URBAN ECOLOGY CENTER
So much life

Preschool Environmental
Education Program
Milwaukee, Wisconsin

by Matt Flower

The Preschool Environmental Education Program (PEEP) is an urban education model based on natural systems for local area child care programs, learning centers, and preschools. This case study gives a detailed overview of the second trip within a three-part PEEP program called Near and Far: Early Adventurers. The first visit takes place in their K–3 classroom, the second outing takes place outside on their school property, and the final trip is to the Urban Ecology Center's outdoor classroom. The purpose of the second trip is to provide fun and age-appropriate outdoor activities that encourage classroom teachers to lead additional excursions on their own throughout the school year. This case study summarizes the unique aspects of the child's experience in an outdoor setting and provides activities that teach children and early childhood educators that nature can be found right outside the school doors. Equipped with the essentials of leading adventurers outside their classroom, early childhood teachers can make the most of a resource some might view as insignificant—the school yard.

UNDERSTANDING EARLY CHILDHOOD EDUCATORS

At times the world of informal, outdoor environmental education is in sharp contrast to the structured, stand-in-line world of classroom teaching. In addition, the areas where outdoor education takes place have relatively loose boundaries, so this type of excursion can be disconcerting to classroom teachers. This, along with the fact that partnering teachers have differing levels of experience, both in the outdoors and in teaching, can produce a myriad of different results if programs are static. Being flexible and accommodating will produce the best results. It's well worth the effort to help teachers that only have their students' best interests at heart to feel comfortable enough to relax and enjoy the experience. Therefore, understanding the perspective of partnering teachers and communicating expectations will help in providing the best experience possible for everyone involved.

PREPARING THE CHILDREN

First and foremost, children cannot enjoy the outdoors if they lack the proper clothing for the weather. Regardless of the reasons why they might not come prepared, it's helpful to always have extra hats, mittens, and boots for participating children. In addition, it's important to help children understand the way weather and comfort correlate to the proper clothing and to teach them the skill of correctly dressing in the right gear. Finally, some children have grown up spending lots of time in nature, while others might have very limited exposure to the outdoors. Determining how comfortable children are in nature is vital to providing an experience that encourages learning and is developmentally appropriate. Regardless of where people are in their experience with nature, it's important to meet them there and lead them in a positive direction.

PREPARING THE NATURE-BASED EARLY CHILDHOOD EDUCATOR

An essential ingredient for leading groups to enjoy nature is having the right attitude—it can transform a walk around the school building into a magical experience that will set the stage for a child's lasting relationship with nature. The other aspect to creating a positive experience is being organized within the spontaneity.

Exploring the site and having an idea of what can be found will be very useful. At the very least, it will inform timing between activities that ensure smooth transitions. In addition, pacing is an element that speaks to engagement and interest. Excited speech and a fun tone encourage children to pay attention and wonder what might possibly

TEACHING MATERIALS LIST

- first aid kit and instant ice packs
- bag for collecting trash
- camera
- thermometer
- small aerial net
- collection container(s)
- puppets: butterfly, flower, hummingbird, bluebird with nest and chicks, woodpecker with nest and chicks, cardinal, chickadee, squirrel, oriole, bee
- fun stuff: lots of sidewalk chalk, simple kite, bubbles, kaleidoscope, magnifying glass, monocular, tree cookies, ribbon, clothespins, rubber fox track, and so on

come next. Being animated conveys excitement and engagement, modeling the behaviors you want them to display.

SAMPLE NATURE-BASED ACTIVITIES FOR URBAN SCHOOL YARDS

SHARE SPOT

A good starting activity is to choose a special spot where children can bring items they discover for sharing with the group. Most would be surprised by the amount of seeds, stones, leaves, and natural materials located on school property. Once collected, these items will spark many wonderful conversations and valuable lessons, including ones with parents. Plus it can be an excellent way to get kids looking and exploring within the natural spaces on the school grounds.

SIDEWALK AND ASPHALT ACTIVITIES

Regardless of the amount of natural space available, most schools have large areas of asphalt and long sections of sidewalk. Some may view these as the opposite of what nature-based education is about, but in fact, they can provide a great way to reinforce nature concepts as well as incorporate health and physical-development goals. By using sidewalk chalk, kids can practice drawing and participate in designing aspects of their games. Plus you can recall memories from the first visit by integrating the puppets used during the initial program. The following examples can be great additions to the mix of activities for children in the school yard, using only sidewalk chalk, puppets, and their imagination:

- Transformation: Draw stages of different life cycles

- Follow Me: Draw tracks/walking patterns of animals
- Migration: Draw nests and pretend to migrate
- Pollination: Draw flowers and pretend to pollinate
- Rainy Day: Draw and act out a basic water cycle
- Adaptations: Draw events for an animal Olympics

SENSORY ACTIVITIES

Concentrating on sensory awareness can be a perfect way to introduce children to the environment. With simple activities that stimulate their attention, a space they've spent many hours in now becomes new and exciting. Season by season, their school yard will provide an ever-changing, outdoor laboratory for their learning experiments.

- Sensory Weather Report: Notice how the weather feels
- Feel the sunshine on your face and smell the fresh air
- Make sounds and walk like native animals
- Flower Fun: Find, smell, and touch

- Feel texture and temperatures of objects and surfaces
- Exploring Wind: Fly a kite and blow bubbles
- Floating: Pretend to float like seeds on the wind
- Flying: Pretend to fly like birds, butterflies, and bees
- Explore puddles and perform water experiments

WILDLIFE ENCOUNTERS

In every urban block, a wildlife population exists but may go unnoticed due to everyone's fast-paced lifestyles. Hopefully, we can help children slow down enough to notice the wildlife living by their school. With frequent observation, patterns emerge and local populations become neighbors just like our human friends on the block.

GIFTS OF A TREE

While even the slightest amount of nature on a school's property can provide hours of discovery, fun, and educational lessons, no other natural organism can compare to the opportunities afforded by a tree! Every school has at least one tree on their property, and many have several beautiful varieties in different stages of growth. Taking time to identify them will provide many wonderful activities that the children will treasure. All trees have fascinating features that make them fun and interesting. Listed below are sample activities that can be easily incorporated into seasonal adventures on school grounds:

- Tree Tag: Identify and name trees for children to run to tag
- Tree Olympics: Compare trees for outstanding characteristics and make tree cookie medals for an awards ceremony
- Leaf Matching: Collect, compare, and contrast different leaves
- Leaf Party: Gather into a group all holding dry leaves, count to three, and throw them straight up; dance and sing, "Leaf party, leaf party, leaf party!"
- Leaf Show: Children present a dry leaf for their ticket to the show; press a leaf between a folded tagboard frame and look through the leaf into the sunlight
- Leaf Shopping List: Pretend to write a shopping list for the kids on the leaf

- Locust Tree Pods: Shake the dried pods like a maraca and dance
- Helicopter Seeds: Gather and throw ash, basswood, or maple samaras in the air to watch them twirl down like a helicopter
- Edible Lessons: Highlight human and wildlife uses for different varieties of trees, such as maple, walnut, apple, serviceberry, hackberry, pine, oak
- Flowers, Buds, Bark, and Seeds: Features for year-round discovery and observation
- Sticks, Branches, and Logs: Build, compare, and investigate
- Decomposer Discovery: Look under bricks, boards, sticks, and logs for decomposers
- Meeting Tree: Choose a special meeting tree where everyone goes if a special sound is made, such as an owl hoot or a coyote howl
- Sounds of Sticks: Drumming on the ground or along a chain-link fence
- Bowling with Natural Objects: Finding pinecones, walnuts, and/or acorns to roll like a bowling ball
- Tree Cookies: Take different-sized tree slices and roll them on the playground
- Family Tree: Use tree cookies to compare ages of people in a child's family
- Tree Jewelry: Draw a tree in different seasons on the cement and place real leaves, seeds, and fruits on the branches

The **PRESCHOOL ENVIRONMENTAL EDUCATION PROGRAM (PEEP)** is the Urban Ecology Center's nature-based early childhood education model for child care programs, learning centers, and preschools. The Urban Ecology Center is in Milwaukee, Wisconsin. It provides environmental education, land stewardship, sustainable food, and other services to a wide range of preschool to senior-citizen audiences across the city.

Bringing the Outdoors In: Using Natural Materials

Dandelion and Snail Preschool
Bringing the Outdoors in:

Twinfield Union School
Plainfield, Vermont

by Harriet Hart

The world of early education is full of games designed to help children practice and acquire certain skills. There are counting games, sorting games, sequencing games, games that use tweezers, games that use fingers, and many more. Most of these games use brightly colored plastic components to engage the children's attention. Many of them require adult supervision in order to facilitate smooth running, turn taking, and to ensure that students follow the rules to meet the intended goals. In our classroom, we have been experimenting with recreating the simplest versions of these activities using natural materials.

On a small table, there are two empty containers, both with a large picture attached to them. The first represents a gray squirrel, and the second represents a child. There is a small basket filled to the top with a mixture of large, dry acorns and uncooked pasta. On the top of the heap lies a pair of tweezers. Students are challenged to use the tweezers to sort the pasta into the child's bucket and the acorns into the squirrel's bucket. Acorns are surprisingly slippery, and the skinnier pasta really tests the students' ability to hold things in their grip. Despite the difficulty of the task, there is often high demand for a chance to engage with this activity. Some of our students sit and determinedly practice their pincer grip; others need more supervision to build their perseverance. Ultimately the context and structure of the game allows it to be accessed without adult intervention. The children have an idea of what success at this game looks like; only the mastery of their own skills stands in their way.

"We need those green things to start," Jamal announced, pointing at the picture of dried pine needles on the pattern card. He pointed with one hand and reached to the sorting tray with another; beside him Henry pulled pine needles from the tray, trying to separate the green bunches. Together, they copied the pattern at the beginning of the strip of white paper. Only when they had completed all three patterns did they attempt to extend the sequences into the remaining white space. "Stick, pinecone, stick, pinecone, STICK!" they say together, picking out the correct object and adding it to the end of the line. Working together, our students engaged in some of the fundamental math principles using natural materials as manipulatives.

The sorting tray includes sticks, spruce cones, pebbles, pine needle bunches, shells, and acorns. The long, laminated pattern cards are 75 percent white space, prompting students to copy the pattern and then continue it on their own. After their initial exploration of the materials, we added blank strips of paper and crayons to allow our higher-level students the opportunity to create and record their own patterns. The activity is structured so that students can access the content on their own or with the help of a friend, at a level that suits them. The pebbles in the sorting tray do not appear in any of the suggested patterns, prompting students to explore their own pattern-producing capabilities.

CONNECTIONS TO STANDARDS

VERMONT EARLY LEARNING STANDARDS

ELEMENT 1: MOTOR DEVELOPMENT AND COORDINATION

Goal 2: Children develop strength, eye-hand coordination, and control of their small or fine-motor muscles. *(Use of tweezers)*

ELEMENT 3: MEASUREMENT, CLASSIFICATION AND DATA, ELEMENT 3A: MEASUREMENT, COMPARISON, CLASSIFICATION, AND TIME

Goal 1: Children develop awareness of the differences of the objects and learn to sort, compare, and classify objects by their attributes and properties. They also develop a rudimentary sense of time based mostly on common routines. *(Sorting acorns from pasta, creating repeating patterns based on attributes)*

DANDELION AND SNAIL PRESCHOOL is the public preschool program at Twinfield Union School in Plainfield, Vermont. Serving children from ages three to five with two half-day programs, the morning class is partnered with Head Start. Twinfield Union School provides free breakfast and lunch for all students.

CHAPTER 9

Gardening

Gardens in schools. Children in gardens. Doesn't this make sense to almost everyone—urban dweller or country cousin, red-state conservative or blue-state liberal, African American or Latino or Caucasian parents? And yet, drive by most early childhood centers and schools and what do you see? Expanses of lawn or asphalt, faceless buildings with little hint of students out in the landscape. Once in a while there might be some ornamental shrubs, a bed of daffodils, perhaps a bean trellis. Thankfully, mercifully for students and teachers, this is changing. From Boston to Washington, DC, to Fort Worth to San Francisco, gardens have sprouted on school yards and at early childhood centers.

It's instructive to realize that garden-based learning is not a new thing. Garden-based learning once flourished in American schools. So what we're actually seeing now is a return to the garden, not some newfangled educational whimsy. As part of the nature-study movement at the end of the nineteenth and beginning of the twentieth centuries, school gardens were heralded as a progressive education innovation that helped "grow a better crop of boys and girls." Innovative schools in Boston, New York, and Philadelphia planted gardens, and the idea spread across the country to Cleveland, Dayton, Saint Louis, Minneapolis, and throughout California (Armitage 2009). By 1910 the US Department of Agriculture (USDA) estimated there were seventy-five thousand school gardens in the country, and two organizations—the School Garden Association of America and the International Children's School Farm League—focused expressly on spreading the school garden movement. H. D. Hemenway, director of the Hartford School of Horticulture and author of *How to Make School Gardens* (1903), exhorted the virtues of school gardening, saying that gardening created in children a love of learning, a love of the country, and it made children truer men and women. School gardens in early childhood programs help to grow truer boys and girls who grow up to be truer men and women.

In urban settings, where access to open space is more challenging, the garden can become the patch of wild space that allows children to connect with nature. Two educators are featured prominently in this chapter. Clare Loughran naturalized the program at the traditional St. George's Episcopal Preschool through a variety of garden experiences in urban New Orleans. She has since moved on to start the New Orleans Nature School, which has "the goal of fostering children's connection to and love of the natural world. One of the first programs of its kind both in the state of Louisiana and the Deep South as a whole, NOLA Nature School is rooted in the philosophy that children are competent and capable constructors of their learning experience and that nature provides a plethora of rich materials with which to do this." She operates her program in a sixty-acre downtown park in the city.

Wendy Robins wove her garden magic working for Explore Ecology and conducting the garden programs at the Open Alternative School in Santa Barbara. Despite its name, there wasn't a lot of openness around this school site, so the garden served as the explorable green space. Brooke Larm outside of Detroit, Wendy Garcia in downtown New Haven, and Kestrel Plump at a school in the North End of Burlington, Vermont (yes, Vermont does have inner-city neighborhoods), all bring nature to inner-city children via their gardens.

PLANTING

It's an interesting phenomenon that, up until recently, a preponderance of nature-based early childhood programs have been in the North, where the growing season can be as short as ninety days. Notice that the good examples of gardening with young children come from New Orleans and Santa Barbara with pretty much year-round growing seasons. (And we're thrilled to see that similar nature preschool programs have cropped up in Atlanta, Miami, Chattanooga, San Antonio, Alabama, and Arizona in the past five years.)

Clare's first article illustrates some of the planting opportunities, from spring bulbs (hyacinth, tulip) to planning a pollinator garden. Clare knows how to take curricular advantage of the planting process. It's not just about sticking things in the ground. It's about identifying the parts of the bulb that will turn into leaves and roots and sensing the difference between the potting soil and the sandier garden soil. And there's a little bit of drawing and a little bit of math mixed in with the science in these activities. Note Clare's ability to speak standardese fluently in her illustration of planting components with the Louisiana Early Learning and Development Standards.

PLAYING, EXPLORING, AND GETTING DIRTY

One of the misconceptions among educators about school gardens is that they are primarily for learning and food production. Yes, *and* they should also be places for digging, getting dirty, playing fantasy games, hiding, and exploring. The next set of articles in this chapter illustrates this rounding out of opportunities in gardens. In Clare's walk around the gardens to come up with a planting plan, the bees attract the children's attention, so the bee in the flower becomes the stimulant for a study of bees. I love that when Jack notices a bumblebee, he declares, "I need my paper," so he can document what he's found. The garden stimulates drawing and writing.

In "Compost Pile Play," Wendy Robins gets at this duality nicely. Yes, compost piles have a biological function, but they're also great places to dig for mini-beasts. As she aptly says, "Holding any living being is magical for these children." She also encourages children to walk and jump along the top of the compost pile. This is a great example of taking advantage of the affordance offered by the pile to challenge students to navigate up and down an uneven slope and bounce up and down on its squishiness. "Mud Paint in the Garden" and "Loofah Gourds" illustrate two sides of another garden coin. The garden provides the unusual affordance of painting with mud, and then the loofahs, created from gourds grown in the garden, can be turned into sponges that can clean up all those muddy tools, tables, and hands. Just as Sarah Sheldon stumbled upon children's fascination with brooms at the Chicago Botanic Garden, Wendy finds that "the children just can't get enough of cleaning with the loofah sponges." Good nature-based educators keep their eyes open for the surprising emergent fascination that they hadn't anticipated.

HARVESTING

In the school gardening community, researchers have uncovered a number of emergent truths. The first finding is that if children are involved in planting the seeds, pulling weeds, picking off the tomato hornworms, and harvesting the vegetables, they are more likely to eat the products of their efforts. It's tough to counteract the tidal wave of junk food that washes over our children—Twinkies, M&M's, sugary sodas, salty chips, Goldfish crackers, and so on. And if children don't grow up in a family with lots of vegetables, they dig in their heels when confronted with broccoli rabe, tomatoes, brussels sprouts, and kale. (Full disclosure, I dig in my heels at raw kale—just too chewy for me. And my motto is "What's wrong with spinach, anyway?") Nonetheless, if children are involved in growing all these vegetables, then they're much more inclined to try them and like them (even kale). That's why one of the parents of a child in Brooke Larm's Tollgate Farm program commented, "She ate tomatoes? How did you do that?"

Much of the food served at Tollgate Farm's early childhood snack program comes from the farm or nearby farms. In addition to the goal of having children become open to a wider range of vegetables, they're also trying to set children on a healthy eating pathway. Having a tasty snack program where vegetables dominate is one small step towards combatting the obesity epidemic in the United States.

Another finding from school gardening and farm-to-school programs is that taste tests encourage children to try, and eventually consume, a larger variety of foods. Often conducted during lunchtime at early childhood centers and elementary schools that serve lunch, small amounts of a food item concocted from produce from the garden is served in tiny paper containers—just a taste. This could be sautéed green beans with a bit of butter and salt, tomato soup with basil and parsley, pureed squash, kale chips, and so on. Each child gets a taste and then records their response on a separate slip of paper. With young children, this might be a visual Likert scale with a smiley face, an expressionless face, and a frowny face to indicate liking, not feeling one way or the other, or disliking the food being taste tested. All children are asked to do the taste test, and one of the findings has been that it's valuable to require children to taste things on at least three different occasions. This helps to overcome the one-and-done mind-set.

Though not set up in a formal taste-test format, Wendy Robins's creating salads activity works in this way. The goal is for each child to create a salad for themselves in the small bowl provided. Some children nibble on the spot, some compose a salad and then add dressing at lunch. They choose sorrel, lettuce, cabbage, broccoli, carrots, cilantro, borage flowers, calendula flowers, broccoli flowers, pineapple guava petals, carrot tops, nasturtium flowers, fava beans, cauliflower, and orange sections. This diversity is a testimonial to expanding the palate of young children.

Kestrel Plump's "Calendula in the Classroom" article suggests yet another arena of classroom activities—concocting herbal products. Many different common school yard "weeds" (think dandelions) and garden herbs are both edible and have medicinal value. Kestrel illustrates how even young children can become fascinated by the process of extracting calendula oil and making a salve. Salsa, pesto, salad dressings, and soups are all within the range of four- and five-year-old chefs supervised by thoughtful teachers. Gardens provide diverse opportunities for working, nibbling, cooking, playing, and discovering.

Planting Spring Bulbs

by Clare Loughran

ST. GEORGE'S
EPISCOPAL SCHOOL
New Orleans, Louisiana

INVESTIGATING BULBS

During our small-group lesson, Miss Clare brought out the bulbs that needed planting in our garden. There were four different types of bulbs; each child chose the bulb that interested them. We looked at the bulbs and compared them to the pictures on the packaging. Lisette took a magnifying glass to get a good look at the tip of her bulb. Martin focused on the roots when making his observational drawing. While Winston was drawing, he noticed that the paper skin from the bulb was moving from the wind. He began taking deep breaths and blew it across the table. He then turned his attention to one of the bulbs on the table. He quickly discovered that the bulb was not as easily moved as the skin. Evangeline watched his attempts with interest.

PREPARING FOR PLANTING

After we examined the bulbs both inside and out, we took a vote to decide which one we wanted to plant. It was a unanimous decision to plant the hyacinth bulb. First we had to prep the flowerpots by adding dirt from our garden supplies. Martin scooped up some dirt from the ground right by our workstation. He noticed something different about it. When asked what was different, he declared that the dirt from the ground was sandy. Evangeline and Martin decided that these bulbs won't like growing in sandy dirt, so we used what was in the bag.

PLANTING THE BULBS

Once the flowerpots were full, we went back to the table to get the bulbs. Winston and Lisette lined them up on the table. We counted how many we had and chose which bulbs would go into each flowerpot. The bulbs had begun to sprout, so we talked about the roots and the green growing part. The children decided the green part should be up and the roots should point down into the dirt. After placing the bulbs in the flowerpot, we covered them with more dirt. Martin wanted some of the green to show "because it's growing!"

The flowerpots were then placed in a sunny location in our butterfly garden. Every day that we pass the plants, we check on the progress and see how much more green is showing.

CONNECTIONS TO STANDARDS

LOUISIANA'S BIRTH TO FIVE EARLY LEARNING & DEVELOPMENT STANDARDS (ELDS)

APPROACHES TO LEARNING

Repeat behaviors to produce desired effect. (2.2) *(Winston blowing paper then trying to blow the bulb across the table)*

MATHEMATICS

Count one to five objects (actual objects or pictures of objects) with one-to-one correspondence or when doing simple routines. (3.4) *(Winston and Lisette counted bulbs before they planted them.)*

SCIENCE

Use all five senses to observe living things, objects, materials, changes that take place, and relationships. (2.1) *(Martin noticed that the dirt from the ground was different than the potting soil.)*
Talk about what they see, hear, and are able to touch in the environment with adult support. *(Martin was able to look at and feel the dirt and then describe the difference.)*

At **ST. GEORGE'S PRESCHOOL** in New Orleans, Louisiana, we cultivate a love of learning and nurture the development of foundational skills across cognitive, social, emotional, and physical domains. Our program offers a secure and exciting environment for children ages one through three to develop their imaginations and grow confident in their abilities.

The Pollinator Garden

by Clare Loughran

EXPLORING THE GARDEN

The Blue Room was put in charge of replanting the flowerbed in the preschool garden. We went on a walk around the school to check out some of the plants that were growing. During a walk through the butterfly garden, Jack noticed large bumblebees buzzing around the flowers. In his excitement, he declared, "I need my paper!" He ran and got his clipboard and a pencil and began to document what he saw. Grayson and Brandt quickly joined in. A discussion ensued about what they were doing and which plants they liked the best. Grayson knew a little something about bees and informed his friends, "Bees can collect nectar, but if you touch them, they can sting you."

INVESTIGATING BEES

After our discussion on bees, Jack, Grayson, and Brandt wanted to learn more about what bees do and why. Jack noticed that the bumblebee didn't have yellow-and-black stripes like the bees he knew about. So we went on the computer and

found out there are many different types of bees. We chose our favorite bees and made a matching game with their pictures. There was also an image that showed the different parts of the bee's body. Finally, we found images of different bees visiting a watermelon flower. The boys were very excited about those pictures because we are growing watermelon in our garden! Then it was time for show-and-tell. Miss Clare read a book about bees, and then the boys presented their images and explained what they were. We kept these resources in the classroom for a couple weeks. They would take them out and oftentimes use the book to match with the laminated pictures.

MAKING A POLLINATOR GARDEN

Bees became so popular that the Blue Room voted unanimously to create a bee garden. We looked at the pictures of plants in the books and also noticed what plants the bees liked most in our butterfly garden. Armed with a list, Miss Clare obtained the requested plants. Then it was time for planting. Grayson began to line up the plants in three groupings. When asked why he chose to put the plants in those groups, he responded, "These plants are big and these are small." "What about

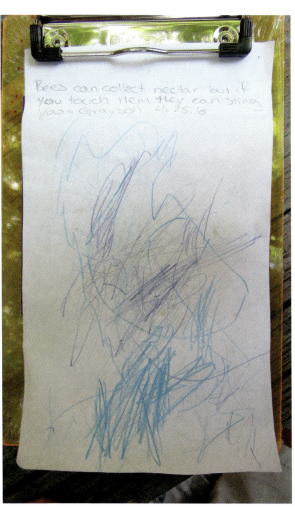

the third group?" "Those are the bees' favorites!" After much consideration the digging began, and in no time our pollinator garden was installed.

CONNECTIONS TO STANDARDS

LOUISIANA'S BIRTH TO FIVE EARLY LEARNING & DEVELOPMENT STANDARDS (ELDS)

APPROACHES TO LEARNING

With prompting and support, develop a simple plan for and work towards the completion of short tasks and activities. (3.3) *(Grayson sorting the plants by size and then deciding where to plant them in the garden)*

MATHEMATICS

Compare sets of objects using *same/different* and *more/less/fewer*. (4.7) *(Luke and Monty used the images that were printed to compare the bees and place in them in pairs that look like each other.)*

SCIENCE

Use prior knowledge and experiences to generate questions, hypothesize, predict, and draw conclusions about living creatures, objects, materials, and changes observed in the environment. (4.4) *(Grayson used prior knowledge of bees to hypothesize what they were doing among the flowers.)*

At **ST. GEORGE'S PRESCHOOL** in New Orleans, Louisiana, we cultivate a love of learning and nurture the development of foundational skills across cognitive, social, emotional, and physical domains. Our program offers a secure and exciting environment for children ages one through three to develop their imaginations and grow confident in their abilities.

Compost Pile Play

ExploreEcology

Santa Barbara, California

by Wendy Robins

PILE PLAY

"I hit the jackpot!" Sloane yelled out as she lifted up an old amaranth stem in the compost pile. Underneath were loads of roly-polys, a few worms, and a bright-orange woodlouse spider. The other children, who were also looking in the compost pile for insects and other creatures, came over and marveled (with loud shrieks), "Look at all those roly-polys!"

This is a typical morning in the garden at Open Alternative School with the TK–K students (four- to six-year-olds) in the garden. One of our favorite things to do is explore the compost pile, no lesson plan necessary. There are small bug-collecting containers, small shovels, and magnifying glasses available if the children chose to use them. Almost everyone picked up a container right away and began to fill it with habitat essentials, such as leaves, wet soil, and pretty flowers (food, water,

and beauty). Austin put a wood chip (shelter) in his "so he has a place to sleep." The children were making homes for the animals they have found, providing what they perceive as the animals' needs. They were recreating a mini-compost-pile habitat inside each container.

COMPOST

The compost pile at Open Alternative Elementary School is a six-by-twenty-five-foot mound of old plants, vegetables, weeds, and food scraps from the garden. A fence provides the back side of the pile; the front side is open to the garden. At times, the pile is five feet high! It is a static pile (not turned very often) that we add to weekly: a mountain of digestion and life.

Holding another living being is magical to these children. They instantly became responsible caretakers and started asking questions such as, "What does my animal like to eat" or "Does it need water?" I helped answer these questions by turning them back to the compost pile and asking them what the pile is made of. Is the compost pile wet? The children also checked out one another's habitats, sometimes moving animals from one cup to another saying, "Now that guy's got a friend."

At the end of our garden time, we often climb up and walk or jump along the compost pile. We call ourselves the "compost machine." The pile challenges the students to navigate up and down its uneven slope. The spring action of the layered plants makes for a natural mini-trampoline that requires balance and strength from each enthusiastic jumper. The action of our feet helps break down the compost pile, making this activity a win for the garden as well as the children!

At the beginning of each year, there are often children who don't want to get dirty, or they immediately try to step on and squish anything that moves. As the year progresses, we eat from the garden, see flowers bloom, listen to birds, and continue to explore our space. In time, the dirt becomes a nonissue and the animals are all respected. It is essential that the adults get dirty, hold bugs, and get excited with every discovery.

EXPLORE ECOLOGY is a nonprofit organization that oversees a garden-based education program in over twenty elementary schools in Santa Barbara County. I work at two schools, seeing children in grades TK–eighth in the garden once each week for thirty to sixty minutes. Sometimes we have a structured lesson, sometimes we perform garden work, and always we explore our beautiful gardens.

Mud Paint in the Garden

by Wendy Robins

EDUCATE · DISCOVER · EMPOWER

Explore Ecology

Santa Barbara, California

yogurt cups; they just have to be strong enough to endure the mixing step. We used old paintbrushes, as they get used pretty roughly against the garden surfaces.

Mud paint can be used on paper (be sure to use thick paper or card stock), but in our garden

Playing with mud is always a wonderful activity; kids love it. Making mud and then painting with it is a process that is fun and combines science, writing, and art. In the garden we have plenty of dirt, but most of the time in Southern California it is dry. Making mud is awesome because we get to be scientists and artists and get messy.

Children choose the dirt they want to use, mix in some water, and then add any additional materials if they wish. Farley said, "I want to make my paint yellow," so she mixed in some flower petals to see if that would work. Many of the children quickly scooped up some dirt that was very close to them, but others searched the garden for just the right soil for their paint. Some of the children made very thick, muddy paint, while others chose to make thin, watery paint. All of the textures and consistencies that the children created worked. Any watertight container can be used to hold the mud paint, such as small plastic bowls or recycled

boxes also are perfect for decorating with mud paint. Some children painted pictures, while others wrote our school name (OAS) or what was growing in the box (beans and loofah gourds).

Some children simply experimented with the mud paint, covering as much wood on the garden boxes as possible; others added flower petals, making more of a collage. We did this on a sunny day, so there was the added magic of watching the water evaporate and seeing the art change right in front of us.

Because we were using brushes, we stayed relatively clean and were able to go back to the classroom without a lot of cleanup. A few children stayed to help me, and we had fun using the spongy inside of the loofah gourds we grew to clean the bowls.

there are many suitable alternatives. Tree stumps are the perfect height for little artists and a great shape for painting faces and suns. Our garden

---

CONNECTIONS TO STANDARDS

CALIFORNIA PRESCHOOL FOUNDATIONS (FROM THE CALIFORNIA DEPARTMENT OF EDUCATION)

SCIENCE

Changes in Nonliving Objects and Materials
2.1 Demonstrate an increased awareness that objects and materials can change in various ways. Explore and describe in greater detail changes in objects and materials (rearrangement of parts; change in color, shape, texture, form, and temperature). *(Mixing dirt with water creates a new material.)*

EARTH SCIENCES

Properties and Characteristics of Earth Materials and Objects
1.1 Demonstrate increased ability to investigate and compare characteristics (size, weight, shape, color, texture) of earth materials such as sand, rocks, soil, water, and air. *(Making mud using various types of dirt, water, and other natural materials)*

WRITING

Children use writing to communicate their ideas.
1.2 Continue to develop writing by using letters or letter-like marks to represent their ideas in English. *(Painting their school name, plant names, and other words in mud paint)*

VISUAL ART

Develop Skills in Visual Art
2.2 Begin to create representative paintings or drawings that approximate or depict people, animals, and objects. *(Painting faces, flowers, and suns with mud in the garden)*

EXPLORE ECOLOGY is a nonprofit organization that oversees a garden-based education program in over twenty elementary schools in Santa Barbara County. I work at two schools, seeing children in grades TK–eighth in the garden once each week for thirty to sixty minutes. Sometimes we have a structured lesson, sometimes we perform garden work, and always we explore our beautiful gardens.

Loofah Gourds: Counting Seeds and Cleaning Tools

Santa Barbara, California

by Wendy Robins

One of my favorite plants in the garden is the fast-growing annual loofah gourd vine that climbs up our trellis, making a tunnel of hanging fruit. "Are those cucumbers?" asked preschooler Joshua on his first day in the garden. When school starts in August, the gourds resemble green cucumbers hanging down, but as the months go by, the gourds get bigger, turn brown, and dry out. We pick them and have hours of fun peeling the gourds, counting the seeds, making them into sponges, and cleaning anything around us that is dirty.

There are not enough dried loofah gourds for each child to have their own to work with, so they take turns clapping the sides and collecting the many (well over one hundred) black seeds that fall out. As one child is knocking the seeds out, the others are sorting them into egg cartons to begin counting how many seeds were in each gourd. Grouping the seeds into tens and getting a total count complements our school's celebration of the one hundredth day of school in early February.

Oftentimes adult assistance is needed to achieve an accurate count; however, the process of counting to ten and then counting by tens is fun practice for our four- to six-year-olds.

While some children were sorting and counting, others were peeling the dry skin off of the inner fibrous sponge. I have already prepared some loofahs to use as sponges (boiled for a few minutes to soften the fibers and cut into smaller sizes). The children couldn't get enough of cleaning with the loofahs. They asked for more dirty tools, and some even stuck their trowels in the dirt so that they could wash them again. "This is just like washing dishes!" exclaimed Lluvia. Our tools, garden sink, and picnic tables sparkle after this activity. A win for the garden and children alike!

CONNECTIONS TO STANDARDS

CALIFORNIA PRESCHOOL FOUNDATIONS (FROM THE CALIFORNIA DEPARTMENT OF EDUCATION)

SOCIAL AND EMOTIONAL

Participate positively and cooperatively as group members. *(Taking turns removing seeds and peel from loofah gourd)*

MATHEMATICS

Children expand their understanding of numbers and quantities in their everyday environment. *(Counting seeds found inside the loofah gourd)*

Understand that putting two groups of objects together will make a bigger group and that a group of objects can be taken apart into smaller groups. *(Sorting seeds into groups of ten in an egg carton then counting the groups of ten)*

LIFE SCIENCES—CHANGES IN LIVING THINGS

Observe and explore growth in humans, animals, and plants and demonstrate an increased understanding that living things change as they grow and go through transformations related to the life cycle. *(Watching the loofah gourd turn from flower to fruit to dry, seed-filled, fibrous, spongy skeleton.)*

EXPLORE ECOLOGY is a nonprofit organization that oversees a garden-based education program in over twenty elementary schools in Santa Barbara County. I work at two schools, seeing children in grades TK–eighth in the garden once each week for thirty to sixty minutes. Sometimes we have a structured lesson, sometimes we perform garden work, and always we explore our beautiful gardens.

Educating for Sustainability in Early Childhood Education: Responsible Consumption

MICHIGAN STATE UNIVERSITY | Extension

Tollgate Farm and Education Center
Novi, Michigan

by Brooke Larm

"She ate tomatoes? How did you do that?" asked a parent of one of the preschoolers in our program. I responded, "Your child cared for the tomatoes by watering and weeding in the garden, harvested the tomatoes, sliced the tomatoes herself using a knife and cutting board, and ground a bit of sea salt on each slice. Of course she had to try them!" For our program, our snack is a time to share in the experience of tasting of the food we worked together to bring from the farm to the table as we develop an appreciation for all of the work that is involved in the process.

While in the garden, children make discoveries and utilize their imaginations in our outdoor environment, where both nature and farm intersect. "Worms grow in the soil," said a child. They dig up earthworms and grubs that reside in the soil, the same soil that grows our tomato plants. They spotted cabbage white butterflies flitting from one plant to the next, exclaiming, "Let's catch them!" as they grabbed nets in an attempt

to inspect one more closely. A child decided to name one Steve, so soon the children proceeded to refer to all of these garden insects as Steve. Their understanding of food systems and the natural world, moderated by their time in the garden, is the key to becoming lifelong, responsible stewards. Examples include a farmer being able to recognize indicators of healthy soil and how to manage pests, such as our "Steves," which happen to be an invasive species.

After our time watering, weeding, and harvesting in the garden, we gathered to share a snack. Snacktime is no longer merely time spent fulfilling the need to nourish and hydrate our bodies but has now become an integral part of our curriculum. We procure our food as locally as possible, with the majority being grown on our own site, a 160-acre farm located in an urban environment outside of Detroit. We collaborate

with our Sustainable Agriculture program in a variety of ways. We utilize the expertise of the staff to support our planting projects. They support us with produce and agricultural products for our consumption, and the Sustainable Agriculture team provides us with opportunities to observe and work alongside them to plant, care for, and harvest crops.

The benefits of this collaboration are bountiful. Children experience the hard work and satisfaction involved in bringing food to the table and therefore show greater adventurousness in tasting a food that isn't typically preferred. For those who taste a food and decide they would rather not eat it, it becomes compost, and once again, children are involved in the process. How can we minimize the waste associated with our snack? Our responsibilities lie not only in how we prepare the snack, but also in how we handle the cleanup.

We utilize cloth napkins, and children bring in reusable water bottles labeled with their names. Children assist with both gathering the cloth napkins to be washed and collecting the food scraps in a compost bin. They carry the scraps to the compost trailer, compost piles, or our vermicomposting bin. Sometimes food scraps are fed to the animals living on the farm. A child who has been exploring these concepts with us through several seasons stated, "When worms die, they turn into compost." By being involved in the authentic task of preparing a snack, children observe and contribute to natural life cycles, in which the death of plants and animals support the growth of new life.

CONNECTIONS TO STANDARDS

NEXT GENERATION SCIENCE STANDARDS (NGSS)

ESS3.A Living things need water, air, and resources from the land, and they live in places that have the things they need. Humans use natural resources for everything they do. *(Caring for plants, discovering animals that exist in a garden, consuming plants to grow and maintain healthy bodies)*
ESS3.C Things that people do to live comfortably can affect the world around them. But they can make choices that reduce their impacts on the land, water, air, and other living things. *(Reducing waste through activities such as utilizing reusable water bottles and composting food scraps)*

Our early childhood education (ECE) programs at **MSU TOLLGATE FARM AND EDUCATION CENTER** focus on an inquiry-based project approach to learning. We provide young children with opportunities to explore local food and our Michigan natural resources to meet the increasing need within our community for learning experiences in the outdoors. We aim to develop a growing understanding of food, community, and ecosystems in order to support a healthy and sustainable future. Children ages three to five years old attend our program one day per week over the course of four to eight weeks during the winter, spring, and fall seasons. Many of our children participate in the program for two to three years.

Calendula in the Classroom at the Sustainability Academy

by Kestrel Plump

Sustainability Academy
at Lawrence Barnes School
Burlington, Vermont

Our exploration of calendula began in the few weeks of school when we were outside in the ABC garden doing a color-matching exercise. The students were happily scampering around the garden, holding up their color tiles to whatever plant life they could reach. I noticed a small group began to gather around some claw-like seeds on a dry flower stalk. As I joined them, I recognized it as calendula. We collected a few small handfuls of seeds and took them inside so the other students could check out our finding and we could all plant them.

I began hatching a plan to make a simple salve. Calendula is one of my go-to herbs with children: the flowers are so bright and inviting, the seeds are weird and full of texture, and it is easy and fun to make medicine from. Calendula is commonly used in creams and soaps for babies and children because the salve it makes is soothing to the skin and promotes cell repair.

Our first step in salve making was to gather and dry flowers. The seeds we planted soon sprouted, but I knew that with the limited amount of light they would get in the winter, the plants would not flower. I decided to bring in a large collection of dried calendula flowers I had at home and set them up for the students to explore. At first

Christopher and Abdiraham stir the beeswax into the oil.

Students transplanting the calendula.

the students pulled apart the flower heads. "Look, there are the seeds!" correctly identified Hushmi, one of the students who had first spied them in the garden. After we had thoroughly dissected the flowers, we packed them into two jars and took turns pouring olive oil over them until it covered all the flower parts. The students watched closely as the oil filled the jar. After every person took their turn pouring, we held the jar up to see how full it was and what the flowers looked like in the oil. "The top is still dry," noted Rajan. "We need more!" Once the jar was full, we put the lid on the jar and set it in the windowsill to infuse over the next few months.

When spring came around, our calendula oil was done infusing and we were ready to make our salve! We took a trip to the kitchen with the necessary supplies. We strained the oil through a washcloth, and students got to squeeze every

last possible drop of oil from the flowers. It was a messy job. Ollie seemed a bit tentative but was soon smiling and squeezing his oily hands. Abdriaham jumped right in with great enthusiasm. "My hands are covered!" he exclaimed gleefully when he was done. Fortunately we had a towel nearby. Next we poured our oil into a small pan. We heated up the oil just enough to melt some beeswax. I turned the burner on low and let it warm up very slowly, hoping that the children would stay interested during this process. We carefully measured the pea-sized chunks of beeswax and added it to the oil. I had two of the older and calmer students come forward and stir the wax in. I needn't have worried about holding their interest: the students were so intrigued by the beeswax pieces slowly becoming invisible as they heated up and blended in with the yellow oil. "What's happening?" "It's disappearing!" "Where is it going?" I explained how the wax was melting and becoming liquid. "Like snow," Abdiraham said wisely. When it was all dissolved, we poured the liquid salve into our collection of baby-food jars (provided by one of the parents). We set them out to cool, and, on our next family day, students took them home with an explanation of what it was and how to use it!

Our final calendula adventure for the year came when we were finally got back in the garden. We transplanted the seedlings that had been growing in our classroom all fall and winter into our garden beds. They were so leggy, but still alive! The kids lined the beds to dig the holes and put them in the ground. Watering them became a highly coveted job. The calendula, like all the other plants in our beds, were left to fend for themselves over the summer. The first year we did it, not only did they survive, but when we came back in the fall, they were flowering! We were able to use those seeds to grow our plants for the classroom this year. If all goes well, they will be there when students return in the fall, full of seeds for our next generation of calendula plants.

CONNECTIONS TO STANDARDS

VERMONT EARLY LEARNING STANDARDS

APPROACHES TO LEARNING DOMAIN

2. Curiosity and Initiative Goal, Indicator D—Engage in activities that are new and unfamiliar. *(Gathering seeds, making infused oil, making salve)*
6. Application Goal, Indicator B—Use prior knowledge to understand new experiences. *(Abdiraham comparing melting snow to melting wax)*

SOCIAL AND EMOTIONAL DEVELOPMENT DOMAIN

4. Interaction with Others Goal, Indicator D—Develop ability to take turns and to interact without being overly submissive or directive. *(Taking turns pouring oil into jar)*

SCIENCE DOMAIN

1. Play Goal, Indicator C—Use Scientific tools as props in their play. *(Using magnifying glasses)*
2. Scientific Knowledge Goal, Indicator C—Investigate changes in materials and cause-effect relationships. *(Different stages of the materials during the oil- and salve-making process)*
3. Scientific Skills and Methods Goal, Indicator A—Explore and describe the natural process of growing, changing, and adapting to the environment. *(Following life stages of calendula's life cycle)*

PHYSICAL DEVELOPMENT

1. Fine-Motor Goal, Indicator B—Use eye-hand coordination to perform fine-motor tasks with a variety of manipulative materials. *(Tweezers to pull apart flowers, plant seeds)*

The **SUSTAINABILITY ACADEMY AT LAWRENCE BARNES** is the country's first sustainability-themed preschool-through-fifth-grade magnet school located in Burlington's Old North End. As of 2013, there were approximately 240 students, 76 percent of whom qualify for free lunch, 18 percent who receive ELL services, and 23 percent who receive special education services. There are fourteen languages other than English spoken as first languages in this diverse community that is a federal refugee resettlement area.

Creating Salads: Picking and Eating Them in the Garden

ExploreEcology

Santa Barbara, California

by Wendy Robins

Throughout the year, we usually end each garden time with a snack, a quick pick of what is in season. It could be a whole tangerine or a petal from an edible flower. As we get closer to the end of the school year and the children's knowledge of and familiarity with the plants in the garden is solid, they are able to wander through the garden picking edibles to create their own personal salad. Each student uses a small bowl (or a large cabbage leaf) to hold their concoction.

They are allowed to pick almost anything they want but only enough to make a small salad for themselves. Before we begin picking, we talk about all that is growing in the garden and available for picking. We also talk about picking

reasonable amounts. The small bowl encourages responsible picking. I suggest that they try to include all parts of a plant, roots to flower. I walk around with them reminding them where the lettuce is and asking if they want to add any edible flowers. Samuel responded, "Oooh, I like broccoli flowers," and Sebastian said, "I'm loving the blue flowers [borage]!" Someone called out from behind the climbing nasturtium, "I need to add spicy flowers, I love the spicy flowers!" As they add more leaves, vegetables, and flowers to their bowls, the salads become works of art.

As the children roamed around the garden, more bits were added to their bowls. Some children ate as they went, tasting their creation

ended. Five- and six-year-olds asking to pick and eat salad: yes!

Our salads contained some or all of the following: sorrel, lettuce, cabbage, broccoli, carrots, cilantro, borage flowers, calendula flowers, broccoli flowers, pineapple guava petals, carrot tops, nasturtium flowers, fava beans, cauliflower, and orange sections.

CONNECTIONS TO STANDARDS

CALIFORNIA PRESCHOOL FOUNDATIONS (FROM THE CALIFORNIA DEPARTMENT OF EDUCATION)

ENGLISH LANGUAGE DEVELOP-MENT-LISTENING

1.2 Follow directions that involve a one- or two-step sequence, relying less on contextual cues. (*Picking leaves then adding vegetables and flowers, picking a reasonable amount*)

HEALTH-NUTRITION

2.1 Demonstrate greater understanding that eating a variety of food helps the body grow and be healthy and choose from a greater variety of foods at mealtimes. (*Picking and eating a variety of vegetables and flowers*)

PHYSICAL

Manipulative Skills
3.2 Show increasing fine-motor manipulative skills using hands and arms such as in-hand manipulation, writing, cutting, and dressing. (*Using hands to gently pick specific leaves, vegetables, and flowers*)

SCIENCE

Life Science
2.2 Develop a greater understanding of the basic needs of humans, animals, and plants (e.g., food, water, sunshine, shelter). (*Helping maintain and grow the garden, eating a variety of healthy food*)

as a real chef would. I asked Sloane what she was eating. "Good stuff!" was her reply. A few of the children wanted to hold onto their full salad bowls until lunchtime so they could add dressing from the cafeteria's salad bar. The connection between the food we grow in the garden and the food that is served in the cafeteria, or at home, is understood and enjoyed by the children. This activity became a favorite and was requested by the children every week they were in the garden until the school year

EXPLORE ECOLOGY is a nonprofit organization that oversees a garden-based education program in over twenty elementary schools in Santa Barbara County. I work at two schools, seeing children in grades TK–eighth in the garden once each week for thirty to sixty minutes. Sometimes we have a structured lesson, sometimes we perform garden work, and always we explore our beautiful gardens.

AFTERWORD

The Path Forward

Here we are. We've traveled hither and yon across America, from urban playgrounds to moose, bear, and unicorn wilderness; from hot and humid New Orleans to cold and brittle Vermont. The movement is moving, creeping along Tennessee trails and into Florida neighborhoods, Seattle parks, the San Antonio Zoo, and Maine intertidal zones. "But how about my backyard?" you're wondering. "Where can I go or what can I do to join in, meet colleagues, learn how to forage for edible mushrooms with children, and develop better personnel policies?" Help is on the way. Take a look at the following organizations as you contemplate ways to incorporate more nature into your students' lives.

NATURAL START

Natural Start is the national network supporting the nature-based early childhood movement. You can find a map of affiliated programs all across North America here—some near you. There's a wonderful array of articles on their website by all the leaders in the field, and they've recently published the *Nature-based Preschool Professional Practices Guidelines*, which provide guidance on how to implement a high-quality program. They also run a national conference in the summer that roams around the county—it's a great networking opportunity. And they conduct valuable webinars throughout the year.

ANTIOCH UNIVERSITY

The Antioch campuses in New England (Keene, New Hampshire) and Santa Barbara, California, offer certificate and master's degree programs in nature-based early childhood. All but one of the contributors to this book are graduates of one of those programs. The courses are either one week long, on the weekends, or online: easy to fit into your busy schedule and in beautiful parts of the country. Courses are tailored specifically to cover all the things you need to know to conduct a good program—business planning, risk management, curriculum development, working with families and communities, landscape design, natural history, movement, and storytelling, from soup to nuts. You'll work with leaders in the field and develop lasting friendships with energetic colleagues. Take just one course, do a certificate program, or engage in a comprehensive master's program.

EASTERN REGIONAL ASSOCIATION OF FOREST AND NATURE SCHOOLS (ERAFANS)

ERAFANS was started by Monica Wiedel-Lubinski, past director of the Irvine Nature Preschool outside of Baltimore. Irvine was an early leader in the nature-preschool movement. ERAFANS conducts teacher professional development courses and workshops all up and down the eastern seaboard, from southern New England to Miami. Check out their wide array of offerings—if you're anywhere east of the Mississippi, there should be an opportunity and an ERAFANS chapter reasonably close by.

REGIONAL NETWORKS

As subsets of the national Natural Start network, there are a variety of regional networks of nature-based early childhood practitioners in different corners of the country. Some of these focus exclusively on young children, and some are expanding their focus up into the elementary grades to support K–6 teachers who want the same kind of naturalized education for their elementary students. Here are five examples of regional networks that provide collegial support.

WASHINGTON NATURE PRESCHOOL ASSOCIATION (WANPA)

This association of nature preschools, pulled together by Kit Harrington, founder of the Fiddleheads Forest School in Seattle, is breaking new ground for the country. Working with their legislators, they have created the first state-approved guidelines for licensing outdoor preschools. This has allowed nature-based programs to expand beyond just half-day programs to offering early morning to late afternoon, full-spectrum childcare programs. And it's provided the opportunity for parents to receive public assistance to support tuition costs for this program. This makes nature-based programming available for children from a wide range of socioeconomic backgrounds. The work of the Washington Nature Preschool Association provides a great step forward towards social justice that can be a model for other states.

NORTHERN ILLINOIS NATURE PRESCHOOL ASSOCIATION (NINPA)

NINPA was organized by Megan Gessler, currently the director of the Little Trees Preschool at the Morton Arboretum on the western edge of Chicagoland. One of Megan's special abilities, now shared broadly by NINPA, is the ability to translate outdoor nature play and learning into "standardese." The NINPA website has a great blog article called "Standards in the Snow," which illustrates how sledding (and other outdoor winter activities) fulfills some of Illinois' Early Learning and Development standards, just like Megan did so well in her articles in this book. They conduct a diverse set of professional development meetings around northern Illinois.

MINNESOTA EARLY CHILDHOOD OUTSIDE (MN ECO)

It's oddly intriguing that nature-based early childhood initiatives tend to take hold more in northern climes. There's a little hotbed of nature preschools in Duluth, Minnesota, one of the colder places in the United States in the wintertime. And nature preschools are taking root in public schools throughout Minnesota. There's a wonderful set of public nature preschool programs in the Prior Lake/Savage school district about a half hour south of the Twin Cities. Anna Dutke, a teacher in this district, has been instrumental in creating Minnesota Early Childhood Outside to weave together the initiatives around the state.

ACADEMY OF CALIFORNIA FOREST KINDERGARTEN TEACHERS

Lia Grippo, Kelly Villaruel, and Erin Boehme are the women behind this California organization that provides in-depth training and networking for forest schoolteachers and early childhood educators with a home base in Santa Barbara. (And they also conduct one of their trainings in Asheville, North Carolina.) This is a particularly good source for compact, intensive teacher professional development in nature connection. Kelly runs a nature preschool for the Wilderness Youth Project, one of the premier nature connection organizations in the country with a focus on nature mentoring. Those folks interested in the nature mentoring work articulated in *Coyote's Guide to Connecting with Nature* would benefit from the Academy's professional development opportunities.

INSIDE-OUTSIDE: NATURE-BASED EDUCATORS OF NEW ENGLAND

There are now about half a dozen Inside-Outside regional chapters of nature-based educators throughout Maine, New Hampshire, Vermont, and Massachusetts. They all offer professional development and conviviality in accessible locations from mid-coast Maine to central Vermont to Cape Cod. Inside-Outside's central organizer is Liza Lowe, founder of Wild Roots Forest School and a faculty member at Antioch New England. This network of regional organizations grew out of the In Bloom conferences (see below) over the past decade. Inside-Outside is an example of the upward infiltration of nature-based early childhood approaches into the elementary grades. It started out as groups of early childhood educators, but as first-, second-, and third-grade teachers started to take their students outside, the Inside-Outside chapters started to focus on the whole spectrum of public elementary school learning.

IN BLOOM CONFERENCES

Antioch University offers four In Bloom conferences each year—one in Santa Barbara in the fall and three (or more) in New England each spring. And Antioch New England faculty have helped the Teton Science School pull together an In Mud conference in Jackson, Wyoming, each April. (Though it's never really quite as muddy in Jackson as it is during mud season in northern New England.) In Bloom conferences offer keynote speakers from across the country and the United Kingdom and workshops by innovative practitioners from all the corners of New England. These one-day events are remarkably cheery, and we strive to have most of the learning occur outside in all weathers. Anne Stires and Eliza Minnucci, pioneers in nature-based learning, are frequent keynote speakers and workshop leaders. You'll laugh and cry and be active and meditative at In Bloom conferences.

And so now you've got no excuse. This book and all these professional development networks and opportunities give you lots of paths to follow out the classroom door and into the great beyond. Happy trails!

What Do We Mean by "Ready"? A Review of Research Behind Nature-Based Early Childhood Education Programs

The emergence of nature preschools and forest kindergartens in North America has generated much interest among parents and educators who are concerned about the changing nature of childhood in the twenty-first century. These people often note the following disturbing trends they see in the lives of pre-K through third-grade children:

1. The "digitalization" of children's lives. Young children spend an average of eight hours a day engaged with screens (television, electronic media, cell phones) and only half an hour per day outdoors. This translates into less social interaction with other children, less physical movement, and the erosion of connectedness with the natural world (Rideout, Foehr, and Roberts 2010). Since most of the screens that children are interacting with are inside buildings, this often leads to . . .

2. The "indoorification" of early childhood, both at home and in school. Children are indoors in confined spaces more of the time, and outside in natural play and learning settings less of the time. This translates into more seat time, less free or guided play, and the decrease in opportunities for gross- and fine-motor development (Louv 2005; Rideout, Foehr, and Roberts 2010). Both of these trends are amplified by . . .

3. The "academification" of early childhood programming. Kindergarten is the new first grade. Preschool is the new kindergarten. This translates into less emphasis on social-emotional school readiness and more emphasis on early literacy and numeracy (Miller and Almon 2009).

The composite effect is that we're raising a generation of young couch potatoes. Our young children are too creeped out to touch earthworms, they don't know where their food comes from, and as they get older, they're afraid to walk in the forest alone. Or, if they are walking in the forest, they can't see the forest for their iPhones.

In response, many parents are attracted to nature-based early childhood education. They like the appeal of children skipping gaily through the forest, jumping in leaf piles, sloshing in puddles, cuddling bunnies.

Parents are interested in the greater emphasis on physical development and social-emotional growth that appears to be occurring in nature-based early childhood programs. The school district of Sooke, near Victoria, British Columbia, started a public school nature-kindergarten program in 2012. In the fall of 2013, when it was evident that there was going to be competition for the limited number of places in the nature-kindergarten program, parents camped out overnight in the registration line in order to get their children into the program—clearly an indication of parental satisfaction with this new approach.

Similarly, when the administrators in the Bullock Creek School District near Midland, Michigan, announced the opening of one section of nature kindergarten in one of the district's elementary schools, the parental response was so great that three sections of nature kindergarten had to be created. A similar interest in Forest Days (one day a week in the woods in Vermont public school kindergartens) has led to the creation of more than thirty such programs throughout Vermont in the past five years. Parents and teachers are voting with their feet in support of this new approach to early childhood education.

In spite of all this early enthusiasm, one persistent question rises to the surface in relation to nature preschools and nature-kindergarten initiatives. Parents are impressed by children's enthusiasm for school, their physical development, the sparkle in their eyes, but they still wonder, "If we put our children in a nature preschool or a forest kindergarten, will they be ready for kindergarten and/or first grade?"

Ah, but perhaps the real question is, "What do we mean by ready?" Readiness for school means lots of things to lots of people, but there are at least two definitive camps or schools of thought: academic readiness—as in, children know their letters and numbers—versus social-emotional readiness—as in, children have good working memories, inhibitory control, and social-interaction skills. Let's explore what we know about these two different versions of *ready*.

To understand this debate, it's useful to put nature-based early childhood initiatives in context. First, it's important to understand some of the research on the long-term effects of preschool and kindergarten education. Second, it's necessary to differentiate between academic- or didactic-oriented early childhood education and play-based early childhood education. Finally, I'll share some of the recent research that compares nature-based early childhood education to high-quality traditional early childhood education.

I. Longitudinal Effects of Preschool Education

Much research exists to support the long-lasting value of preschool education. The much-publicized *Lifetime Effects: The High/Scope Perry Preschool Study Through Age 40* (Schweinhart et al. 2005) compared the longitudinal effects of a high-quality preschool program versus no preschool experience at all. Three- and four-year-old children were randomly divided into two groups—one that received a high-quality preschool program and a comparison group who received no preschool program. Ninety-seven percent of the study participants were interviewed at age forty, and data was gathered from the participants' school, social services, and arrest records. "The study found that adults at age 40 who had the preschool program had higher earnings, were more likely to hold a job, had committed fewer crimes, and were more likely to have graduated from high school than adults who did not have preschool." This research has been used to justify the substantial social benefits of publicly funded preschool programs.

There's a similar litany of other research that supports the longitudinal benefits of preschool education on students that shows the rate of return on educational investment is greatest between zero and five years of age. For instance, a report called *The Business Case for Early Childhood Investments* by ReadyNation says that "an overview of 56 studies across 23 countries in Europe, Asia, Africa and Central and South America found impacts of early childhood programs on health, IQ and emotional development." This is the rationale behind the national Head Start program and the reason why many states are starting to mandate preschool for four-year-olds within the public school system.

IMPACTS OF PLAY-BASED PRESCHOOL ON SCHOOL PERFORMANCE

Assuming that we know preschool experience is valuable (Schweinhart et al. 2005), what makes for the most effective approach to preschool education? Researchers have asked whether academically oriented versus play-based preschool programs are more effective. Writing in the *International Journal of Environmental Research and Public Health* in an article titled "Risky Play and Children's Safety: Balancing Priorities for Optimal Child Development," Dr. Mariana Brussoni and other public health physicians cite a US study in which sixty-eight disadvantaged children (ages three to four) were randomly assigned to participate in one of three preschool programs.

> Two of the classes included at least 21% free play and a child-initiated activity component. The third class focused on direct instruction of academic skills and allowed for only 2% of free play activities. When tested at age 15, children in the latter class were significantly more likely than the other classes to experience misconduct, and less likely to participate in active sports or contribute to their family or community. Furthermore, at age 23, problems worsened with significantly higher levels of work suspensions and arrests (Weikart 1998). These findings underline that free play is fundamental to healthy child development, and that restriction of free play in the preschool years might potentially have lifelong repercussions. (Brussoni et al. 2012, 3136)

This emphasis on the benefits of free play and child-initiated activity aligns with the core conviction that self-directed nature play and child-initiated activity are integral components of nature-based early childhood programs. Since it appears that play-based early childhood has long-term impacts on healthy child development and the development of adult social skills, researchers have gone on to question the impact of play-based early childhood programs on academic success in the elementary grades.

Rebecca Marcon (2002) at the University of North Florida conducted research examining three different approaches to preschool instruction and their influence on later school success. The programs ranged from academically oriented at one end of the continuum to play-based at the other end. The study included an examination of student report-card grades, retention rates, and special education placement of 160 children at the end of third grade and 183 children at the end of fourth grade. The sample was mostly African American children, with 75 percent of the children qualifying for free and reduced lunch. The study found that by the end of third grade, there were no substantial differences in school performance, but by the end of fourth grade, the children in the academically oriented preschool program had significantly lower grades compared with the children in a play-based classrooms. "Children's later school success appears to have been enhanced by more active, child-initiated early learning experiences. Their progress may have been slowed by overly academic preschool experiences that introduced formalized learning experiences too early for most children's developmental status" (page 1).

In other words, through the end of third grade, there was no difference in academic success as a function of being in a more play-based preschool program. But by the end of fourth grade, the children from a more play-based preschool program were performing better than the children from more direct-instruction preschools. How could this be? Marcon speculates that beginning in fourth grade, teachers expect students to be more independent learners. They are required to take on more responsibility and show more initiative. Thus, teaching is less didactic and more driven by the individual students. Therefore, she contends, motivated and self-initiating students do better at this point, as these were skills they developed in more play-based preschool programs. "This is the point at which Elkind (1986) and Zigler (1987) worried that short-term academic gains produced by overly didactic, formal instructional practices for young children would be offset by long-term stifling of children's motivation. Important lessons about independence and self-initiative are being learned in the early childhood years. Overly teacher-directed approaches that tell young children what to do, when to do it, and how to do it most likely curtail development of initiative during the preschool years" (2002, 23).

Marcon is suggesting an important point here. Perhaps the fostering of independence and self-initiative are more important in preschool than the early teaching of academic skills. Moreover, perhaps this early teaching stifles children's motivation and does them a disservice in the long term. This concept of "disservice" is addressed in a recent press release by the Gesell Institute in New Haven, Connecticut, in which executive director Marcy Guddemi summarizes the problem of an undue emphasis on early academics:

> Good quality early childhood programs from age 3 to grade 3 are essential because they provide the proper *experiences* and exploration which allows a child to access his or her greatest potential, relative to the developmental level they are at. These programs are not to help children learn more letters earlier or faster, but to learn to negotiate and problem solve with peers and engage in the work of making sense of their world alongside teachers who are experienced, patient, and creative role models. Unfortunately, in an effort to close achievement gaps, both schools and parents endorse the "earlier is better myth," believing that by "learning" academic skills earlier, developmental success will follow. Gesell's recent data proves the opposite—that developmental abilities must emerge before an academic curriculum has meaning for the child and that it stimulates a corresponding motivation to learn. (Gesell Institute 2012, 2)

The report titled *Crisis in the Kindergarten: Why Children Need to Play in School* produced by the Alliance for Childhood cites a German study with similar findings.

> Long-term research casts doubt on the assumption that starting earlier on the teaching of phonics and other discrete skills leads to better results. For example, most of the play-based kindergartens in Germany were changed into centers for cognitive achievement during a wave of educational "reform" in the 1970s. But research comparing 50 play-based classes with 50 early-learning centers found that by age ten the children who had played in kindergarten excelled over the others in a host of ways. They were more advanced in reading and mathematics and they were better adjusted socially and emotionally in school. They excelled in creativity and intelligence, oral expression, and "industry." As a result of this study German kindergartens returned to being play-based again. (Miller and Almon 2009, 2)

The crux, therefore, is that play-based programs that help children learn to negotiate, problem solve, and engage in making sense of the world are more important than learning more letters and numbers faster.

II. Nature-Based Early Childhood Programs Compared to High-Quality Traditional Early Childhood Programs

Assuming that we now agree that play-based programs are more effective than academic programs at getting children "ready" for kindergarten, the question then becomes, "Is there any advantage to a nature-based program versus a traditional program if both programs are play-based?" First let's define what we mean by *nature-based programs*.

In an article currently moving towards publication by Rachel Larimore, David Sobel, and Rachel Becker Klein titled "Expansion of a Nature-Based Preschool Program into the K-5 Curriculum: A Case Study Exploring Potential Child Outcomes and Administrative Successes," these parameters are provided:

> Nature-based early childhood education (NbECE) is a broad term that encompasses any program model that provides young children ages 0-8 extensive daily outdoor time over the course of a school year and the curriculum's organizing concept is nature (Larimore

2016; Sobel, 2014). Under this larger umbrella of NbECE are programs such as nature-based preschools, forest preschools, forest kindergartens, and nature kindergartens. (We define) nature-based preschools as high-quality, licensed early childhood programs for 3-5 year olds, with at least 25-50% of the class day held outside each day, including time beyond the designated play area, nature infused into the indoor spaces, and with nature as the driving theme of the curriculum (Bailie, 2010; Green Hearts, 2014; Larimore, 2011a, 2011b; Moore, 2014). We distinguish this program model from forest preschools, sometimes referred to as forest kindergartens, by their longer periods of time outdoors (70-100%) and very limited use, if any, of indoor space (Larimore 2016; Sobel 2015). (Larimore, Sobel, and Becker-Klein, unpublished)

To translate this back to parental decision-making, this leads us to the next question of "Will my child be just as ready if I send her to a nature preschool or a kindergarten where she's playing and learning in the woods (for part of the day) compared to a program where she's playing and learning indoors most of the day in the drama and arts corner in the classroom?" The following comment from the superintendent of the Bullock Creek Schools in 2016 near Midland, Michigan, is illustrative of this question. He describes his own parental choice about whether his children should participate in the nature kindergarten in his district:

> [When it started] I was dour towards nature-based. My own kids, who are now in first and third grade—we could have put them in the nature kindergarten. Instead, we chose the traditional approach. Now, I regret that decision. If I could meet with every parent considering kindergarten, I would try to convince them that there are lots of positives in that approach. If I knew then what I know now, I'd put my own kids in nature kindergarten. (Larimore and Sobel 2016, 17)

Qualitative research conducted in preschools and kindergartens in Michigan have found five areas in which parents, teachers, and administrators report that children in nature preschools and kindergartens seem to be equivalently or more ready than children in traditional programs. Nature preschool and kindergarten programs appear to

- provide opportunities for a full range of physical development through regularly scheduled hikes and the creation of naturalized play areas;

- increase students' motivation and enthusiasm for school through program design that aligns with children's interests;

- create the foundation for STEM (science, technology, engineering, math) learning through providing opportunities for problem solving and sustained inquiry;

- enhance language development through grounding literacy in natural learning experiences; and

- develop executive functions (working memory, cognitive flexibility, inhibitory control, and self-regulation) through thoughtfully designed outdoor activities and challenges.

First I'm going to discuss some quantitative and qualitative findings about physical development, motivation and enthusiasm, and STEM learning. Then I'm going to bring you up to date on recent research on language development and executive function. The focus on language development and executive function is my way of addressing these two conceptions of readiness— the academic preparedness conception represented by language development and the social-emotional preparedness conception as represented by executive function.

PHYSICAL DEVELOPMENT

There's not much quantitative research on physical development in the US, but there are a few studies from Europe and Canada. This is reflective of the European emphasis being less on academic achievement and more on how nature-based programming develops children's physical and social skills. In a report on Swedish Forest Schools, Juliet Robertson (2008) summarizes some of the findings based on comparisons of forest kindergartens with conventional (more indoors) early childhood programs. She indicates that at the I Ur och Skur nursery (a forest kindergarten), (a) the sickness/absence rate was 5 percent less than at the traditional nursery, (b) the children had better concentration, (c) the children had better motor functions, and (d) the children played more imaginatively and for longer sustained periods.

Conversely at the traditional nursery, (a) the dominant outdoor activity was cycling, and play seldom got to a stage where roles and action had a lot of scope; (b) play was interrupted, either by other children who disturbed it or by the staff; and (c) staff stepped in more to intervene when conflict arose.

Some of these findings are reinforced by studies of Norwegian children (Fjørtoft 2001) with access to forest areas for nature play versus children with access to only a conventional playground. The study focused on the physical development of children that played in a forested area one to two hours a day compared with children that played on a conventional playground for the same amount of time. The motor development of the forest area children increased more in nine months than the conventional playground children. The findings related particularly to greater development in balance and coordination.

The improvements in motor development were objectively assessed through beginning- and end-of-the-year administrations of the Eurofit Motor Fitness Test—a standardized measure of children's physical fitness that measures balance, strength, endurance, and speed. All the children with access to uneven ground, natural climbing, and balancing challenges in the natural-play settings developed greater physical competence through their self-directed play.

Similarly, researchers at the University of Victoria in British Columbia compared growth in physical development in nature-based and conventional kindergarten programs in the Sooke, British Columbia, public schools. The nature kindergarten children spent most of every morning in a forest area adjacent to the school grounds. The researchers found that children in the nature kindergarten group had significantly more locomotor skills growth over the course of the year than children in the conventional kindergarten as measured on the Test of Gross Motor Development-2 standardized assessment (Temple, Müller, and Smith 2015).

MOTIVATION AND ENTHUSIASM

There's an interesting resonance between two qualitative studies conducted in Michigan and Vermont that independently found recurrent comments about children's enthusiasm for school as a function of nature-based programming. For a case study titled "Nature Cements the New Learning" (Sobel and Larimore 2018), we interviewed parents, teachers, and administrators about the impact of the nature kindergarten program implemented in Fall 2012 and the nature first-grade program implemented in Fall 2015 in the Bullock Creek, Michigan, public schools. These programs were implemented in the public schools in part because of parent enthusiasm about the Chippewa Nature Preschool located in the same community. Administrators and teachers also recognized that the increase in prescriptive curriculum and increased amounts of seatwork in kindergarten was doing a disservice to their five-year-old children. This comment below from a parent suggests the general sentiment we found:

My son is in nature kindergarten right now. My daughter loved it [three years ago]. For both of my kids, it lets them still have that creativity, where usually [the curriculum is] so structured. Nature kindergarten brings that out in them. I don't see that it is distracting from learning. My son loves the outside, so his ability to talk about nature is phenomenal.

It was quite a difference when my daughter transitioned into first grade. That was tough! They sat there all day, and she honestly did not like school that much in the first grade . . . [Now, it's] great to know that next year my son will have nature first grade as well. (Sobel and Larimore 2018, 13)

Parents saw the difference in the school experience for their kindergartners and wanted the experience to continue for their first graders. This motivation for school is reflected in attendance records as well. At Bullock Creek in the 2012–2013 school year, the first year of nature kindergarten, kindergarten attendance was 88 percent. In the 2013–2014 school year, the attendance rate was 95 percent—a significant increase. If children are enthusiastic about school, they're less likely to find reasons to be absent.

Similarly, the Forest Days Case Studies research project of three different Forest Days programs in Vermont and New Hampshire by Amy Powers of PEER Associates (2017) identified similar comments from parents, teachers, and administrators. Forest Days are one day a week in the woods in public school kindergarten classrooms. In the section of the reports on cross-cutting findings, Powers reported that "students at all sites showed evidence of an enhanced enthusiasm for going to school. Examples offered included students at multiple sites proudly bringing visitors on weekends or after school to see their outdoor classroom, students laying out clothes the night before in anticipation of the forest day, and higher attendance rates on forest days" (page 24).

At one of the sites, Mt. Lebanon Elementary in Lebanon, New Hampshire, the teacher noted the following:

The most significant benefit to kids I've seen has been their enjoyment of school—enjoyment of school in its purest form. When we're up there they show just total joy at being outside. Even in the trickiness of a cold or wet day, they are overwhelmingly asking to go outside. When we have choice time, kids ask, can we go outside instead? If it's motivating kids to come to school, to enjoy being in school, that's huge. (Powers 2017, 20)

A father of a child at this school related the common story of asking his children, "What did you do today at school?" and getting the reply "Nothing." But, he said, on Wednesdays (the forest day), there's always an enthusiastic sharing of the day's doings. He values a newsletter that comes home with pictures and stories of the day and says his son "circles his picture, tells about what they're doing, reminds him to do a tick check. He's always really proud to tell me what he did that day" (page 21).

STEM LEARNING

In our qualitative studies of nature preschool, kindergarten, and first grade in Midland, Michigan, parents and early childhood professionals who visit the program comment consistently on the striking examples of problem solving and self-directed inquiry that they observe. In the current atmosphere of concern for encouraging a disposition to science, technology, engineering, and math learning, it makes sense to look at how those dispositions are cultivated in early childhood programs.

In the film *School's Out: Lessons from a Forest Kindergarten* (Molomot 2013), there's a scene in which a group of children is trying to design a pathway so a ball will travel a curved path down a hill rather than run straight down the hill. The underlying question is, "How can we change the direction of travel so the ball follows the curve to our desired destination?" What an excellent engineering challenge! The boys scavenge branches from the surrounding woods to create barriers to deflect the path of the ball. The ball hops over the barrier. They need to figure out how to slow the speed of the ball and create higher barriers. The boys are deeply invested in solving this very real-world problem.

Two related observations of children at the Chippewa Nature Center (CNC) preschool suggest similar problem-solving experiences. One visiting early childhood administrator made a comparison between what she sees at CNC versus other early childhood programs.

> There could be more inquiry-based language outside, and a greater length of engagement of outdoor play at CNC compared to indoor programs. They are examining under a rock for thirty minutes. In high-quality programs inside and out we have open-ended activities, but the Chippewa children appear to do more problem solving. They are trying to figure out how to move rocks. "How do we move these rocks? I wonder what rope might do, we can tie rope to the rock. It's not moving, what else could we do?" It's problem solving, it's inquiry, it's hypothesis. I don't see as much testing inside the classroom, it is more pretend play. (Sobel and Larimore 2018, 18)

Whereas the above experience was self-directed, the teachers at CNC also create experiences that lead to inquiry. It's been a regular activity for teachers to have a road-killed deer carcass placed in the woods so they could observe what happens to it with the children. They visit it regularly and also set up a motion-sensor trail camera to record visitations to the carcass. The teachers describe,

> Right after the deer was dumped, we saw it was newly dead, and we visited it about once a week to see what it looked like as it decomposed. They were asking many questions: "Why is it disappearing? What's eating it?" We watched it all the way down to a pile of fur and bones strewn through the woods. They got to see coyotes dragging it away, scavengers like hawks and skunks pecking at it.

> This process opens up the dialogue. We don't have a [predetermined] word list. Instead the words emerge out of the process. We use technical terms like *decomposition, decomposers, predators, prey*—all scientific words that usually don't come up till fifth or sixth grade. And the children start to understand cycles because they've seen them. They're developing their own definitions based on those experiences.

This combination of self-directed and teacher-initiated scientific inquiry lays the foundation for an interest in STEM learning in the elementary grades.

III. Are They Ready? Language Development and Executive Function

Though much of the research is primarily qualitative and anecdotal, there seems to be emergent agreement that nature-based early childhood programs are perhaps more effective than traditional programs in encouraging physical development, generating enthusiasm for school, and providing opportunities for problem solving with concrete materials that create a disposition to STEM learning. These factors appeal to parents, but there's still that niggling question about readiness for school. Parents still say, "Well yes, that's all well and good, but will my child be academically ready for kindergarten or first grade?" And early childhood professionals still want to know if children's executive functions are being developed in these settings. To answer these questions, two different research projects in Michigan and Minnesota have been conducted in the past few years.

MICHIGAN AND MINNESOTA RESEARCH

Our previous studies identified recurrent comments about the increase in children's science vocabularies in nature preschool and kindergarten. Recall the previously cited comment by one public school kindergarten teacher:

> I'm surprised at the size of their vocabulary—it's amazing—and they're just getting this at school. Bears going through torpor, frogs in brumation. Insects—it's not just a bug—they know the body parts, and the functions of the body parts. Then this relates back to writing. In winter, when we're reading the *All About Book*, the children are recalling body parts and then they don't just talk about it, they write about it. (Sobel and Larimore 2018).

This greater scientific vocabulary included words such as *hibernation*, *vernal pools*, *talons*, *abdomen*, *thorax*, *decomposition*, *carcass*, *exoskeleton*, and *metamorphosis*.

On the basis of these previous studies, we designed a study to determine if we could quantify some of the qualitative findings. The purpose of the study was to compare development in children attending a nature-based preschool versus children attending a traditional university preschool using measures of language and literacy, reasoning, and executive function. To accomplish these goals, we conducted direct assessment of child outcomes in the fall and spring of the 2016–2017 school year.

Both of these Michigan-based preschools received five-star ratings as part of Michigan's Quality Rating Improvement System. The nature-based preschool had extensive outdoor time and integration of nature indoors, while the other was a traditional preschool with limited outdoor time. The study included 139 three- to five-year-old children from the two different program approaches (82 nature-based, 57 traditional). Average ages, demographics, parent education levels, and boy/girl populations were similar. The average number of hours in school was greater in the traditional preschool, six to fifty hours per week, versus the nature preschool's six to twelve hours per week. Direct assessments were used to measure child outcomes in the fall and spring of the 2016–2017 school year, and a parent questionnaire was used to collect demographic information.

To measure language and literacy in children, we used three assessments: the Test of Preschool Early Literacy (TOPEL) (Lonigan et al. 2007), the Quick Letter Name Knowledge (Tortorelli, Bowles, and Skibbe 2017), and the Letter-Sound knowledge (Piasta et al. 2016).

To measure reasoning in children, we used the Mouse House Task (Sodian, Zaitchik, and Carey 1991).

To measure executive function in children, we used three assessments: two from the National Institute of Health Toolbox—the Flanker Inhibitory Control and Attention Test (Weintraub et al. 2013) and the Picture Sequence Memory Test (Weintraub et al. 2013). We also used the Head-Toes-Knees-Shoulders (HTKS) Task (McClelland et al., in development.) (I'll elaborate below on components of executive function and how it's measured.)

The results from this research were as follows:

1. Growth in language and literacy skills was comparable in both settings.

2. Children developed reasoning skills at similar rates in both the traditional and nature-based classrooms.

3. Some aspects of executive function, including performance on the picture sequence memory task, showed statistically equivalent growth for both groups of children.

4. Other aspects of executive function, including performance on the Flanker and HTKS tasks, were associated with greater growth for children in the traditional preschool classrooms.

What do we make of these Michigan results? In response to the original question, "If we put our children in a nature preschool, will they be ready for the academic and social challenges of kindergarten?" the answer appears to be a qualified yes. Let's unpack the concept of "ready." For the parents who ask whether their children will be academically ready—will they know their ABCs, will they have early literacy skills, will they be able to differentiate sounds, the answer is yes. The results on the TOPEL, the Letter Name, and the Letter-Sound measures all indicate that children in the nature preschool develop these early literacy skills at the same rate as the children in the high-quality traditional preschool. It's important to see this measure within the context of the number of hours of preschool per week. The nature-based children are in their program six to twelve hours per week depending on the particular session in which they are enrolled. The traditional preschool children attend school from six to fifty hours a week, although at one of the two sites, most children attended school for approximately twenty-two hours per week.

Therefore, even though the average amount of time in program at the nature-based preschool is less than at the traditional preschool, the increase in early literacy skills is essentially the same. This is in addition to the greater opportunities for physical development, exploration in the natural world, and exposure to bracing fresh air available in the nature preschool setting.

The development in reasoning skills, as measured with the Mouse House task, indicated no significant difference between the nature-based preschool children and the traditional preschool children. We were a bit surprised that the nature-based preschool children's scores didn't increase more, because we hypothesized that nature-based preschool children would show even greater growth. However, we weren't entirely pleased with the assessment itself, and we are interested in seeking out other assessments of science thinking and reasoning with very young children.

The executive function findings were somewhat puzzling. Executive function is a composite construct that includes the subcomponents of working memory, inhibitory control and attention, self-regulation, and cognitive flexibility. In regard to working-memory skills, as measured by the NIH Picture Memory Sequence Test, the children who attended nature-based preschool showed similar growth compared to children who attended the traditional preschool. However, children in the nature-based preschool developed fewer skills related to self-regulation (as measured by the HTKS assessment) and less inhibitory/attentional control (as measured by the NIH Flanker assessment) over the course of the school year when compared to children attending the traditional preschool.

TRANSLATING EXECUTIVE FUNCTION INTO LAYMEN'S TERMS

Before proceeding to talk about the Minnesota research, let's step back for a moment and examine the construct of executive function and translate the somewhat jargon-y academic terms into something we can all understand. Much research over the past few decades points to the development of executive functioning in young children as a more important and productive goal than the development of early literacy and numeracy skills. Executive function, it turns out, appears to be a better predictor of long-term academic and social success than early reading and writing. Therefore, focusing on the development of these executive function skills—working memory, cognitive flexibility, inhibitory control, and self-regulation—may be more appropriate early childhood program goals than learning letters and numbers.

Since these are squirmy concepts to wrap one's head around, let's define these subcomponents and translate them into illustrative childhood games.

Working memory is the ability to briefly hold information in mind for the purpose of completing a task. Think of the children's game Concentration as an illustration of working memory. You have to remember where the picture of the ant was when you turned it over a couple of turns ago to match it with the other ant picture you now have in your hand.

Inhibitory control (sometimes referred to as *self-regulation*) is the ability to stop thoughts and actions at the appropriate time, set priorities, and generally have a considered response rather than give in to impulses. Think of the children's game Simon Says as an illustration of inhibitory control and self-regulation. When the leader says "Touch your nose" and also touches her nose without saying "Simon says," the child has to inhibit their mimetic response and not touch their nose. In that case, they have self-regulated.

Cognitive flexibility is the ability to respond appropriately to changing situations and apply different rules in different settings. Let's use the children's game Head-Toes-Knees-Shoulders (HTKS), which has been adapted as an executive function measure, to illustrate cognitive flexibility. The children's game is straightforward: when the leader says "Touch your head" and models that gesture, the child touches her head. When the leader says "Touch your toes," the child does the same. In the executive function assessment, children are first taught the above instructions and then told they will play a silly version of the game. The leader says, "When I say touch your head, I want you to touch your toes." And vice versa. Then the knees-shoulders pair is taught and reversed. The child has to keep both pairs in mind and remember to do the opposite of what is asked in response to each command. This ability to learn one set of rules and then switch to another set of rules is an illustration of cognitive flexibility (D'Amore, Charles, and Louv 2015).

Executive function changes rapidly from three to six years old, and disadvantaged children notably show lower-than-average scores in executive function for their age. Some early childhood programs, such as Tools of the Mind, have been shown to help remediate executive function deficiencies through a carefully planned curriculum that scaffolds extensive dramatic play.

In wondering whether any aspects of the curriculum in nature-based programs might address executive function intentionally, we asked Chippewa Nature Preschool teachers for examples of executive-function instruction. The teachers described a variety of ways in which children were developing these skills. One teacher said,

> The first thing that comes to mind [regarding self-regulation] is risk assessment. Our kids are assessing their own risk daily. [We ask] "Do you feel comfortable doing that?" Today we were out climbing on fallen logs. We had a child that climbed up to the top but wasn't sure how to get back down. I watched her; she put a foot down [but found it not safe] and then found a different ledge. That child at the beginning of this year would have reached out for help. She has learned how to control her body and have self-confidence.

We then pushed a bit further and asked, "Can you give us explicit examples of activities that you conduct that actively help children develop the subcomponents of working memory, inhibitory control, and cognitive flexibility?" We were surprised at the array of very specific activities that clearly target these skills. Here's a sample below.

Code Word (working memory and inhibitory control): Every day the teachers develop a code word to release the children from the circle to go to the gate. This occurs after group meeting as a transition to go on the hike. They choose a science word like *insect*, and then they say a variety of words that sound like the word but aren't the word. The children can only leave when they hear "Ready, set, insect." First the teacher says, "Ready, set, go," and the children have to restrain the impulse to get up. Then, "Ready, set, ant," which also doesn't count because ants are insects, but the code word here is the actual word. Then the teachers will use a word that sounds a lot like the code word: "Ready, set, inside," or, more subtly, "Ready, set, inspect." The children have to attend to the subtle distinction between the sound of *inspect* and *insect*. Kids start suggesting words—sometimes it's unrelated like *pizza*—but other times it rhymes, which suggests that they're developing language differentiation skills.

Freeze Song (cognitive flexibility): The teachers play a game called Freeze Song while outside. They play music from a portable music device. When the music plays, the children dance, and when the music stops, they freeze. It's like the movement pattern in Musical Chairs. Then the teachers switch the pattern. (In executive-function terms, this is known as *rule switching*.) When music is playing, children have to freeze. When the music is silent, they dance.

Goodbye Song (working memory and cognitive flexibility): The CNC preschool has a program-wide goodbye song that is sung every day at the end of the class sessions. There are a number of verses that are taught in a very specific order, and there are hand gestures that go with each verse. Once the children know all the verses, the teachers start to change it up. Teachers will say, "This time we're going to switch the butterfly and ladybug verses." Or, "This time we're going to sing all of the verses backwards." Or, "This time we're going to do it silently and just do the hand gestures." Or, "This time make sure you do a different hand gesture than the normal one for that verse." They ask the children to come up with variations as well, and all the rule changing requires the children to develop cognitive flexibility.

Trail Walks (inhibitory control): The teachers described a great deal of inhibition control that occurs on the trail. When children see a squirrel, their first impulse is to run after it. Rather, the teachers explain that if the children want to get close to see the squirrel, then they have to get really quiet and walk very, very slowly towards the squirrel. Similarly, the teachers often have children play Red Light, Green Light on the trail. Or they will challenge the children in a game like Blind Cat. The "cat" stands with eyes closed in the center of the circle in a part of the woods filled with fallen, crunchy leaves. The children try to creep forward as silently as possible (inhibitory control) to get close enough to pet the cat. If the cat hears a noise, she points in the direction of the child making the noise, who then has to return to the circle and start again.

On the basis on these CNC descriptions, and comparable elements at programs around the country, researchers have speculated that nature-based programs may be particularly effective at helping children develop executive function—therefore our inclusion of executive-function assessments in the Michigan study and the rationale behind the following study.

MINNESOTA RESEARCH

A recent Minnesota study focused on comparing executive function in nature preschool and traditional preschool children in Duluth-area programs. The research, conducted by Julie Ernst and Jenna Zamzow at the University of Minnesota Duluth was designed similarly to the Michigan study in that children in four nature preschool programs were compared with children in two nonnature preschool programs. Age, demographics, and quality of preschool were all similar. The instrument used for comparison was the Minnesota Executive Function Scale developed by Stephanie Carlson at the University of Minnesota. It is conducted on an iPad and requires that children sort items on the screen using changing, and increasingly more challenging, sets of rules.

It's similar to the HTKS task, but the scoring is built into the program and the researcher doesn't need to score the children's sometimes confusing responses as in HTKS. It only takes about five to ten minutes to administer the assessment.

I'll spare you all the statistical details and provide the summary from the master's project currently being finalized. The author, Jenna Zamzow, says,

> Collectively, the results of these comparisons suggest that preschool participation, whether that be in nature or non-nature preschools, can support the development of executive function skills beyond what is typically seen in growth from cognitive maturation. All four nature preschools showed greater growth than what would be expected through cognitive maturation. One of the two control preschools showed greater growth than would be expected. (The other showed growth comparable to the expected maturational growth.) Thus these findings lend practical significance to the statistically significant growth found in each of the four nature preschools. (2019)

What do we make of these Minnesota and Michigan results? In regard to the original "Will my child be ready?" question, we can answer a somewhat more assured, but still qualified, yes. From the perspective of academics and reading readiness, the Michigan study suggests that nature preschool children will be just as ready as children in a high-quality university early childhood program. From the perspective of social-emotional readiness and executive function, the Minnesota study suggests that nature preschool children will be just as ready as children in comparable traditional early childhood programs.

A study published in a recent issue of the *International Journal of Early Childhood Environmental Education*, "Nature-Based Education and Kindergarten Readiness," resonates interestingly with these findings (Cordiano et al. 2019).

The objectives of this study were to better understand the learning process that occurs in a nature-based preprimary program and to compare the experience of a nature-based preprimary program with that of a high-quality traditional preprimary program. A unique aspect of this study is that both preschool programs were located in the same school and drew students from the same community, ensuring that the groups were matched on important variables such as location, socioeconomic status, and parents' levels of education.

Faculty at Case Western Reserve conducted the research, and the study subjects were twenty-six half-day preschool children at an independent school in Cleveland. Fourteen children were enrolled in a traditional preschool program; twelve children were in an almost completely outdoors preschool program. The demographics of both groups were similar, about half white and half non-white. Parents and teachers were asked to complete forms at the beginning and end of the year using six different assessment measures, including the Penn Interactive Peer Play Scale, the Preschool and Kindergarten Behavior Scales, the Pretend Play Scale, Kindergarten Readiness Measures, Children's Attitudes Toward School, and Children's Attitudes Toward Nature. The Kindergarten Readiness Measure used is most analogous to the AimswebPlus assessment used in our Michigan study.

The researchers found that "children in both types of preschool programs achieved expected developmental gains in their behavior, early academic skills, and social-emotional functioning over the year prior to kindergarten. In most areas and generally overall, the two groups ended the year with equal levels of preparedness for kindergarten in the domains of social-emotional functioning, academic readiness, and pretend play" (Cordiano et al. 2019, 31).

And in the conclusion, the authors summarize that, similar to what we have found in our research, nature preschool students perform similarly, on standard measures of school readiness, to children in traditional programs. These findings will help parents choose nature-based preschool programs with confidence, "knowing that the learning that takes place outdoors provides similar academic and social-emotional benefits as the learning that takes place in a traditional setting" (Cordiano et al. 2019, 33).

Consider these findings within the context of the qualitative findings. A significant majority of parents, teachers, and administrators report that children enjoy substantial physical development, elevated enthusiasm for school, and positive inclinations towards STEM learning. Moreover, we've overlooked one of the significant goals of all these programs—laying the foundation for bonding with nature that hopefully leads to environmental behaviors and ethics later in life. There is a significant body of literature that suggests that nature play is a contributor to environmental behaviors. As Louise Chawla and Victoria Derr (2012) say in their landmark chapter, "The Development of Conservation Behaviors in Childhood and Youth," "research has linked a background of childhood play in nature with every form of care for the environment: informed citizen action, volunteerism, public support for pro-environmental policies, environmental career choices, and private-sphere behaviors like buying green products, conserving energy, and recycling" (Chawla and Derr 2012, 30).

In environmental circles, the truth is that many folks could care less about early literacy readiness. They believe in nature preschools because they are convinced that nature play and learning experiences are making children citizens of the planet. I confess that I'm of this mind-set as well. But if nature-based early childhood is going to appeal to the masses, if we want to run it up the flagpole in Peoria to see if people will salute, we need to address these conventional school aspirations. We're comfortably on the path to being able to say that nature-based early childhood does a whole lot of good for kids, and they'll be just as ready for kindergarten and first grade as their peers in traditional programs. And I like harking back to Charlie Schwedler, the Bullock Creek, Michigan, superintendent under whose watch the nature-kindergarten program was started. In response to our quest for data, he said,

> I don't care what you guys say, I know that there is more to things than testing. This is so good for these kids, and they are not outside enough and this puts them outside.

To quote Spiderman, "'Nuff said."

References

Antioch University New England and High Cairn Productions, producers. 2017. *The Best Day Ever: Forest Days in Vermont Kindergartens* (film). https://video.vermontpbs.org/video/best-day-ever-forest-kindergartens-in-vermont-tgjldc/.

Armitage, Kevin C. 2009. *The Nature Study Movement: The Forgotten Popularizer of American's Conservation Ethic.* Lawrence, KS: University Press of Kansas.

Brussoni, Mariana, Lise L. Olsen, Ian Pike, and David A. Sleet. 2012. "Risky Play and Children's Safety: Balancing Priorities for Optimal Child Development." *International Journal of Environmental Research and Public Health* 9 (9): 3134–48.

Chawla, Louise, and Victoria Derr. 2012. "The Development of Conservation Behaviors in Childhood and Youth." In *Oxford Handbook of Environmental and Conservation Psychology*, edited by Susan D. Clayton. 1–45. Oxford, UK: Oxford University Press.

Cordiano, Tori S., Alexis Lee, Joshua Wilt, Audrey Elszasz, Lisa K. Damour, and Sandra W. Russ. 2019. "Nature-Based Education and Kindergarten Readiness: Nature-Based and Traditional Preschoolers Are Equally Prepared for Kindergarten." *International Journal of Early Childhood Environmental Education* 6 (3): 18–36. https://eric.ed.gov/?id=EJ1225659.

D'Amore, C., Charles, C., and Louv, R. 2015. "Thriving through Nature: Fostering Children's Executive Function Skills." Children & Nature Network. www.childrenandnature.org.

Fjørtoft, Ingunn. 2001. "The Natural Environment as a Playground for Children: The Impact of Outdoor Play Activities in Pre-primary School Children." *Early Childhood Education Journal* 29 (3): 111–17.

Gesell Institute. 2012. "Gesell Executive Director Speaks at Global Summit in DC." Press release, April 4, 2012. New Haven, CT. www.gesellinstitute.org/pages/press-releases.

Gibson, James J. 1979. *The Ecological Approach to Visual Perception.* Boston: Houghton Mifflin.

Hawkins, David. (1969.) 2007. "The Bird in the Window." In *The Informed Vision: Essays on Learning and Human Nature*, 77–98. New York: Algora.

Hemenway, H. D. 1903. *How to Make School Gardens: A Manual for Teachers and Pupils.* New York: Doubleday, Page and Co.

Larimore, Rachel A. 2011. *Establishing a Nature-based Preschool.* Fort Collins, CO: National Association for Interpretation.

———. 2016. "Defining Nature-based Preschools." *International Journal of Early Childhood Education* 4 (1): 32–36.

Larimore, R., and Sobel, D. 2016. *Nature Cements the New Learning: A Case Study of Expanding a Nature-based Early Childhood Program from Preschool into the K-5 Curriculum in Public Schools in Midland, Michigan.* Keene, NH: Antioch University.

Larimore, Rachel, David Sobel, and Rachel Becker-Klein. *Expansion of a Nature-Based Preschool Program into the K-5 Curriculum: A Case Study Exploring Child Outcomes and Administrative Successes.* Unpublished.

Louv, Richard. 2005. *Last Child in the Woods: Saving Our Children from Nature-Deficit Disorder.* Chapel Hill, NC: Algonquin.

Marcon, Rebecca A. 2002. "Moving Up the Grades: Relationship between Preschool Model and Later School Success." *Early Childhood Research and Practice* 4 (1).

Miller, Edward, and Joan Almon. 2009. *Summary and Recommendations of Crisis in the Kindergarten: Why Children Need to Play in School.* College Park, MD: Alliance for Childhood.

Minnucci, Eliza, and Meghan Teachout. 2018. *A Forest Days Handbook: Program Design for School Days Outside.* Brattleboro, VT: Antioch University and Green Writers Press.

Molomot, Lisa, director. 2013. *School's Out: Lessons from a Forest Kindergarten.* Linden Tree Films.

ParticipACTION. 2015. *The Biggest Risk is Keeping Kids Indoors: The 2015 ParticipACTION Report Card on Physical Activity for Children and Youth.* Toronto: ParticipACTION. https://participaction.cdn.prismic.io/participaction%2F61cf55e8-c1c0-42c7-ba6b-1480fd2c29b9_participaction-2015-report-card-full.pdf.

Powers, Amy. 2017. *Forest Days Case Studies: Hartland Elementary, Vermont; Ludlow Elementary, Vermont; Mount Lebanon Elementary, New Hampshire.* Richmond, VT: PEER Associates. https://drive.google.com/file/d/0B4Azl0bN2dL9a3NOcU4yZkktd2s/view.

ReadyNation: Council for a Strong America. *Business Case for Early Childhood Investments.* Washington, D.C. https://strongnation.s3.amazonaws.com/documents/318/4e8aa99a-873d-4bc5-ba14-638029d4b622.pdf?1506694511.

Rideout, Victoria J., Ulla G. Foehr, and Donald F. Roberts. 2010. *Generation M2: Media in the Lives of 8- to 18-Year-Olds.* Menlo Park, CA: Kaiser Family Foundation. www.kff.org/wp-content/uploads/2013/04/8010.pdf.

Robertson, Juliet. 2008. *Swedish Forest Schools.* Aberdeenshire, Scotland: Creative Learning Star Company. https://creativestarlearning.co.uk/wp-content/uploads/2013/06/Rain-or-shine-Swedish-Forest-Schools.pdf.

Schweinhart, Lawrence J., Jeanne Montie, Zongping Xiang, W. Steven Barnett, Clive R. Belfield, and Milagros Nores. 2005. *Lifetime Effects: The High/Scope Perry Preschool Study Through Age 40.* Ypsilanti, MI: High/Scope Press.

Sobel, David. 2008. *Childhood and Nature: Design Principles for Educators.* Portland, ME: Stenhouse Publishers.

———. 2015. *Nature Preschools and Forest Kindergartens: The Handbook for Outdoor Learning.* St. Paul, MN: Redleaf Press.

Sobel, David, and Larimore, Rachel. 2018. "Nature Cements the New Learning: Expanding Nature-based Learning into the K-5 Curriculum." *Research Handbook on Children and Nature: Assemblages of Childhood and Nature Research.* New York: Springer International.

The Strong National Museum of Play. 2008. "Stick." National Toy Hall of Fame. www. toyhalloffame.org/toys/stick.

Temple, Viviene A., Ulrich Müller, and Beverly Smith. 2015. *Evaluation of Nature Kindergarten Project Results*. Centre for Early Childhood Research and Policy. Victoria, BC: University of Victoria.

Weikart, David P. 1998. "Why Curriculum Matters in Early Childhood Education." *Educational Leadership: Journal of Association of Supervision and Curriculum Development, N.E.A.* 55 (6).

Young, Jon, Ellen Haas, and Evan McGown. 2011. *Coyote's Guide to Connecting with Nature*. Shelton, WA: OWLink Media.

Zamzow, Jenna. 2019. "Supporting School Readiness Naturally: Investigating Executive Function Growth in Nature Preschools." Master's thesis, University of Minnesota Duluth.

Index of Newsletter Topics

ACTIVITIES

TOPIC	PAGE	CURRICULUM CONNECTION
animal drills	51–52	safety and procedures
animal homes	23–26, 212–214	fine motor, gross motor, language and literacy, social/emotional, STEM
alphabet and letters	125–129	art and dramatic play, language and literacy
animal tracks, poop, and signs	94, 112–115, 138, 186–195, 198–199	STEM
counting and numbers	136–151, 191, 200, 217–218	cognitive development, STEM
critical thinking	76, 112–113, 118, 165	cognitive development
data collection	138–141	cognitive development, STEM
death in nature	119–121, 187, 221	language and literacy, social/emotional, STEM
dramatic play	31–32, 33–35, 58–59, 109–110, 112, 116–118, 120, 122–124, 168, 191–193	art and dramatic play, language and literacy, social/emotional, STEM
drawing and painting	8, 13, 49, 111, 114, 125–126, 136–137, 170–171, 189–190, 198, 206, 215–216	art and dramatic play, fine motor, language and literacy, STEM
engineering and construction	21–26, 60, 74–76, 141, 163–169, 177–181	fine motor, gross motor, social/emotional, STEM
English language learning	130–131	language and literacy
experiments and experimental design	25, 40, 171–181, 198–199	cognitive development, STEM
exploring	46–50, 51–52, 93–94, 95, 109, 112, 119, 136–138, 144–145, 163–166, 198	gross motor, cognitive development, STEM
fire (pretend)	33–35, 122–124, 168	art and dramatic play, language and literacy, social/emotional
forts and structures	21–26, 28, 60, 167–169	fine motor, gross motor, social/emotional, STEM
free play	49–50, 131, 177, 186	teaching and curriculum

friction, forces, and gravity	172–174, 179–181	STEM
gardening and gardens	38, 85, 144–151, 206–227	art and dramatic play, fine motor, social/emotional, STEM
journaling	8, 111, 114, 130–131	language and literacy
measuring	40–41, 140–141, 146–154, 165–166, 177, 224	STEM
mud and puddles	10, 31–32, 38, 62, 126, 152, 199, 215–216	art and dramatic play, gross motor, language and literacy, STEM
music and songs	36–37, 90–91, 93, 96–97, 99–100, 109, 112, 130–131, 165, 189–190	art and dramatic play, language and literacy
naturalist thinking and behaviors	8, 29–30, 87–88, 92–94, 108–111, 186–188, 191–193, 199	cognitive development, social/emotional, STEM
patterns and symmetry	8, 41, 140–141, 155–157, 198, 200–201	fine motor, social/emotional, STEM
reflection, opportunities for	8, 49–50, 77–79, 94, 98, 118	cognitive development, language and literacy, social/emotional
research projects and investigation	35, 112–115, 122–124, 142–143, 163–166, 170–181, 189–190, 199, 206–208, 209–211	language and literacy, STEM
rough-and-tumble play	55–57, 73	gross motor, social/emotional
seeds	85, 95, 125, 146–148, 185, 198–199, 217–218, 222	STEM
sensory experiences	8, 152–154, 165, 198–199, 215–216	fine motor, STEM
shadows	170–171	STEM
sorting	58, 146–148, 200–201, 210, 217–218	STEM
sticks	7, 11, 21, 23–26, 51, 58, 60–61, 72–76, 90, 94, 125, 137, 155–156, 163–169, 179–181, 199, 201	gross motor, social/emotional, STEM
storytelling	35, 58–59, 93, 95–100, 109–111, 116–121	art and dramatic play, language and literacy, social/emotional
stretching and yoga	38–39, 93	gross motor, social/emotional
tools and utensils	8, 13, 31–32, 36–37, 38–39, 40–41, 60, 75, 113, 163–166, 217–218	fine motor, gross motor, STEM